Contractarianism/Contractualism

Blackwell Readings in Philosophy
Series Editor: Steven M. Cahn

Blackwell Readings in Philosophy are concise, chronologically arranged collections of primary readings from classical and contemporary sources. They represent core positions and important developments with respect to key philosophical concepts. Edited and introduced by leading philosophers, these volumes provide valuable resources for teachers and students of philosophy, and for all those interested in gaining a solid understanding of central topics in philosophy.

Contractarianism/ Contractualism

Edited by

Stephen Darwall

Blackwell
Publishing

350 Main Street, Malden, MA 02148-5018, USA
108 Cowley Road, Oxford OX4 1JF, UK
550 Swanston Street, Carlton, Victoria 3053, Australia
Kurfürstendamm 57, 10707 Berlin, Germany

First published 2003 by Blackwell Publishers Ltd, a Blackwell Publishing company

Library of Congress Cataloging-in-Publication Data

Contractarianism, contractualism/edited by Stephen Darwall.
p. cm. – (Blackwell readings in philosophy ; 8)
Includes bibliographical references and index.
ISBN 0-631-23109-9 (alk. paper) – ISBN 0-631-23110-2 (pbk. : alk. paper)
1. Contracts.   2. Contractarianism (Ethics)   I. Darwall, Stephen L., 1946–
II. Series.

BJ1500 C65 C66 2002
171'.7 – dc21
2002066427

A catalogue record for this title is available from the British Library.

Set in 10/12½ Palatino
by SNP Best-set Typesetter Ltd., Hong Kong

For further information on
Blackwell Publishing, visit our website:
http://www.blackwellpublishing.com

Contents

Acknowledgments

I am indebted to Steven Cahn for initially suggesting the idea of this anthology, to Jeff Dean for patiently shepherding me through the production process, to Blackwell's anonymous referees for very helpful comments, to Anthony Grahame for expert copy-editing, and to Sue London for yeoman work in copying.

The editor and publisher gratefully acknowledge the following for permission to reproduce copyright material:

Chapter 1: Thomas Hobbes, *Leviathan*, edited by Edwin Curley. Copyright © Hackett Publishing Company, Inc. 1994. Reprinted by permission of Hackett Publishing Company, Inc. All rights reserved;

Chapter 2: Jean-Jacques Rousseau, "On the Social Contract" from *The Social Contract and other later political writings*, edited by Victor Gourevitch. Reproduced by permission of Cambridge University Press and the editor;

Chapter 3: Immanuel Kant, from *The Groundwork of the Metaphysics of Morals*, translated and edited by Mary Gregor (1997). Reproduced by permission of Cambridge University Press;

Chapter 4: David Gauthier, "Why Contractarianism?" from *Contractarianism and Rational Choice*, edited by Peter Vallentyne (1991). Reproduced by permission of Cambridge University Press and the author;

Chapter 5: David Gauthier, reprinted from *Morals by Agreement* (1986). Copyright © David Gauthier. Reproduced by permission of Oxford University Press;

Chapter 6: Gilbert Harman, "Convention" from *The Nature of Morality* (1977). Reproduced by permission of Oxford University Press Inc.;

Chapter 7: John Rawls, reprinted by permission of the publisher from *A Theory of Justice* by John Rawls, pp. 11–22, 60–5, 118–22, 136–42, 150–61, 251–7. Cambridge, Mass. : The Belknap Press of Harvard University Press. Copyright © 1971, 1999 by the President and Fellows of Harvard College;

Chapter 8: John Rawls, "Kantian Constructivism in Moral Theory" from *Journal of Philosophy* 77 (1980). Reproduced by permission of the journal and author;

Chapter 9: T. M. Scanlon, "Contractualism and Utilitarianism" from *Utilitarianism and Beyond* (1982), edited by Amartya Sen and Bernard Williams. Reproduced by permission of Cambridge University Press and the author;

Chapter 10: Gary Watson, "Some Considerations in Favor of Contractualism" from *Rational Commitment, and Morality,* edited by Christopher Morris and Jules Coleman (1998). Reproduced by permission of Cambridge University Press and the author;

The publisher apologizes for any errors or omissions in the above list and would be grateful if notified of any corrections that should be incorporated in future reprints or editions of this book.

Introduction

The normative ethical theories called "contractarian" or "contractualist" derive from a conception of morality modeled on, and perhaps presupposed in, mutually agreeable reciprocity or cooperation between equals. The idea is that morality is deeply implicated in the very notion of agreement, and vice versa, so that whether an action is right or wrong must depend on whether the act accords with or violates principles that are, or would be, the object of a suitable agreement between equals. This general idea can be developed in a variety of ways, depending on how one characterizes the relevant agreement, the parties to it and their equality, and the conditions under which it is made. One broad distinction is that between *contractarianism*, where the parties' equality is merely *de facto* and their choice of principles rationally self-interested, and *contractualism*, which proceeds from an ideal of *reasonable* reciprocity or fairness between *moral* equals.

It may seem odd to think that the validity of a moral principle could depend in any way on a choice or agreement. But only rarely do contractarians or contractualists claim that moral standards depend on *actual* agreements.[1] More frequently what they hold is that moral principles are those that *would* be rationally or reasonably chosen or agreed to under certain ideal, counterfactual conditions.

Contractarianism

The classic statement of contractarianism was provided by Thomas Hobbes in *Leviathan*.[2] Hobbes begins by considering the situation of an agent deliberating independently of others, from the perspective of his own desires or interests. Each person, he thinks, sees what he desires as good and so as giving him reasons to realize it. But what results if all of us, together, pursue our respective desires and interests? Although each person's pursuing his interests may result in their actually being best promoted, *given* the conduct of others, it doesn't follow that *everyone's* pursuing his own interests, rather than acting on some principle other than self-interest, will actually result in everyone's (or even anyone's) interests being best promoted. In situations where this is not the case, where the collective pursuit of self-interest leads to an outcome that is worse for each, we have what is known as a *collective action problem*.

This is illustrated by the game-theoretic example known as Prisoner's Dilemma, in which two individuals are jailed on suspicion of robbery. The district attorney tells each that she lacks enough evidence to convict either of robbery, but can easily convict both of breaking and entering with a sentence of one year. She offers each a deal: if one confesses and his partner doesn't, the confessor will go free and the partner will get twenty years. If both confess, both get five years.

Suppose that each cares only about doing the least time. The structure of the situation then is as follows. If A confesses but B does not, then A gets his first-ranked outcome and B his fourth-ranked (worst) outcome. And vice versa, if B confesses but A does not, then the outcomes are reversed: fourth-ranked for A and first-ranked for B. If both confess, both get their third-ranked outcome. And if both don't confess, both get their second-ranked.

What should each do? Reason first from A's perspective. B will act independently of A and either confess or not. It seems, therefore, that A should confess, since whatever B does, A will do better if he (A) confesses. If B confesses, then A will get his third- as opposed to his fourth-best outcome by confessing. And if B doesn't confess, then A will get his first- as opposed to his second-best outcome by confessing. So A should confess. A will do better by confessing, whatever B does.

But B's situation is exactly analogous to A's, so any reasons for A to confess apply equally to B. So if A would do best to confess, then so would B. It may now be evident why this is called a collective action *problem*. A's and B's actions, although both likeliest to achieve the agent's best outcome when taken individually, taken together yield an outcome that is worse for each. If each does what would be best for himself, given the actions of the other, then both will confess. But that yields each's third-ranked outcome, whereas they could have both achieved their second-ranked outcomes by not confessing. Although the jailhouse context gives it a strange ring, not confessing is actually the *cooperative* strategy for A and B. If A and B could cooperate to their mutual advantage, they would both not confess and end up with their second-ranked outcome rather than the third-ranked outcome that independently promoting their interests will achieve.

People *cooperate* when they forego the pursuit of their own independent interests and follow rules or roles, the collective following of which promotes everyone's interests better than would have been done by everyone pursuing her own interests *independently*. Obviously, cooperation is required for many things that are valuable in life, perhaps especially in complex modern societies, in which we cannot assume that genuinely common interests, shaped by common cultural or religious tradition, will stretch across all areas of significant interaction. *Morality* can be thought of as an especially broad and pervasive form of cooperation. Principles of moral right and wrong can then be understood as rules, specifying requirements, permissions, and so on, that underlie the broadest possible cooperation, namely a cooperative scheme that involves not just this or that group, community, or political unit, but all competent human or rational agents.[3]

According to contractarianism, therefore, whether an action is right or wrong is determined by rules of cooperation of this broadest sort. Take, for example, the rule that it is wrong not to come to the aid of others in need, so long as the sacrifice involved is not too great (say, so long as it is not above some level α and/or the ratio of sacrifice to need is not above some level β). Because we all depend on each other in a variety of ways (this is the *de facto* equality referred to above), there arguably exist some α and β, such that it would promote everyone's interests more for everyone to follow the resulting rule, than it would for everyone to pursue her own interests independently. If that is so, contractarianism will hold that it would be wrong not to follow this rule.

To a first approximation, then, contractarianism holds that what it is right to do depends on what rules it would be in everyone's interest for all to accept and be guided by in their deliberations and moral practice. However, what if various *different* possible rules for a given kind of situation have the property that everyone's interests would be promoted better by everyone's following that rule than they would be if everyone attempted to promote her own interests independently? Here is where the idea of an agreement or contract enters the contractarian picture. Taking as a benchmark the "no agreement" point in which all regard themselves as bound by nothing but their own interests and values, contractarians treat the question of which principles we actually are morally bound by as the solution to a rational bargaining problem from this benchmark, in which we all have a greater interest in agreeing to *some* mutually advantageous principles, thereby avoiding the "no agreement" point, but have differing interests in exactly which principles are actually agreed.[4] How favorably the resultant principles treat the different negotiating agents will depend on who has the most to lose if there is no agreement. Consider, for example, what principle of mutual aid would be agreed to. If those with fewer resources and greater vulnerabilities have more to lose from the lack of agreement than those with greater resources and fewer vulnerabilities, then rational bargaining may lead to a less onerous principle of mutual aid than would result if everyone were as vulnerable as those with less.

This, then, is contractarianism's basic framework for assessing moral issues. To work out our moral obligations in a specific kind of case we have to think about what agreement on principles for dealing with the issue would result from a negotiation from the "no agreement" point in which each attempts to advance his or her own interests and values. It is important to appreciate, nonetheless, that in actually acting on the principles that *would* be agreed, the parties are *not* simply promoting their interests; they are cooperating. Cooperation promotes everyone's advantage, but, as in Prisoner's Dilemma, it does so by requiring individuals to *restrict* the promotion of their own interests. Each would prefer schemes in which the necessary sacrifices are borne in greater measure by others, but is prepared to do her part as required by principles of cooperation that everyone could rationally agree to.

Contractualism

Contractualism has a similar structure. It too understands principles of right conduct as the object of a rational agreement. But whereas contractarianism takes moral principles to result from rationally self-interested bargaining, contractualism sees the relevant agreement as governed by a moral ideal of equal respect, one that would be inconsistent, indeed, with bargaining over fundamental terms of association in the way contractarianism proposes. From contractualism's point of view, the problem with contractarianism is that it seems to assume that individuals have, in effect, a moral claim to the resources they could command if there were no agreed rules of cooperation. Otherwise, contractualists think, the rules that result by bargaining from that position can have no moral force. But why assume that people have such a moral claim? From a moral point of view this seems entirely arbitrary, unless some background theory of natural rights is assumed. And contractarianism can't justify *that* assumption without circularity if its own moral force already depends on it.[5]

The animating idea of contractualism can be seen in the "kingdom of ends" formulation of Immanuel Kant's Categorical Imperative. Kant maintains that anyone subject to the moral law must be able to be regarded also as "giving the law."[6] Only thus can the moral law be thought of as a common law for a community of free moral agents, subject only to laws they themselves legislate. This is a version of Rousseau's idea of legitimate political community as an association in which each, "uniting with all, nevertheless obeys only himself."[7] According to Rousseau, a community of free equals is possible only if their laws express what he calls the "general will," the will of each *as* a free and equal member. Similarly, Kant understands the moral law to be "made" by each moral agent if each would "legislate" it *as* a free and equal member of the "kingdom of ends." Here we have the central difference from contractarianism. Moral principles of right are not rules that individuals would prescribe, and attempt to gain acceptance for, from their *different* individual perspectives, bargaining out of self-interest. They are, rather, rules individuals would prescribe (and agree to) from a common perspective as one free and equal person among others.

But how, more specifically, is this perspective to be understood? Kant gives some hints, saying that we can conceive a "systematic union of rational beings under common objective laws," only if we "abstract from the personal differences of rational beings as well as from all the content of their private ends."[8] This suggests John Rawls's idea that principles of justice are those it would be rational to choose in an "original position" behind a "veil of ignorance" regarding any features that individuate different persons or their societies.[9] In particular, the choosing parties must be ignorant of their individual resources, abilities, talents, gender, race, socioeconomic position, *and* their own interests or individual values. Rawls argues that, so understood, the parties can nonetheless be assumed to take an interest in their ability autonomously to choose and pursue their interests (whatever these turn out to be). They value the "primary goods" that are necessary for these: freedom, opportunities, wealth, and the "social bases" of self-respect.

Rawls's idea then is that justice is determined by whichever principles it would be rational to choose from the original position, that is, *as* one free and equal person among others. Rawls does assume that this choice is self-interested within the constraints placed by the veil, but this does not reduce moral reasoning to self-interest in any way. Suppose the parties were motivated, not by self-interest, but by concern for a single other individual. Since the veil of ignorance deprives them of any information that would let them tailor principles to any *particular* person's interest, there is no functional difference between assuming the parties to be self-interested and assuming them to be trustees for another individual. The original position is, in effect, the perspective of *a*, that is, *an arbitrary*, free and equal individual.

Rawls put his ideas forward as a theory of *justice* – "justice as fairness," he called it – and more recently he has stressed that it is to be understood as a political, rather than a more general moral, theory.[10] But in his earlier work, he suggested that it might also be conceived as a moral theory: "rightness as fairness."[11]

A second contractualist approach can be motivated by thinking about what it is to make a claim on someone as an equal. When one person claims something of another in this way, she attempts to give that person a reason based in her needs as an equal. It is as if she says, "This is a reasonable claim for you to grant to me, as you can see were you to put yourself in my shoes and consider that it would be reasonable for you to make it of me." Such a claim implicitly invokes the idea of principles of conduct that reciprocally recognizing equals can accept or, at least, not reasonably reject. In developing such a contractualist approach, T. M. Scanlon assumes a community whose members wish to be able to justify their conduct to each other by principles that others could not reasonably reject, insofar as they also have this aim.[12] Principles of moral right and wrong can then be thought of as norms that structure a mutually accountable community of equals.

To apply this criterion, we must make judgments about what is reasonable. How can we do this? There seems no alternative to putting ourselves into others' shoes and seeing whether we would regard a certain claim, or objection against a proposed principle, as one we would reasonably make if in their situation. This is a complex judgment. It is not simply the prediction that we would make the same claim or objection. We might think that we would, but that it would be unreasonable. To make the requisite judgment, it seems, we must attempt to enter into the other's perspective impartially, as anyone, to see whether we would endorse the claim or objection as a reasonable one to make to another, reciprocally recognizing equal.

The readings that follow fall into three main categories. The first consists of classical sources of contractarianism and contractualism in the writings of Hobbes, Rousseau, and Kant. Second, there are important contemporary statements of contractarianism by David Gauthier and Gilbert Harman, and of contractualism by John Rawls and T. M. Scanlon. Finally, there is a discussion of the attractions of the general contractualist approach by Gary Watson.

Notes

1 One exception is Gilbert Harman. See his "Moral Relativism Defended," *The Philosophical Review* 84 (1975): 3–22, and the selection in this volume.

2 Originally published in 1651. For a discussion of Hobbes's ethical philosophy see my *Philosophical Ethics* (Boulder, CO: Westview Press, 1998).

3 Hobbes's view was that cooperation among large groups is impossible without political authority, since the threat of sanctions is necessary to give everyone the assurance that others will do their part in the cooperative scheme. His point was not, however, that the threat of sanctions was what gave everyone reason to comply with mutually advantageous rules. If people forego what would otherwise promote their interests in order to avoid sanctions, they are not cooperating but simply taking account of the sanctions in promoting their interests. Hobbes's view was that people have a reason to *cooperate*, that is, to *forego* their own individual interest, when the scheme of cooperation is mutually advantageous in the way we have described. He thought, however, that the rationality of cooperation is conditional on the assurance that others will cooperate also. What sanctions do is give everyone the rational assurance that others will be doing their part. Importantly, therefore, Hobbes thought that everyone *would* have a reason actually to follow the rules against their own interest (as in Prisoner's Dilemma) *if* they could be assured of the compliance of others *and* that the existence of *this* truth does not depend on political authority in any way. What we need political institutions for is the assurance to give this truth practical effect by guaranteeing the condition of the reason it hypothesizes.

4 The most prominent statement of this view can be found in David Gauthier. Since Hobbes believed that absolute political authority was required to give moral norms practical effect, there is no similar role for bargaining in his theory. It is the sovereign's will that determines which more nuanced specifications of mutually advantageous rules have moral force.

5 This problem emerges from another direction if we consider how individuals might get from self-interested practical reasoning to contractarian moral reasoning. If each agent reasons in terms of her own independent interests, then, from a situation in which there are no established rules of cooperation, she will think it rational to bargain to an agreement with others to be bound by certain rules. But how can this give her a reason actually to follow the rules? The reasons of interest she has for agreeing to follow the rules can't give her a reason actually to follow them since the whole point and function of rules of cooperation requires that they *constrain* her pursuit of her interests. For her to be able to reason as these rules require, she must already accept

moral reasons of cooperation. It may even be that it is in her interest to be someone who does accept contractarian moral reasons of cooperation, but while this would give her reasons to *want* to accept the moral reasons, she couldn't accept the moral reasons *for these reasons*.

6   Immanuel Kant, *Groundwork of the Metaphysics of Morals* (originally published in 1785), Ak., p. 431 (in the standard [German] edition of Kant's works, published by the Prussian [later German] Academie; the canonical reference is Ak., p. 431; p. 82 in this volume). For a discussion of Kant's ethical philosophy, see my *Philosophical Ethics* (Boulder, CO: Westview Press, 1998).

7   Jean-Jacques Rousseau, *The Social Contract and Other Later Political Writings*, Victor Gourevitch, ed. (Cambridge: Cambridge University Press, 1997), p. 49 (p. 63 in this volume).

8   Kant, *Groundwork*, Ak., p. 433 (p. 84 in this volume).

9   John Rawls, *A Theory of Justice* (Cambridge, MA: Belknap Press of Harvard University Press, 1971), see esp. pp. 136–42 (pp. 183–8 in this volume).

10   John Rawls, *Political Liberalism* (New York: Columbia University Press, 1993).

11   Rawls, *A Theory of Justice*, p. 111.

12   In addition to the selection in this volume, see T. M. Scanlon, *What We Owe to Each Other* (Cambridge, MA: Belknap Press of Harvard University Press, 1998), esp. pp. 147–257.

Part I

Classical Sources:
Contractarianism

1

From *Leviathan*

Thomas Hobbes

Part I
Of Man

Chapter I
Of Sense

[1] Concerning the thoughts of man, I will consider them first *singly*, and afterwards in *train*, or dependence upon one another. *Singly*, they are every one a *representation* or *appearance*, of some quality or other accident, of a body without us, which is commonly called an *object*. Which object worketh on the eyes, ears, and other parts of a man's body, and by diversity of working produceth diversity of appearances.

[2] The original of them all is that which we call SENSE. (For there is no conception in a man's mind which hath not at first, totally or by parts, been begotten upon the organs of sense.) The rest are derived from that original.

[3] To know the natural cause of sense is not very necessary to the business now in hand, and I have elsewhere written of the same at large. Nevertheless, to fill each part of my present method, I will briefly deliver the same in this place.

[4] The cause of sense is the external body, or object, which presseth the organ proper to each sense, either immediately, as in the taste and touch, or mediately, as in seeing, hearing, and smelling; which pressure, by the mediation of nerves and other strings and membranes of the body, continued inwards to the brain and heart, causeth there a resistance, or counter-pressure, or endeavour of the heart to deliver itself; which

Thomas Hobbes, *Leviathan*, Edwin Curley, ed. (Indianapolis, IN: Hackett Publishing Co., Inc., 1994), pp. 6–7, 22–35, 74–105.

endeavour, because *outward*, seemeth to be some matter without. And this *seeming*, or *fancy*, is that which men call *sense*; and consisteth, as to the eye, in a *light* or *colour figured*; to the ear, in a *sound*; to the nostril, in an *odour*; to the tongue and palate, in a *savour*; and to the rest of the body, in *heat, cold, hardness, softness*, and such other qualities as we discern by *feeling*. All which qualities called *sensible* are in the object that causeth them but so many several motions of the matter, by which it presseth our organs diversely. Neither in us that are pressed are they anything else but divers motions (for motion produceth nothing but motion). But their appearance to us is fancy, the same waking that dreaming. And as pressing, rubbing, or striking the eye, makes us fancy a light, and pressing the ear, produceth a din, so do the bodies also we see, or hear, produce the same by their strong, though unobserved action. For if those colours and sounds were in the bodies, or objects, that cause them, they could not be severed from them, as by glasses, and in echoes by reflection, we see they are, where we know the thing we see is in one place, the appearance in another. And though at some certain distance the real and very object seem invested with the fancy it begets in us, yet still the object is one thing, the image or fancy is another. So that sense in all cases, is nothing else but original fancy, caused (as I have said) by the pressure, that is, by the motion, of external things upon our eyes, ears, and other organs thereunto ordained.

[5]   But the philosophy-schools, through all the universities of Christendom, grounded upon certain texts of *Aristotle*, teach another doctrine, and say, for the cause of *vision*, that the thing seen sendeth forth on every side a *visible species* (in English, a *visible show, apparition*, or *aspect*, or *a being seen*), the receiving whereof into the eye is *seeing*. And for the cause of *hearing*, that the thing heard sendeth forth an *audible species*, that is, an *audible aspect*, or *audible being seen*, which entering at the ear maketh *hearing*. Nay for the cause of *understanding* also, they say the thing understood sendeth forth *intelligible species*, that is, an *intelligible being seen*, which coming into the understanding makes us understand. I say not this as disapproving the use of universities; but because I am to speak hereafter of their office in a commonwealth, I must let you see on all occasions by the way, what things would be amended in them, amongst which the frequency of insignificant speech is one.

Chapter V
Of Reason, and Science

[1]   When a man *reasoneth*, he does nothing else but conceive a sum total from *addition* of parcels, or conceive a remainder from *subtraction* of one

sum from another; which (if it be done by words) is conceiving of the consequence of the names of all the parts to the name of the whole, or from the names of the whole and one part to the name of the other part. And though in some things (as in numbers) besides *adding* and *subtracting* men name other operations, as *multiplying* and *dividing*, yet they are the same; for multiplication is but adding together of things equal, and division, but subtracting of one thing as often as we can. These operations are not incident to numbers only, but to all manner of things that can be added together and taken one out of another. For as arithmeticians teach to add and subtract in *numbers*, so the geometricians teach the same in *lines*, *figures* (solid and superficial), *angles*, *proportions*, *times*, degrees of *swiftness*, *force*, *power*, and the like; the logicians teach the same in *consequences of words*, adding together *two names* to make an *affirmation*, and *two affirmations* to make a *syllogism*; and *many syllogisms* to make a *demonstration*; and from the *sum*, or *conclusion*, of a *syllogism* they subtract one *proposition* to find the other. Writers of politics add together *pactions* to find men's *duties*; and lawyers, *laws* and *facts*, to find what is *right* and *wrong* in the actions of private men. In sum, in what matter soever there is place for *addition* and *subtraction*, there also is place for *reason*; and where these have no place, there *reason* has nothing at all to do.

[2]   Out of all which we may define (that is to say determine) what that is which is meant by this word *reason*, when we reckon it amongst the faculties of the mind. For REASON, in this sense, is nothing but *reckoning* (that is, adding and subtracting) of the consequences of general names agreed upon for the *marking* and *signifying* of our thoughts; I say *marking* them when we reckon by ourselves, and *signifying*, when we demonstrate or approve our reckonings to other men.

[3]   And as in arithmetic, unpractised men must, and professors themselves may, often err and cast up false, so also in any other subject of reasoning, the ablest, most attentive, and most practised men may deceive themselves and infer false conclusions; not but that reason itself is always right reason, as well as arithmetic is a certain and infallible art, but no one man's reason, nor the reason of any one number of men, makes the certainty, no more than an account is therefore well cast up, because a great many men have unanimously approved it. And therefore, as when there is a controversy in an account, the parties must by their own accord set up for right reason the reason of some arbitrator or judge to whose sentence they will both stand, or their controversy must either come to blows or be undecided, for want of a right reason constituted by nature, so is it also in all debates of what kind soever. And when men that think themselves wiser than all others clamour and demand right reason for judge,

yet seek no more but that things should be determined by no other men's reason but their own, it is as intolerable in the society of men as it is in play, after trump is turned, to use for trump on every occasion that suit whereof they have most in their hand. For they do nothing else, that will have every of their passions, as it comes to bear sway in them, to be taken for right reason, and that in their own controversies, bewraying their want of right reason by the claim they lay to it.

[4] The use and end of reason is not the finding of the sum and truth of one or a few consequences, remote from the first definitions and settled significations of names, but to begin at these, and proceed from one consequence to another. For there can be no certainty of the last conclusion without a certainty of all those affirmations and negations on which it was grounded and inferred. As when a master of a family, in taking an account, casteth up the sums of all the bills of expense into one sum, and not regarding how each bill is summed up by those that give them in account, nor what it is he pays for, he advantages himself no more than if he allowed the account in gross, trusting to every of the accountants' skill and honesty, so also in reasoning of all other things, he that takes up conclusions on the trust of authors, and doth not fetch them from the first items in every reckoning (which are the significations of names settled by definitions), loses his labour, and does not know anything, but only believeth.

[5] When a man reckons without the use of words, which may be done in particular things (as when upon the sight of any one thing, we conjecture what was likely to have preceded, or is likely to follow upon it), if that which he thought likely to follow, follows not, or that which he thought likely to have preceded it, hath not preceded it, this is called ERROR, to which even the most prudent men are subject. But when we reason in words of general signification, and fall upon a general inference which is false, though it be commonly called *error*, it is indeed an ABSURDITY, or senseless speech. For error is but a deception, in presuming that somewhat is past, or to come, of which, though it were not past, or not to come, yet there was no impossibility discoverable. But when we make a general assertion, unless it be a true one, the possibility of it is inconceivable. And words whereby we conceive nothing but the sound are those we call *absurd*, *insignificant*, and *nonsense*. And therefore if a man should talk to me of a *round quadrangle*, or *accidents of bread in cheese*, or *immaterial substances*, or of *a free subject*, *a free will*, or any *free*, but free from being hindered by opposition, I should not say he were in an error, but that his words were without meaning, that is to say, absurd.

[6]   I have said before (in the second chapter [¶10]) that a man did excel all other animals in this faculty: that when he conceived anything whatsoever, he was apt to inquire the consequences of it, and what effects he could do with it. And now I add this other degree of the same excellence: that he can by words reduce the consequences he finds to general rules, called *theorems*, or *aphorisms*; that is, he can reason, or reckon, not only in number, but in all other things whereof one may be added unto or subtracted from another.

[7]   But this privilege is allayed by another, and that is by the privilege of absurdity, to which no living creature is subject but man only. And of men, those are of all most subject to it that profess philosophy. For it is most true that *Cicero* saith of them somewhere: that there can be nothing so absurd, but may be found in the books of philosophers. And the reason is manifest. For there is not one of them that begins his ratiocination from the definitions, or explications of the names they are to use; which is a method that hath been used only in geometry, whose conclusions have thereby been made indisputable.

[8]   The first cause of absurd conclusions I ascribe to the want of method, in that they begin not their ratiocination from definitions, that is, from settled significations of their words, as if they could cast account without knowing the value of the numeral words, *one, two*, and *three*.

[9]   And whereas all bodies enter into account upon diverse considerations (which I have mentioned in the precedent chapter [¶¶15–18]), these considerations being diversely named, diverse absurdities proceed from the confusion and unfit connexion of their names into assertions. And therefore,

[10]   The second cause of absurd assertions I ascribe to the giving of names of *bodies* to *accidents*, or of *accidents* to *bodies*, as they do that say *faith is infused* or *inspired*, when nothing can be *poured* or *breathed* into anything but body, and that *extension* is *body*, that *phantasms* are *spirits*, &c.

[11]   The third I ascribe to the giving of the names of the *accidents* of *bodies without us* to the *accidents* of our *own bodies*, as they do that say the *colour is in the body, the sound is in the air*, &c.

[12]   The fourth, to the giving of the names of *bodies* to *names* or *speeches*, as they do that say that *there be things universal*, that *a living creature is genus*, or *a general thing*, &c.

[13]   The fifth, to the giving of the names of *accidents* to *names* and *speeches*, as they do that say *the nature of a thing is its definition, a man's command is his will*, and the like.

[14]   The sixth, to the use of metaphors, tropes, and other rhetorical figures, instead of words proper. For though it be lawful to say (for example) in common speech *the way goeth, or leadeth hither, or thither, the proverb says this or that* (whereas ways cannot go, nor proverbs speak), yet in reckoning and seeking of truth such speeches are not to be admitted.

[15]   The seventh, to names that signify nothing, but are taken up and learned by rote from the schools, as *hypostatical, transubstantiate, consubstantiate, eternal-now,* and the like canting of schoolmen.

[16]   To him that can avoid these things it is not easy to fall into any absurdity, unless it be by the length of an account, wherein he may perhaps forget what went before. For all men by nature reason alike, and well, when they have good principles. For who is so stupid as both to mistake in geometry, and also to persist in it when another detects his error to him?

[17]   By this it appears that reason is not, as sense and memory, born with us, nor gotten by experience only, as prudence is, but attained by industry, first in apt imposing of names, and secondly by getting a good and orderly method in proceeding from the elements, which are names, to assertions made by connexion of one of them to another, and so to syllogisms, which are the connexions of one assertion to another, till we come to a knowledge of all the consequences of names appertaining to the subject in hand; and that is it men call SCIENCE. And whereas sense and memory are but knowledge of fact, which is a thing past and irrevocable, *Science* is the knowledge of consequences, and dependence of one fact upon another, by which, out of that we can presently do, we know how to do something else when we will, or the like, another time; because when we see how anything comes about, upon what causes, and by what manner, when the like causes come into our power, we see how to make it produce the like effects.

[18]   Children therefore are not endued with reason at all till they have attained the use of speech, but are called reasonable creatures for the possibility apparent of having the use of reason in time to come. And the most part of men, though they have the use of reasoning a little way, as in numbering to some degree, yet it serves them to little use in common life, in which they govern themselves, some better, some worse, according to their differences of experience, quickness of memory, and inclinations to several ends, but specially according to good or evil fortune, and the errors of one another. For as for *science*, or certain rules of their actions, they are so far from it that they know not what it is. Geometry they have thought conjuring; but for other sciences, they who have not been taught the beginnings and some progress in them, that they may see how

they be acquired and generated, are in this point like children, that having no thought of generation are made believe by the women that their brothers and sisters are not born, but found in the garden.

[19]   But yet they that have no *science* are in better and nobler condition with their natural prudence than men that by mis-reasoning, or by trusting them that reason wrong, fall upon false and absurd general rules. For ignorance of causes and of rules does not set men so far out of their way as relying on false rules, and taking for causes of what they aspire to, those that are not so, but rather causes of the contrary.

[20]   To conclude, the light of human minds is perspicuous words, but by exact definitions first snuffed and purged from ambiguity; *reason* is the *pace*; increase of *science*, the *way*; and the benefit of mankind, the *end*. And on the contrary, metaphors, and senseless and ambiguous words, are like *ignes fatui* [a fool's fire], and reasoning upon them is wandering amongst innumerable absurdities; and their end, contention and sedition, or contempt.

[21]   As much experience is *prudence*, so is much science *sapience*. For though we usually have one name of wisdom for them both, yet the Latins did always distinguish between *prudentia* and *sapientia*, ascribing the former to experience, the latter to science. But to make their difference appear more clearly, let us suppose one man endued with an excellent natural use and dexterity in handling his arms, and another to have added to that dexterity an acquired science of where he can offend or be offended by his adversary in every possible posture or guard; the ability of the former would be to the ability of the latter as prudence to sapience; both useful, but the latter infallible. But they that trusting only to the authority of books follow the blind blindly are like him that, trusting to the false rules of a master of fence, ventures presumptuously upon an adversary that either kills or disgraces him.

[22]   The signs of science are some, certain and infallible, some, uncertain. Certain, when he that pretendeth the science of anything can teach the same, that is to say, demonstrate the truth thereof perspicuously to another; uncertain, when only some particular events answer to his pretence, and upon many occasions prove so as he says they must. Signs of prudence are all uncertain, because to observe by experience and remember all circumstances that may alter the success is impossible. But in any business whereof a man has not infallible science to proceed by, to forsake his own natural judgment and be guided by general sentences read in authors (and subject to many exceptions) is a sign of folly, and generally scorned by the name of pedantry. And even of those men themselves that in councils of the commonwealth love to show their reading of

politics and history, very few do it in their domestic affairs, where their particular interest is concerned, having prudence enough for their private affairs; but in public they study more the reputation of their own wit than the success of another's business.

Chapter VI
Of the Interiour Beginnings of Voluntary Motions, Commonly Called the PASSIONS, and the Speeches by Which They Are Expressed

[1]   There be in animals two sorts of *motions* peculiar to them: one called *vital*, begun in generation and continued without interruption through their whole life, such as are the *course* of the *blood*, the *pulse*, the *breathing*, the *concoction*, *nutrition*, *excretion*, &c., to which motions there needs no help of imagination; the other is *animal motion*, otherwise called *voluntary motion*, as to *go*, to *speak*, to *move* any of our limbs, in such manner as is first fancied in our minds. That sense is motion in the organs and interior parts of man's body, caused by the action of the things we see, hear, &c, and that fancy is but the relics of the same motion, remaining after sense, has been already said in the first and second chapters. And because *going*, *speaking*, and the like voluntary motions depend always upon a precedent thought of *whither*, *which way*, and *what*, it is evident that the imagination is the first internal beginning of all voluntary motion. And although unstudied men do not conceive any motion at all to be there, where the thing moved is invisible, or the space it is moved in is (for the shortness of it) insensible, yet that doth not hinder, but that such motions are. For let a space be never so little, that which is moved over a greater space whereof that little one is part must first be moved over that. These small beginnings of motion within the body of man, before they appear in walking, speaking, striking, and other visible actions, are commonly called ENDEAVOUR.

[2]   This endeavour, when it is toward something which causes it, is called APPETITE or DESIRE, the latter being the general name, and the other oftentimes restrained to signify the desire of food, namely *hunger* and *thirst*. And when the endeavour is fromward something, it is generally called AVERSION. These words, *appetite* and *aversion*, we have from the *Latins*, and they both of them signify the motions, one of approaching, the other of retiring. So also do the Greek words for the same, which are *horme* and *aphorme*. For nature itself does often press upon men those truths which afterwards, when they look for somewhat beyond nature, they

stumble at. For the Schools find in mere appetite to go, or move, no actual motion at all; but because some motion they must acknowledge, they call it metaphorical motion, which is but an absurd speech; for though words may be called metaphorical, bodies and motions cannot.

[3]   That which men desire they are also said to LOVE, and to HATE those things for which they have aversion. So that desire and love are the same thing, save that by desire we always signify the absence of the object; by love, most commonly the presence of the same. So also by aversion we signify the absence, and by hate, the presence of the object.

[4]   Of appetites and aversions some are born with men, as appetite of food, appetite of excretion and exoneration (which may also and more properly be called aversions from somewhat they feel in their bodies) and some other appetites, not many. The rest, which are appetites of particular things, proceed from experience and trial of their effects upon themselves or other men. For of things we know not at all, or believe not to be, we can have no further desire than to taste and try. But aversion we have for things, not only which we know have hurt us, but also that we do not know whether they will hurt us or not.

[5]   Those things which we neither desire nor hate we are said to *contemn*, CONTEMPT being nothing else but an immobility or contumacy of the heart in resisting the action of certain things, and proceeding from that the heart is already moved otherwise, by other more potent objects, or from want of experience of them.

[6]   And because the constitution of a man's body is in continual mutation, it is impossible that all the same things should always cause in him the same appetites and aversions; much less can all men consent in the desire of almost any one and the same object.

[7]   But whatsoever is the object of any man's appetite or desire that is it which he for his part calleth *good*; and the object of his hate and aversion, *evil*; and of his contempt, *vile* and *inconsiderable*. For these words of good, evil, and contemptible are ever used with relation to the person that useth them, there being nothing simply and absolutely so, nor any common rule of good and evil to be taken from the nature of the objects themselves, but from the person of the man (where there is no commonwealth), or (in a commonwealth) from the person that representeth it, or from an arbitrator or judge whom men disagreeing shall by consent set up, and make his sentence the rule thereof.

[8]   The Latin tongue has two words whose significations approach to those of good and evil, but are not precisely the same; and those are *pulchrum* and *turpe*. Whereof the former signifies that which by some apparent signs promiseth good; and the latter, that which promiseth evil.

But in our tongue we have not so general names to express them by. But for *pulchrum* we say, in some things, *fair*; in others, *beautiful*, or *handsome*, or *gallant*, or *honourable*, or *comely*, or *amiable*; and for *turpe*, *foul*, *deformed*, *ugly*, *base*, *nauseous*, and the like, as the subject shall require; all which words, in their proper places, signify nothing else but the *mien*, or countenance, that promiseth good and evil. So that of good there be three kinds: good in the promise, that is *pulchrum*; good in effect, as the end desired, which is called *jucundum, delightful*; and good as the means, which is called *utile, profitable*; and as many of evil; for *evil* in promise is that they call *turpe*; evil in effect and end is *molestum, unpleasant, troublesome*; and evil in the means *inutile, unprofitable, hurtful*.

[9]   As in sense that which is really within us is (as I have said before) only motion caused by the action of external objects (but in appearance, to the sight, light and colour, to the ear, sound, to the nostril, odour, &c.), so when the action of the same object is continued from the eyes, ears, and other organs to the heart, the real effect there is nothing but motion or endeavour, which consisteth in appetite or aversion, to or from the object moving. But the appearance, or sense of that motion, is that we either call DELIGHT, or TROUBLE OF MIND.

[10]   This motion which is called appetite, and for the appearance of it *delight* and *pleasure*, seemeth to be a corroboration of vital motion, and a help thereunto; and therefore such things as caused delight were not improperly called *jucunda* (*a juvando*, from helping or fortifying); and the contrary, *molesta, offensive*, from hindering and troubling the motion vital.

[11]   *Pleasure*, therefore, or *delight*, is the appearance, or sense, of good; and *molestation* or *displeasure*, the appearance, or sense, of evil. And consequently all appetite, desire, and love is accompanied with some delight more or less; and all hatred and aversion, with more or less displeasure and offence.

[12]   Of pleasures or delights, some arise from the sense of an object present, and those may be called *pleasures of sense* (the word *sensual*, as it is used by those only that condemn them, having no place till there be laws). Of this kind are all onerations and exonerations of the body, as also all that is pleasant in the *sight, hearing, smell, taste, or touch*. Others arise from the expectation that proceeds from foresight of the end or consequence of things, whether those things in the sense please or displease. And these are *pleasures of the mind* of him that draweth those consequences, and are generally called Joy. In the like manner displeasures are some in the sense, and called PAIN; others in the expectation of consequences, and are called GRIEF.

[13]   These simple passions, called *appetite, desire, love, aversion, hate, joy,* and *grief,* have their names for diverse considerations diversified. As first, when they one succeed another, they are diversely called from the opinion men have of the likelihood of attaining what they desire. Secondly, from the object loved or hated. Thirdly, from the consideration of many of them together. Fourthly, from the alteration or succession itself.

[14]   For *appetite* with an opinion of attaining is called HOPE.

[15]   The same without such opinion, DESPAIR.

[16]   *Aversion* with opinion of *hurt* from the object, FEAR.

[17]   The same with hope of avoiding that hurt by resistance, COURAGE.

[18]   Sudden *courage,* ANGER.

[19]   Constant *hope,* CONFIDENCE of ourselves.

[20]   Constant *despair,* DIFFIDENCE of ourselves.

[21]   *Anger* for great hurt done to another, when we conceive the same to be done by injury, INDIGNATION.

[22]   *Desire* of good to another, BENEVOLENCE, GOOD WILL, CHARITY. If to man generally, GOOD NATURE.

[23]   *Desire* of riches, COVETOUSNESS, a name used always in signification of blame, because men contending for them are displeased with one another's attaining them, though the desire in itself be to be blamed or allowed, according to the means by which those riches are sought.

[24]   Desire of office or precedence, AMBITION, a name used also in the worse sense, for the reason before mentioned.

[25]   *Desire* of things that conduce but a little to our ends, and fear of things that are but of little hindrance, PUSILLANIMITY.

[26]   *Contempt* of little helps and hindrances, MAGNANIMITY.

[27]   *Magnanimity* in danger of death or wounds, VALOUR, FORTITUDE.

[28]   *Magnanimity* in the use of riches, LIBERALITY.

[29]   *Pusillanimity,* in the same, WRETCHEDNESS, MISERABLENESS, or PARSIMONY; as it is liked or disliked.

[30]   *Love* of persons for society, KINDNESS.

[31]   *Love* of persons for pleasing the sense only, NATURAL LUST.

[32]   *Love* of the same, acquired from rumination, that is, imagination of pleasure past, LUXURY.

[33]   *Love* of one singularly, with desire to be singularly beloved, THE PASSION OF LOVE. The same, with fear that the love is not mutual, JEALOUSY.

[34]   *Desire,* by doing hurt to another, to make him condemn some fact of his own, REVENGEFULNESS.

[35] *Desire* to know why, and how, Curiosity, such as is in no living creature but *man*, so that man is distinguished, not only by his reason, but also by this singular passion from other *animals*, in whom the appetite of food and other pleasures of sense by predominance take away the care of knowing causes, which is a lust of the mind that by a perseverance of delight in the continual and indefatigable generation of knowledge exceedeth the short vehemence of any carnal pleasure.

[36] *Fear* of power invisible, feigned by the mind, or imagined from tales publicly allowed, Religion; not allowed, Superstition. And when the power imagined is truly such as we imagine, True Religion.

[37] *Fear* without the apprehension of why or what, Panic Terror, called so from the fables, that make *Pan* the author of them; whereas in truth there is always in him that so feareth first, some apprehension of the cause, though the rest run away by example, every one supposing his fellow to know why. And therefore this passion happens to none but in a throng, or multitude of people.

[38] *Joy* from apprehension of novelty, Admiration; proper to man, because it excites the appetite of knowing the cause.

[39] *Joy* arising from imagination of a man's own power and ability is that exultation of the mind which is called Glorying; which, if grounded upon the experience of his own former actions, is the same with *confidence*; but if grounded on the flattery of others, or only supposed by himself, for delight in the consequences of it, is called Vainglory; which name is properly given, because a well grounded *confidence* begetteth attempt, whereas the supposing of power does not, and is therefore rightly called *vain*.

[40] *Grief* from opinion of want of power is called Dejection of mind.

[41] The *vain-glory* which consisteth in the feigning or supposing of abilities in ourselves (which we know are not) is most incident to young men, and nourished by the histories or fictions of gallant persons; and is corrected oftentimes by age and employment.

[42] *Sudden glory* is the passion which maketh those *grimaces* called Laughter, and is caused either by some sudden act of their own that pleaseth them, or by the apprehension of some deformed thing in another, by comparison whereof they suddenly applaud themselves. And it is incident most to them that are conscious of the fewest abilities in themselves, who are forced to keep themselves in their own favour by observing the imperfections of other men. And therefore much laughter at the defects of others is a sign of pusillanimity. For of great minds one of the proper works is to help and free others from scorn, and compare themselves only with the most able.

[43]   On the contrary, *sudden dejection* is the passion that causeth WEEPING, and is caused by such accidents as suddenly take away some vehement hope, or some prop of their power; and they are most subject to it that rely principally on helps external, such as are women and children. Therefore some weep for the loss of friends; others for their unkindness; others for the sudden stop made to their thoughts of revenge, by reconciliation. But in all cases, both laughter and weeping are sudden motions, custom taking them both away. For no man laughs at old jests, or weeps for an old calamity.

[44]   *Grief* for the discovery of some defect of ability is SHAME, or the passion that discovereth itself in BLUSHING, and consisteth in the apprehension of some thing dishonourable; and in young men is a sign of the love of good reputation and commendable; in old men it is a sign of the same, but because it comes too late, not commendable.

[45]   The *contempt* of good reputation is called IMPUDENCE.

[46]   *Grief* for the calamity of another is PITY, and ariseth from the imagination that the like calamity may befall himself; and therefore is called also COMPASSION, and in the phrase of this present time a FELLOW-FEELING; and therefore for calamity arriving from great wickedness, the best men have the least pity; and for the same calamity, those have least pity that think themselves least obnoxious to the same.

[47]   *Contempt*, or little sense, of the calamity of others is that which men call CRUELTY, proceeding from security of their own fortune. For, that any man should take pleasure in other men's great harms without other end of his own I do not conceive it possible.

[48]   *Grief* for the success of a competitor in wealth, honour, or other good, if it be joined with endeavour to enforce our own abilities to equal or exceed him, is called EMULATION; but joined with endeavour to supplant or hinder a competitor, ENVY.

[49]   When in the mind of man appetites and aversions, hopes and fears, concerning one and the same thing arise alternately, and diverse good and evil consequences of the doing or omitting the thing propounded come successively into our thoughts, so that sometimes we have an appetite to it, sometimes an aversion from it, sometimes hope to be able to do it, sometimes despair or fear to attempt it, the whole sum of desires, aversions, hopes and fears, continued till the thing be either done or thought impossible, is that we call DELIBERATION.

[50]   Therefore of things past, there is no *deliberation*, because manifestly impossible to be changed; nor of things known to be impossible, or thought so, because men know or think such deliberation vain. But of things impossible which we think possible, we may deliberate, not

knowing it is in vain. And it is called *deliberation*, because it is a putting an end to the *liberty* we had of doing or omitting, according to our own appetite or aversion.

[51]   This alternate succession of appetites, aversions, hopes and fears is no less in other living creatures than in man; and therefore beasts also deliberate.

[52]   Every *deliberation* is then said to *end*, when that whereof they deliberate is either done or thought impossible, because till then we retain the liberty of doing or omitting, according to our appetite or aversion.

[53]   In deliberation, the last appetite or aversion immediately adhering to the action, or to the omission thereof, is that we call the WILL, the act (not the faculty) of *willing*. And beasts that have *deliberation* must necessarily also have *will*. The definition of the *will* given commonly by the Schools, that it is a *rational appetite*, is not good. For if it were, then could there be no voluntary act against reason. For a *voluntary act* is that which proceedeth from the *will*, and no other. But if instead of a rational appetite, we shall say an appetite resulting from a precedent deliberation, then the definition is the same that I have given here. *Will* therefore *is the last appetite in deliberating*. And though we say in common discourse, a man had a will once to do a thing, that nevertheless he forbore to do, yet that is properly but an inclination, which makes no action voluntary; because the action depends not of it, but of the last inclination or appetite. For if the intervenient appetites make any action voluntary, then by the same reason all intervenient aversions should make the same action involuntary; and so one and the same action should be both voluntary and involuntary.

[54]   By this it is manifest that not only actions that have their beginning from covetousness, ambition, lust, or other appetites to the thing propounded, but also those that have their beginning from aversion or fear of those consequences that follow the omission are *voluntary actions*.

[55]   The forms of speech by which the passions are expressed are partly the same and partly different from those by which we express our thoughts. And first, generally all passions may be expressed *indicatively*, as *I love, I fear, I joy, I deliberate, I will, I command*; but some of them have particular expressions by themselves, which nevertheless are not affirmations (unless it be when they serve to make other inferences besides that of the passion they proceed from). Deliberation is expressed *subjunctively*, which is a speech proper to signify suppositions, with their consequences, as *if this be done, then this will follow*, and differs not from

the language of reasoning, save that reasoning is in general words, but deliberation for the most part is of particulars. The language of desire and aversion is *imperative*, as *do this, forbear that*, which, when the party is obliged to do or forbear, is *command*; otherwise *prayer*, or else *counsel*. The language of vain-glory, of indignation, pity and revengefulness, *optative*; but of the desire to know there is a peculiar expression, called *interrogative*, as *what is it, when shall it, how is it done*, and *why so?* other language of the passions I find none; for cursing, swearing, reviling, and the like, do not signify as speech, but as the actions of a tongue accustomed.

[56]   These forms of speech, I say, are expressions, or voluntary significations, of our passions; but certain signs they be not, because they may be used arbitrarily, whether they that use them have such passions or not. The best signs of passions present are in the countenance, motions of the body, actions, and ends or aims which we otherwise know the man to have.

[57]   And because in deliberation the appetites and aversions are raised by foresight of the good and evil consequences and sequels of the action whereof we deliberate, the good or evil effect thereof dependeth on the foresight of a long chain of consequences, of which very seldom any man is able to see to the end. But for so far as a man seeth, if the good in those consequences be greater than the evil, the whole chain is that which writers call *apparent* or *seeming good*. And contrarily, when the evil exceedeth the good, the whole is *apparent* or *seeming evil*; so that he who hath by experience or reason the greatest and surest prospect of consequences deliberates best himself, and is able, when he will, to give the best counsel unto others.

[58]   *Continual success* in obtaining those things which a man from time to time desireth, that is to say, continual prospering, is that men call FELICITY; I mean the felicity of this life. For there is no such thing as perpetual tranquillity of mind, while we live here; because life itself is but motion, and can never be without desire, nor without fear, no more than without sense. What kind of felicity God hath ordained to them that devoutly honour Him, a man shall no sooner know than enjoy, being joys that now are as incomprehensible as the word of school-men *beatifical vision* is unintelligible.

[59]   The form of speech whereby men signify their opinion of the goodness of anything is PRAISE. That whereby they signify the power and greatness of anything is MAGNIFYING. And that whereby they signify the opinion they have of a man's felicity is by the Greeks called *makarismos*,

for which we have no name in our tongue. And thus much is sufficient for the present purpose, to have been said of the Passions.

Chapter XIII
Of the Natural Condition *of* Mankind, *As Concerning Their Felicity, and Misery*

[1]   Nature hath made men so equal in the faculties of body and mind as that, though there be found one man sometimes manifestly stronger in body or of quicker mind than another, yet when all is reckoned together the difference between man and man is not so considerable as that one man can thereupon claim to himself any benefit to which another may not pretend as well as he. For as to the strength of body, the weakest has strength enough to kill the strongest, either by secret machination, or by confederacy with others that are in the same danger with himself.

[2]   And as to the faculties of the mind – setting aside the arts grounded upon words, and especially that skill of proceeding upon general and infallible rules called science (which very few have, and but in few things), as being not a native faculty (born with us), nor attained (as prudence) while we look after somewhat else – I find yet a greater equality amongst men than that of strength. For prudence is but experience, which equal time equally bestows on all men in those things they equally apply themselves unto. That which may perhaps make such equality incredible is but a vain conceit of one's own wisdom, which almost all men think they have in a greater degree than the vulgar, that is, than all men but themselves and a few others whom, by fame or for concurring with themselves, they approve. For such is the nature of men that howsoever they may acknowledge many others to be more witty, or more eloquent, or more learned, yet they will hardly believe there be many so wise as themselves. For they see their own wit at hand, and other men's at a distance. But this proveth rather that men are in that point equal, than unequal. For there is not ordinarily a greater sign of the equal distribution of anything than that every man is contented with his share.

[3]   From this equality of ability ariseth equality of hope in the attaining of our ends. And therefore, if any two men desire the same thing, which nevertheless they cannot both enjoy, they become enemies; and in the way to their end, which is principally their own conservation, and sometimes their delectation only, endeavour to destroy or subdue one another. And from hence it comes to pass that, where an invader hath no

more to fear than another man's single power, if one plant, sow, build, or possess a convenient seat, others may probably be expected to come pre-pared with forces united, to dispossess and deprive him, not only of the fruit of his labour, but also of his life or liberty. And the invader again is in the like danger of another.

[4]   And from this diffidence of one another, there is no way for any man to secure himself so reasonable as anticipation, that is, by force or wiles to master the persons of all men he can, so long till he see no other power great enough to endanger him. And this is no more than his own conservation requireth, and is generally allowed. Also, because there be some that taking pleasure in contemplating their own power in the acts of conquest, which they pursue farther than their security requires, if others (that otherwise would be glad to be at ease within modest bounds) should not by invasion increase their power, they would not be able, long time, by standing only on their defence, to subsist. And by consequence, such augmentation of dominion over men being necessary to a man's con-servation, it ought to be allowed him.

[5]   Again, men have no pleasure, but on the contrary a great deal of grief, in keeping company where there is no power able to over-awe them all. For every man looketh that his companion should value him at the same rate he sets upon himself, and upon all signs of contempt, or under-valuing, naturally endeavours, as far as he dares (which amongst them that have no common power to keep them in quiet, is far enough to make them destroy each other), to extort a greater value from his contemners, by damage, and from others, by the example.

[6]   So that in the nature of man we find three principal causes of quarrel: first, competition; secondly, diffidence; thirdly, glory.

[7]   The first maketh men invade for gain; the second, for safety; and the third, for reputation. The first use violence to make themselves masters of other men's persons, wives, children, and cattle; the second, to defend them; the third, for trifles, as a word, a smile, a different opinion, and any other sign of undervalue, either direct in their persons, or by reflection in their kindred, their friends, their nation, their profession, or their name.

[8]   Hereby it is manifest that during the time men live without a common power to keep them all in awe, they are in that condition which is called war, and such a war as is of every man against every man. For WAR consisteth not in battle only, or the act of fighting, but in a tract of time wherein the will to contend by battle is sufficiently known. And therefore, the notion of *time* is to be considered in the nature of war, as it is in the nature of weather. For as the nature of foul weather lieth not in

a shower or two of rain, but in an inclination thereto of many days together, so the nature of war consisteth not in actual fighting, but in the known disposition thereto during all the time there is no assurance to the contrary. All other time is PEACE.

[9]   Whatsoever therefore is consequent to a time of war, where every man is enemy to every man, the same is consequent to the time wherein men live without other security than what their own strength and their own invention shall furnish them withal. In such condition there is no place for industry, because the fruit thereof is uncertain, and consequently, no culture of the earth, no navigation, nor use of the commodities that may be imported by sea, no commodious building, no instruments of moving and removing such things as require much force, no knowledge of the face of the earth, no account of time, no arts, no letters, no society, and which is worst of all, continual fear and danger of violent death, and the life of man, solitary, poor, nasty, brutish, and short.

[10]   It may seem strange, to some man that has not well weighed these things, that nature should thus dissociate, and render men apt to invade and destroy one another. And he may, therefore, not trusting to this inference made from the passions, desire perhaps to have the same confirmed by experience. Let him therefore consider with himself – when taking a journey, he arms himself, and seeks to go well accompanied; when going to sleep, he locks his doors; when even in his house, he locks his chests; and this when he knows there be laws, and public officers, armed, to revenge all injuries shall be done him – what opinion he has of his fellow subjects, when he rides armed; of his fellow citizens, when he locks his doors; and of his children and servants, when he locks his chests. Does he not there as much accuse mankind by his actions, as I do by my words? But neither of us accuse man's nature in it. The desires and other passions of man are in themselves no sin. No more are the actions that proceed from those passions, till they know a law that forbids them – which till laws be made they cannot know. Nor can any law be made, till they have agreed upon the person that shall make it.

[11]   It may peradventure be thought, there was never such a time nor condition of war as this; and I believe it was never generally so, over all the world. But there are many places where they live so now. For the savage people in many places of *America* (except the government of small families, the concord whereof dependeth on natural lust) have no government at all, and live at this day in that brutish manner as I said before. Howsoever, it may be perceived what manner of life there would be where there were no common power to fear, by the manner of life which

men that have formerly lived under a peaceful government use to degenerate into, in a civil war.

[12]   But though there had never been any time wherein particular men were in a condition of war one against another, yet in all times kings and persons of sovereign authority, because of their independency, are in continual jealousies and in the state and posture of gladiators, having their weapons pointing and their eyes fixed on one another, that is, their forts, garrisons, and guns upon the frontiers of their kingdoms, and continual spies upon their neighbours, which is a posture of war. But because they uphold thereby the industry of their subjects, there does not follow from it that misery which accompanies the liberty of particular men.

[13]   To this war of every man against every man, this also is consequent: that nothing can be unjust. The notions of right and wrong, justice and injustice, have there no place. Where there is no common power, there is no law; where no law, no injustice. Force and fraud are in war the two cardinal virtues. Justice and injustice are none of the faculties neither of the body, nor mind. If they were, they might be in a man that were alone in the world, as well as his senses and passions. They are qualities that relate to men in society, not in solitude. It is consequent also to the same condition that there be no propriety, no dominion, no *mine* and *thine* distinct, but only that to be every man's that he can get, and for so long as he can keep it. And thus much for the ill condition which man by mere nature is actually placed in, though with a possibility to come out of it, consisting partly in the passions, partly in his reason.

[14]   The passions that incline men to peace are fear of death, desire of such things as are necessary to commodious living, and a hope by their industry to obtain them. And reason suggesteth convenient articles of peace, upon which men may be drawn to agreement. These articles are they which otherwise are called the Laws of Nature, whereof I shall speak more particularly in the two following chapters.

Chapter XIV
Of the First and Second Natural Laws and of Contracts

[1]   The RIGHT OF NATURE, which writers commonly call *jus naturale*, is the liberty each man hath to use his own power, as he will himself, for the preservation of his own nature, that is to say, of his own life, and consequently of doing anything which, in his own judgment and reason, he shall conceive to be the aptest means thereunto.

[2]   By LIBERTY is understood, according to the proper signification of the word, the absence of external impediments, which impediments may oft take away part of a man's power to do what he would, but cannot hinder him from using the power left him, according as his judgment and reason shall dictate to him.

[3]   A LAW OF NATURE (*lex naturalis*) is a precept or general rule, found out by reason, by which a man is forbidden to do that which is destructive of his life or taketh away the means of preserving the same, and to omit that by which he thinketh it may be best preserved. For though they that speak of this subject use to confound *jus* and *lex* (*right* and *law*), yet they ought to be distinguished, because RIGHT consisteth in liberty to do or to forbear, whereas LAW determineth and bindeth to one of them; so that law and right differ as much as obligation and liberty, which in one and the same matter are inconsistent.

[4]   And because the condition of man (as hath been declared in the precedent chapter) is a condition of war of everyone against everyone (in which case everyone is governed by his own reason and there is nothing he can make use of that may not be a help unto him in preserving his life against his enemies), it followeth that in such a condition every man has a right to everything, even to one another's body. And therefore, as long as this natural right of every man to everything endureth, there can be no security to any man (how strong or wise soever he be) of living out the time which nature ordinarily alloweth men to live. And consequently it is a precept, or general rule, of reason *that every man ought to endeavour peace, as far as he has hope of obtaining it, and when he cannot obtain it, that he may seek and use all helps and advantages of war.* The first branch of which rule containeth the first and fundamental law of nature, which is *to seek peace, and follow it.* The second, the sum of the right of nature, which is *by all means we can, to defend ourselves.*

[5]   From this fundamental law of nature, by which men are commanded to endeavour peace, is derived this second law: *that a man be willing, when others are so too, as far-forth as for peace and defence of himself he shall think it necessary, to lay down this right to all things, and be contented with so much liberty against other men, as he would allow other men against himself.* For as long as every man holdeth this right of doing anything he liketh, so long are all men in the condition of war. But if other men will not lay down their right as well as he, then there is no reason for anyone to divest himself of his; for that were to expose himself to prey (which no man is bound to), rather than to dispose himself to peace. This is that law of the Gospel: "whatsoever you require that others should do to you, that do ye to them." And that law of all men: *quod tibi fieri non vis, alteri ne feceris.*

[6]   To *lay down* a man's *right* to anything is to *divest* himself of the *liberty* of hindering another of the benefit of his own right to the same. For he that renounceth or passeth away his right giveth not to any other man a right which he had not before (because there is nothing to which every man had not right by nature), but only standeth out of his way, that he may enjoy his own original right without hindrance from him, not without hindrance from another. So that the effect which redoundeth to one man by another man's defect of right is but so much diminution of impediments to the use of his own right original.

[7]   Right is laid aside either by simply renouncing it or by transferring it to another. By *simply* RENOUNCING, when he cares not to whom the benefit thereof redoundeth. By TRANSFERRING, when he intendeth the benefit thereof to some certain person or persons. And when a man hath in either manner abandoned or granted away his right, then is he said to be OBLIGED or BOUND not to hinder those to whom such right is granted or abandoned from the benefit of it; and [it is said] that he *ought*, and it is his DUTY, not to make void that voluntary act of his own, and that such hindrance is INJUSTICE, and INJURY, as being *sine jure* [without right], the right being before renounced or transferred. So that *injury* or *injustice*, in the controversies of the world, is somewhat like to that which in the disputations of scholars is called absurdity. For as it is there called an *absurdity* to contradict what one maintained in the beginning, so in the world it is called injustice and injury voluntarily to undo that which from the beginning he had voluntarily done.

The way by which a man either simply renounceth or transferreth his right is a declaration, or signification by some voluntary and sufficient sign or signs, that he doth so renounce or transfer, or hath so renounced or transferred the same, to him that accepteth it. And these signs are either words only, or actions only, or (as it happeneth most often) both words and actions. And the same are the BONDS by which men are bound and obliged, bonds that have their strength, not from their own nature (for nothing is more easily broken than a man's word) but from fear of some evil consequence upon the rupture.

[8]   Whensoever a man transferreth his right or renounceth it, it is either in consideration of some right reciprocally transferred to himself or for some other good he hopeth for thereby. For it is a voluntary act, and of the voluntary acts of every man the object is some *good to himself*. And therefore there be some rights which no man can be understood by any words or other signs to have abandoned or transferred. As, first, a man cannot lay down the right of resisting them that assault him by force, to take away his life, because he cannot be understood to aim thereby at any

good to himself. [Second], the same may be said of wounds, and chains, and imprisonment, both because there is no benefit consequent to such patience (as there is to the patience of suffering another to be wounded or imprisoned), as also because a man cannot tell, when he seeth men proceed against him by violence, whether they intend his death or not. [Third] and lastly, the motive and end for which this renouncing and transferring of right is introduced, is nothing else but the security of a man's person, in his life and in the means of so preserving life as not to be weary of it. And therefore if a man by words or other signs seem to despoil himself of the end for which those signs were intended, he is not to be understood as if he meant it, or that it was his will, but that he was ignorant of how such words and actions were to be interpreted.

[9]   The mutual transferring of right is that which men call CONTRACT.

[10]   There is difference between transferring of right to the thing and transferring (or tradition, that is, delivery) of the thing itself. For the thing may be delivered together with the translation of the right (as in buying and selling with ready money, or exchange of goods or lands); and it may be delivered some time after.

[11]   Again, one of the contractors may deliver the thing contracted for on his part, and leave the other to perform his part at some determinate time after (and in the meantime be trusted); and then the contract on his part is called PACT, or COVENANT; or both parts may contract now, to perform hereafter, in which cases he that is to perform in time to come, being trusted, his performance is called *keeping of promise*, or *faith*, and the failing of performance (if it be voluntary) *violation of faith*.

[12]   When the transferring of right is not mutual, but one of the parties transferreth in hope to gain thereby friendship or service from another (or from his friends), or in hope to gain the reputation of charity or magnanimity, or to deliver his mind from the pain of compassion, or in hope of reward in heaven, this is not contract, but GIFT, FREE-GIFT, GRACE, which words signify one and the same thing.

[13]   Signs of contract are either *express* or *by inference*. Express are words spoken with understanding of what they signify; and such words are either of the time *present* or *past* (as, *I give, I grant, I have given, I have granted, I will that this be yours*), or of the future (as, *I will give, I will grant*), which words of the future are called PROMISE.

[14]   Signs by inference are: sometimes the consequence of words, sometimes the consequence of silence; sometimes the consequence of actions, sometimes the consequence of forbearing an action; and generally a sign by inference of any contract is whatsoever sufficiently argues the will of the contractor.

[15]   Words alone, if they be of the time to come, and contain a bare promise, are an insufficient sign of a free-gift, and therefore not obligatory. For if they be of the time to come (as, *tomorrow I will give*), they are a sign I have not given yet, and consequently that my right is not transferred, but remaineth till I transfer it by some other act. But if the words be of the time present or past (as, *I have given, or do give to be delivered tomorrow*), then is my tomorrow's right given away today; and that by the virtue of the words, though there were no other argument of my will. And there is a great difference in the signification of these words: *volo hoc tuum esse cras* and *cras dabo* (that is, between *I will that this be thine tomorrow* and *I will give it thee tomorrow*); for the word *I will* in the former manner of speech signifies an act of the will present, but in the latter it signifies a promise of an act of the will to come; and therefore the former words, being of the present, transfer a future right; the latter, that be of the future, transfer nothing.

But if there be other signs of the will to transfer a right besides words, then though the gift be free, yet may the right be understood to pass by words of the future (as, if a man propound a prize to him that comes first to the end of a race, the gift is free, and though the words be of the future, yet the right passeth; for if he would not have his words so be understood, he should not have let them run).

[16]   In contracts the right passeth, not only where the words are of the time present or past, but also where they are of the future, because all contract is mutual translation, or change of right; and therefore he that promiseth only (because he hath already received the benefit for which he promiseth) is to be understood as if he intended the right should pass; for unless he had been content to have his words so understood, the other would not have performed his part first. And for that cause, in buying and selling, and other acts of contract, a promise is equivalent to a covenant, and therefore obligatory.

[17]   He that performeth first in the case of a contract is said to MERIT that which he is to receive by the performance of the other, and he hath it as *due*. Also when a prize is propounded to many, which is to be given to him only that winneth (or money is thrown amongst many, to be enjoyed by them that catch it), though this be a free gift, yet so to win (or so to catch) is to *merit*, and to have it as DUE. For the right is transferred in the propounding of the prize (and in throwing down the money), though it be not determined to whom but by the event of the contention.

But there is between these two sorts of merit, this difference: that in contract I merit by virtue of my own power, and the contractor's need; but in this case of free gift, I am enabled to merit only by the benignity of the giver; in contract I merit at the contractor's hand that he should depart with his right; in this case of gift, I merit not that the giver should part with his right, but that when he has parted with it, it should be mine rather than another's.

And this I think to be the meaning of that distinction of the Schools between *meritum congrui* and *meritum condigni*. For God Almighty having promised Paradise to those men (hoodwinked with carnal desires) that can walk through this world according to the precepts and limits prescribed by him, they say: he that shall so walk shall merit Paradise *ex congruo*. But because no man can demand a right to it, by his own righteousness or any other power in himself, but by the free grace of God only, they say: no man can merit Paradise *ex condigno*. This, I say, I think is the meaning of that distinction; but because disputers do not agree upon the signification of their own terms of art longer than it serves their turn, I will not affirm anything of their meaning. Only this I say: when a gift is given indefinitely, as a prize to be contended for, he that winneth meriteth, and may claim the prize as due.

[18] If a covenant be made wherein neither of the parties perform presently, but trust one another, in the condition of mere nature (which is a condition of war of every man against every man) upon any reasonable suspicion it is void; but if there be a common power set over them both, with right and force sufficient to compel performance, it is not void. For he that performeth first has no assurance the other will perform after, because the bonds of words are too weak to bridle men's ambition, avarice, anger, and other passions, without the fear of some coercive power; which in the condition of mere nature, where all men are equal and judges of the justness of their own fears, cannot possibly be supposed. And therefore, he which performeth first does but betray himself to his enemy, contrary to the right (he can never abandon) of defending his life and means of living.

[19] But in a civil estate, where there is a power set up to constrain those that would otherwise violate their faith, that fear is no more reasonable; and for that cause, he which by the covenant is to perform first is obliged so to do.

[20] The cause of fear which maketh such a covenant invalid must be always something arising after the covenant made (as some new fact or other sign of the will not to perform), else it cannot make the covenant void. For that which could not hinder a man from promising, ought not to be admitted as a hindrance of performing.

[21] He that transferreth any right transferreth the means of enjoying it, as far as lieth in his power. As he that selleth land is understood to

transfer the herbage and whatsoever grows upon it; nor can he that sells a mill turn away the stream that drives it. And they that give to a man the right of government in sovereignty are understood to give him the right of levying money to maintain soldiers, and of appointing magistrates for the administration of justice.

[22]   To make covenants with brute beasts is impossible because, not understanding our speech, they understand not, nor accept of, any translation of right, nor can translate any right to another; and without mutual acceptation, there is no covenant.

[23]   To make covenant with God is impossible, but by mediation of such as God speaketh to (either by revelation supernatural or by his lieutenants that govern under him and in his name); for otherwise we know not whether our covenants be accepted or not. And therefore, they that vow anything [OL (*Opera latina*, the collection of Hobbes's Latin works): to God] contrary to any law of nature vow in vain, as being a thing unjust to pay such vow. And if it be a thing commanded by the law of nature, [OL: they vow in vain;] it is not the vow, but the law that binds them.

[24]   The matter or subject of a covenant is always something that falleth under deliberation (for to covenant is an act of the will; that is to say an act, and the last act, of deliberation) and is therefore always understood to be something to come, and which is judged possible for him that covenanteth to perform.

[25]   And therefore, to promise that which is known to be impossible is no covenant. But if that prove impossible afterwards which before was thought possible, the covenant is valid and bindeth, though not to the thing itself, yet to the value; or, if that also be impossible, to the unfeigned endeavour of performing as much as is possible (for to more no man can be obliged).

[26]   Men are freed of their covenants two ways: by performing or by being forgiven. For performance is the natural end of obligation; and forgiveness, the restitution of liberty (as being a retransferring of that right in which the obligation consisted).

[27]   Covenants entered into by fear, in the condition of mere nature, are obligatory. For example, if I covenant to pay a ransom, or service, for my life, to an enemy, I am bound by it. For it is a contract wherein one receiveth the benefit of life; the other is to receive money, or service, for it; and consequently, where no other law (as in the condition of mere nature) forbiddeth the performance, the covenant is valid. Therefore prisoners of war, if trusted with the payment of their ransom, are obliged to pay it; and if a weaker prince make a disadvantageous peace with a stronger, for fear, he is bound to keep it, unless (as hath been said before

[¶20]) there ariseth some new and just cause of fear, to renew the war. And even in commonwealths, if I be forced to redeem myself from a thief by promising him money, I am bound to pay it, till the civil law discharge me. For whatsoever I may lawfully do without obligation, the same I may lawfully covenant to do through fear; and what I lawfully covenant, I cannot lawfully break.

[28]   A former covenant makes void a later. For a man that hath passed away his right to one man today, hath it not to pass tomorrow to another; and therefore the later promise passeth no right, but is null.

[29]   A covenant not to defend myself from force by force is always void. For (as I have showed before) no man can transfer or lay down his right to save himself from death, wounds, and imprisonment (the avoiding whereof is the only end of laying down any right), and therefore the promise of not resisting force in no covenant transferreth any right, nor is obliging. For though a man may covenant thus *unless I do so, or so, kill me*, he cannot covenant thus *unless I do so, or so, I will not resist you, when you come to kill me*. For man by nature chooseth the lesser evil, which is danger of death in resisting, rather than the greater, which is certain and present death in not resisting. And this is granted to be true by all men, in that they lead criminals to execution and prison with armed men, notwithstanding that such criminals have consented to the law by which they are condemned.

[30]   A covenant to accuse oneself, without assurance of pardon, is likewise invalid. For in the condition of nature, where every man is judge, there is no place for accusation; and in the civil state the accusation is followed with punishment, which being force, a man is not obliged not to resist. The same is also true of the accusation of those by whose condemnation a man falls into misery (as, of a father, wife, or benefactor). For the testimony of such an accuser, if it be not willingly given, is presumed to be corrupted by nature, and therefore not to be received; and where a man's testimony is not to be credited, he is not bound to give it. Also accusations upon torture are not to be reputed as testimonies. For torture is to be used but as means of conjecture and light in the further examination and search of truth; and what is in that case confessed tendeth to the ease of him that is tortured, not to the informing of the torturers, and therefore ought not to have the credit of a sufficient testimony; for whether he deliver himself by true or false accusation, he does it by the right of preserving his own life.

[31]   The force of words being (as I have formerly noted) too weak to hold men to the performance of their covenants, there are in man's nature

but two imaginable helps to strengthen it. And those are either a fear of the consequence of breaking their word, or a glory or pride in appearing not to need to break it. This latter is a generosity too rarely found to be presumed on, especially in the pursuers of wealth, command, or sensual pleasure (which are the greatest part of mankind).

The passion to be reckoned upon is fear, whereof there be two very general objects: one, the power of spirits invisible; the other, the power of those men they shall therein offend. Of these two, though the former be the greater power, yet the fear of the latter is commonly the greater fear. The fear of the former is in every man his own religion, which hath place in the nature of man before civil society. The latter hath not so, at least not place enough to keep men to their promises, because in the condition of mere nature the inequality of power is not discerned but by the event of battle.

So that before the time of civil society, or in the interruption thereof by war, there is nothing can strengthen a covenant of peace agreed on, against the temptations of avarice, ambition, lust, or other strong desire, but the fear of that invisible power which they every one worship as God and fear as a revenger of their perfidy. All therefore that can be done between two men not subject to civil power is to put one another to swear by the God he feareth; which *swearing*, or OATH, is a *form of speech, added to a promise, by which he that promiseth signifieth that unless he perform, he renounceth the mercy of his God, or calleth to him for vengeance on himself.* Such was the heathen form *Let* Jupiter *kill me else, as I kill this beast.* So is our form *I shall do thus, and thus, so help me God.* And this, with the rites and ceremonies which everyone useth in his own religion, that the fear of breaking faith might be the greater.

[32]   By this it appears that an oath taken according to any other form or rite than his that sweareth is in vain, and no oath, and that there is no swearing by anything which the swearer thinks not God. For though men have sometimes used to swear by their kings, for fear or flattery, yet they would have it thereby understood they attributed to them divine honour. And that swearing unnecessarily by God is but prophaning of his name, and swearing by other things, as men do in common discourse, is not swearing, but an impious custom, gotten by too much vehemence of talking.

[33]   It appears also that the oath adds nothing to the obligation. For a covenant, if lawful, binds in the sight of God without the oath as much as with it; if unlawful, bindeth not at all, though it be confirmed with an oath.

Chapter XV
Of Other Laws of Nature

[1]   From that law of nature by which we are obliged to transfer to another such rights as, being retained, hinder the peace of mankind, there followeth a third, which is this *that men perform their covenants made*, without which covenants are in vain, and but empty words, and the right of all men to all things remaining, we are still in the condition of war.

[2]   And in this law of nature consisteth the fountain and original of JUSTICE. For where no covenant hath preceded, there hath no right been transferred, and every man has right to everything; and consequently, no action can be unjust. But when a covenant is made, then to break it is *unjust*; and the definition of INJUSTICE is no other than *the not performance of covenant*. And whatsoever is not unjust, is *just*.

[3]   But because covenants of mutual trust where there is a fear of not performance on either part (as hath been said in the former chapter [xiv, 18–20]) are invalid, though the original of justice be the making of covenants, yet injustice actually there can be none till the cause of such fear be taken away, which, while men are in the natural condition of war, cannot be done. Therefore, before the names of just and unjust can have place, there must be some coercive power to compel men equally to the performance of their covenants, by the terror of some punishment greater than the benefit they expect by the breach of their covenant, and to make good that propriety which by mutual contract men acquire, in recompense of the universal right they abandon; and such power there is none before the erection of a commonwealth. And this is also to be gathered out of the ordinary definition of justice in the Schools; for they say that *justice is the constant will of giving to every man his own*. And therefore where there is no *own*, that is, no propriety, there is no injustice; and where there is no coercive power erected, that is, where there is no commonwealth, there is no propriety, all men having right to all things; therefore where there is no commonwealth, there nothing is unjust. So that the nature of justice consisteth in keeping of valid covenants; but the validity of covenants begins not but with the constitution of a civil power sufficient to compel men to keep them; and then it is also that propriety begins.

[4]   The fool hath said in his heart: "there is no such thing as justice"; and sometimes also with his tongue, seriously alleging that: "every man's conservation and contentment being committed to his own care, there could be no reason why every man might not do what he thought conduced thereunto, and therefore also to make or not make, keep or not keep, covenants was not against reason, when it conduced to one's

benefit." He does not therein deny that there be covenants, and that they are sometimes broken, sometimes kept, and that such breach of them may be called injustice, and the observance of them justice; but he questioneth whether injustice, taking away the fear of God (for the same fool hath said in his heart there is no God), may not sometimes stand with that reason which dictateth to every man his own good; and particularly then, when it conduceth to such a benefit as shall put a man in a condition to neglect, not only the dispraise and revilings, but also the power of other men.

"The kingdom of God is gotten by violence; but what if it could be gotten by unjust violence? were it against [OL: right] reason so to get it, when it is impossible to receive hurt by it [OL: but only the supreme good]? and if it be not against reason, it is not against justice; or else justice is not to be approved for good."

From such reasoning as this, successful wickedness hath obtained the name of virtue, and some that in all other things have disallowed the violation of faith, yet have allowed it when it is for the getting of a kingdom. And the heathen that believed that *Saturn* was deposed by his son *Jupiter* believed nevertheless the same *Jupiter* to be the avenger of injustice, somewhat like to a piece of law in *Coke's* Commentaries on *Littleton*, where he says: if the right heir of the crown be attainted of treason, yet the crown shall descend to him, and *eo instante* [immediately] the attainder be void; from which instances a man will be very prone to infer that "when the heir apparent of a kingdom shall kill him that is in possession, though his father, you may call it injustice, or by what other name you will, yet it can never be against reason, seeing all the voluntary actions of men tend to the benefit of themselves, and those actions are most reasonable that conduce most to their ends." This specious reasoning is nevertheless false.

[5]   For the question is not of promises mutual where there is no security of performance on either side (as when there is no civil power erected over the parties promising), for such promises are no covenants, but either where one of the parties has performed already, or where there is a power to make him perform, there is the question whether it be against reason, that is, against the benefit of the other to perform or not. And I say it is not against reason. For the manifestation whereof we are to consider: first, that when a man doth a thing which, notwithstanding anything can be foreseen and reckoned on, tendeth to his own destruction (howsoever some accident which he could not expect, arriving, may turn it to his benefit), yet such events do not make it reasonably or wisely done. Secondly, that in a condition of war wherein every man to every man (for

want of a common power to keep them all in awe) is an enemy, there is no man can hope by his own strength or wit to defend himself from destruction without the help of confederates (where everyone expects the same defence by the confederation that anyone else does); and therefore, he which declares he thinks it reason to deceive those that help him can in reason expect no other means of safety than what can be had from his own single power. He, therefore, that breaketh his covenant, and consequently declareth that he thinks he may with reason do so, cannot be received into any society that unite themselves for peace and defence but by the error of them that receive him; nor when he is received, be retained in it without seeing the danger of their error; which errors a man cannot reasonably reckon upon as the means of his security; and therefore, if he be left or cast out of society, he perisheth; and if he live in society, it is by the errors of other men, which he could not foresee nor reckon upon; and consequently [he has acted] against the reason of his preservation, and so as all men that contribute not to his destruction forbear him only out of ignorance of what is good for themselves.

[6]   As for the instance of gaining the secure and perpetual felicity of heaven by any way, it is frivolous, there being but one way imaginable, and that is not breaking, but keeping of covenant.

[7]   And for the other instance of attaining sovereignty by rebellion, it is manifest that, though the event follow, yet because it cannot reasonably be expected (but rather the contrary), and because (by gaining it so) others are taught to gain the same in like manner, the attempt thereof is against reason. Justice, therefore, that is to say, keeping of covenant, is a rule of reason by which we are forbidden to do anything destructive to our life, and consequently a law of nature.

[8]   There be some that proceed further, and will not have the law of nature to be those rules which conduce to the preservation of man's life on earth, but to the attaining of an eternal felicity after death, to which they think the breach of covenant may conduce, and consequently be just and reasonable (such are they that think it a work of merit to kill, or depose, or rebel against the sovereign power constituted over them by their own consent). But because there is no natural knowledge of man's estate after death, much less of the reward that is then to be given to breach of faith, but only a belief grounded upon other men's saying that they know it supernaturally, or that they know those that knew them that knew others that knew it supernaturally, breach of faith cannot be called a precept of reason or nature.

[9]   Others, that allow for a law of nature the keeping of faith, do nevertheless make exception of certain persons (as heretics and such as use not

to perform their covenant to others); and this also is against reason. For if any fault of a man be sufficient to discharge our covenant made, the same ought in reason to have been sufficient to have hindered the making of it.

[10]   The names of just and unjust, when they are attributed to men, signify one thing; and when they are attributed to actions, another. When they are attributed to men, they signify conformity or inconformity of manners to reason. But when they are attributed to actions, they signify the conformity or inconformity to reason, not of manners or manner of life, but of particular actions. A just man, therefore, is he that taketh all the care he can that his actions may be all just; and an unjust man is he that neglecteth it. And such men are more often in our language styled by the names of righteous and unrighteous, than just and unjust, though the meaning be the same. Therefore a righteous man does not lose that title by one or a few unjust actions that proceed from sudden passion or mistake of things or persons; nor does an unrighteous man lose his character for such actions as he does or forbears to do for fear, because his will is not framed by the justice, but by the apparent benefit of what he is to do. That which gives to human actions the relish of justice is a certain nobleness or gallantness of courage (rarely found) by which a man scorns to be beholden for the contentment of his life to fraud or breach of promise. This justice of the manners is that which is meant where justice is called a virtue, and injustice a vice.

[11]   But the justice of actions denominates men, not just, but *guiltless*; and the injustice of the same (which is also called injury) gives them but the name of *guilty*.

[12]   Again, the injustice of manners is the disposition or aptitude to do injury, and is injustice before it proceed to act and without supposing any individual person injured. But the injustice of an action (that is to say injury) supposeth an individual person injured, namely, him to whom the covenant was made; and therefore, many times the injury is received by one man, when the damage redoundeth to another. As when the master commandeth his servant to give money to a stranger; if it be not done, the injury is done to the master, whom he had before covenanted to obey, but the damage redoundeth to the stranger, to whom he had no obligation, and therefore could not injure him. And so also in commonwealths, private men may remit to one another their debts, but not robberies or other violences whereby they are endamaged; because the detaining of debt is an injury to themselves, but robbery and violence are injuries to the person of the commonwealth.

[13]   Whatsoever is done to a man conformable to his own will, signified to the doer, is no injury to him. For if he that doeth it hath not

passed away his original right to do what he please by some antecedent covenant, there is no breach of covenant, and therefore no injury done him. And if he have, then his will [i.e., that of the person acted on] to have it done being signified, is a release of that covenant; and so again there is no injury done him.

[14] Justice of actions is by writers divided into *commutative* and *distributive*; and the former they say consisteth in proportion arithmetical; the latter, in proportion geometrical. Commutative, therefore, they place in the equality of value of the things contracted for; and distributive, in the distribution of equal benefit to men of equal merit (as if it were injustice to sell dearer than we buy, or to give more to a man than he merits). The value of all things contracted for is measured by the appetite of the contractors; and therefore the just value is that which they be contented to give. And merit (besides that which is by covenant, where the performance on one part meriteth the performance of the other part, and falls under justice commutative, not distributive) is not due by justice, but is rewarded of grace only.

And therefore this distinction, in the sense wherein it useth to be expounded, is not right. To speak properly, commutative justice is the justice of a contractor, that is, a performance of covenant (in buying and selling, hiring and letting to hire, lending and borrowing, exchanging, bartering, and other acts of contract). [15] And distributive justice [is] the justice of an arbitrator, that is to say, the act of defining what is just. Wherein (being trusted by them that make him arbitrator) if he perform his trust, he is said to distribute to every man his own; and this is indeed just distribution, and may be called (though improperly) distributive justice (but more properly, equity, which also is a law of nature, as shall be shown in due place [¶24]).

[16]   As justice dependeth on antecedent covenant, so does GRATITUDE depend on antecedent grace, that is to say, antecedent free-gift; and is the fourth law of nature, which may be conceived in this form *that a man which receiveth benefit from another of mere grace endeavour that he which giveth it have no reasonable cause to repent him of his good will.* For no man giveth but with intention of good to himself, because gift is voluntary, and of all voluntary acts the object is to every man his own good; of which, if men see they shall be frustrated, there will be no beginning of benevolence or trust; nor, consequently, of mutual help, nor of reconciliation of one man to another; and therefore they are to remain still in the condition of war, which is contrary to the first and fundamental law of nature, which commandeth men to *seek peace.* The breach of this law is called *ingratitude*, and hath the same relation to grace that injustice hath to obligation by covenant.

[17]   A fifth law of nature is COMPLAISANCE, that is to say, *that every man strive to accommodate himself to the rest.* For the understanding whereof we may consider that there is, in men's aptness to society, a diversity of nature rising from their diversity of affections, not unlike to that we see in stones brought together for building of an edifice. For as that stone which (by the asperity and irregularity of figure) takes more room from others than itself fills, and (for the hardness) cannot be easily made plain, and thereby hindereth the building, is by the builders cast away as unprofitable and troublesome, so also a man that (by asperity of nature) will strive to retain those things which to himself are superfluous and to others necessary, and (for the stubbornness of his passions) cannot be corrected, is to be left or cast out of society as cumbersome thereunto. For seeing every man, not only by right, but also by necessity of nature, is supposed to endeavour all he can to obtain that which is necessary for his conservation, he that shall oppose himself against it for things superfluous is guilty of the war that thereupon is to follow; and, therefore, doth that which is contrary to the fundamental law of nature, which commandeth *to seek peace.* The observers of this law may be called SOCIABLE (the Latins call them *commodi*); the contrary, *stubborn, insociable, froward, intractable.*

[18]   A sixth law of nature is this *that upon caution of the future time, a man ought to pardon the offences past of them that, repenting, desire it.* For PARDON is nothing but granting of peace, which (though granted to them that persevere in their hostility be not peace but fear, yet) not granted to them that give caution of the future time is sign of an aversion to peace; and therefore contrary to the law of nature.

[19]   A seventh is *that in revenges* (that is, retribution of evil for evil) *men look not at the greatness of the evil past, but the greatness of the good to follow.* Whereby we are forbidden to inflict punishment with any other design than for correction of the offender, or direction of others. For this law is consequent to the next before it, that commandeth pardon upon security of the future time. Besides, revenge without respect to the example and profit to come is a triumph, or glorying, in the hurt of another, tending to no end (for the end is always somewhat to come); and glorying to no end is vain-glory, and contrary to reason; and to hurt without reason tendeth to the introduction of war, which is against the law of nature, and is commonly styled by the name of *cruelty.*

[20]   And because all signs of hatred or contempt provoke to fight, insomuch as most men choose rather to hazard their life than not to be revenged, we may in the eighth place, for a law of nature, set down this precept *that no man by deed, word, countenance, or gesture, declare hatred*

or contempt of another. The breach of which law is commonly called *contumely*.

[21]   The question 'who is the better man?' has no place in the condition of mere nature, where (as has been shewn before) all men are equal. The inequality that now is, has been introduced by the laws civil. I know that *Aristotle* (in the first book of his Politics [ch. iii–vii], for a foundation of his doctrine) maketh men by nature, some more worthy to command (meaning the wiser sort, such as he thought himself to be for his philosophy), others to serve (meaning those that had strong bodies, but were not philosophers as he), as if master and servant were not introduced by consent of men, but by difference of wit; which is not only against reason, but also against experience. For there are very few so foolish that had not rather govern themselves than be governed by others; nor when the wise in their own conceit contend by force with them who distrust their own wisdom, do they always, or often, or almost at any time, get the victory. If nature therefore have made men equal, that equality is to be acknowledged; or if nature have made men unequal, yet because men that think themselves equal will not enter into conditions of peace but upon equal terms, such equality must be admitted. And therefore for the ninth law of nature, I put this *that every man acknowledge other for his equal by nature*. The breach of this precept is *pride*.

[22]   On this law dependeth another: *that at the entrance into conditions of peace, no man require to reserve to himself any right which he is not content should be reserved to every one of the rest*. As it is necessary, for all men that seek peace, to lay down certain rights of nature (that is to say, not to have liberty to do all they list), so is it necessary, for man's life, to retain some (as, right to govern their own bodies, [right to] enjoy air, water, motion, ways to go from place to place, and all things else without which a man cannot live, or not live well). If in this case, at the making of peace, men require for themselves that which they would not have to be granted to others, they do contrary to the precedent law, that commandeth the acknowledgment of natural equality, and therefore also against the law of nature. The observers of this law are those we call *modest*, and the breakers *arrogant* men. The Greeks call the violation of this law *pleonexia*, that is, a desire of more than their share.

[23]   Also *if a man be trusted to judge between man and man*, it is a precept of the law of nature that *he deal equally between them*. For without that, the controversies of men cannot be determined but by war. He, therefore, that is partial in judgment doth what in him lies to deter men from the use of judges and arbitrators; and consequently (against the fundamental law of nature), is the cause of war.

[24]   The observance of this law (from the equal distribution to each man of that which in reason belongeth to him) is called EQUITY, and (as I have said before) distributive justice; the violation [is called] *acception of persons (prosopolepsia)*.

[25]   And from this followeth another law: *that such things as cannot be divided be enjoyed in common, if it can be; and if the quantity of the thing permit, without stint; otherwise proportionably to the number of them that have right*. For otherwise the distribution is unequal, and contrary to equity.

[26]   But some things there be that can neither be divided nor enjoyed in common. Then the law of nature which prescribeth equity requireth *that the entire right (or else, making the use alternate, the first possession) be determined by lot*. For equal distribution is of the law of nature, and other means of equal distribution cannot be imagined.

[27]   Of *lots* there be two sorts: *arbitrary* and *natural*. Arbitrary is that which is agreed on by the competitors; natural is either *primogeniture* (which the Greek calls *kleronomia*, which signifies, *given by lot*) or *first seizure*.

[28]   And therefore those things which cannot be enjoyed in common, nor divided, ought to be adjudged to the first possessor; and in some cases to the first-born, as acquired by lot.

[29]   It is also a law of nature *that all men that mediate peace be allowed safe conduct*. For the law that commandeth peace, as the *end*, commandeth intercession, as the *means*; and to intercession the means is safe conduct.

[30]   And because (though men be never so willing to observe these laws) there may nevertheless arise questions concerning a man's action (first, whether it were done or not done; secondly, if done, whether against the law or not against the law; the former whereof is called a question *of fact*; the latter a question *of right*), therefore unless the parties to the question covenant mutually to stand to the sentence of another, they are as far from peace as ever. This other to whose sentence they submit is called an ARBITRATOR. And therefore it is of the law of nature *that they that are at controversy, submit their right to the judgment of an arbitrator*.

[31]   And seeing every man is presumed to do all things in order to his own benefit, *no man is a fit arbitrator in his own cause*; and if he were never so fit, yet (equity allowing to each party equal benefit) if one be admitted to be judge, the other is to be admitted also; and so the controversy, that is, the cause of war, remains, against the law of nature.

[32]   For the same reason no man in any cause ought to be received for arbitrator, to whom greater profit, or honour, or pleasure apparently ariseth out of the victory of one party, than of the other; for he hath taken (though an unavoidable bribe, yet) a bribe; and no man can be obliged to

trust him. And thus also the controversy, and the condition of war remaineth, contrary to the law of nature.

[33]   And in a controversy of *fact* the judge (being to give no more credit to one [litigant] than to the other, if there be no other arguments) must give credit to a third [a non-litigant witness], or to a third and fourth; or more; for else the question is undecided, and left to force, contrary to the law of nature.

[34]   These are the laws of nature dictating peace for a means of the conservation of men in multitudes; and which only concern the doctrine of civil society. There be other things tending to the destruction of particular men (as drunkenness and all other parts of intemperance), which may therefore also be reckoned amongst those things which the law of nature hath forbidden; but are not necessary to be mentioned, nor are pertinent enough to this place.

[35]   And though this may seem too subtle a deduction of the laws of nature to be taken notice of by all men (whereof the most part are too busy in getting food, and the rest too negligent, to understand), yet to leave all men inexcusable they have been contracted into one easy sum, intelligible even to the meanest capacity, and that is *Do not that to another, which thou wouldst not have done to thyself*; which sheweth him that he has no more to do in learning the laws of nature but (when, weighing the actions of other men with his own, they seem too heavy) to put them into the other part of the balance, and his own into their place, that his own passions and self-love may add nothing to the weight; and then there is none of these laws of nature that will not appear unto him very reasonable.

[36]   The laws of nature oblige *in foro interno*, that is to say, they bind to a desire they should take place; but *in foro externo*, that is, to the putting them in act, not always. For he that should be modest and tractable, and perform all he promises, in such time and place where no man else should do so, should but make himself a prey to others, and procure his own certain ruin, contrary to the ground of all laws of nature, which tend to nature's preservation. And again, he that having sufficient security that others shall observe the same laws towards him, observes them not himself, seeketh not peace, but war, and consequently the destruction of his nature by violence.

[37]   And whatsoever laws bind *in foro interno* may be broken, not only by a fact contrary to the law, but also by a fact according to it, in case a man think it contrary. For though his action in this case be according to the law, yet his purpose was against the law, which, where the obligation is *in foro interno*, is a breach.

[38]   The laws of nature are immutable and eternal; for injustice, ingratitude, arrogance, pride, iniquity, acception of persons, and the rest, can never be made lawful. For it can never be that war shall preserve life, and peace destroy it.

[39]   The same laws, because they oblige only to a desire and endeavour (I mean an unfeigned and constant endeavour) are easy to be observed. For in that they require nothing but endeavour, he that endeavoureth their performance fulfilleth them; and he that fulfilleth the law is just.

[40]   And the science of them [the laws of nature] is the true and only moral philosophy. For moral philosophy is nothing else but the science of what is *good* and *evil* in the conversation and society of mankind. *Good* and *evil* are names that signify our appetites and aversions, which in different tempers, customs, and doctrines of men are different; and divers men differ not only in their judgment on the senses (of what is pleasant and unpleasant to the taste, smell, hearing, touch, and sight), but also of what is conformable or disagreeable to reason in the actions of common life. Nay, the same man in divers times differs from himself, and one time praiseth (that is, calleth good) what another time he dispraiseth (and calleth evil); from whence arise disputes, controversies, and at last war. And therefore so long a man is in the condition of mere nature (which is a condition of war) as private appetite is the measure of good and evil; and consequently, all men agree on this, that peace is good; and therefore also the way or means of peace (which, as I have shewed before, are *justice, gratitude, modesty, equity, mercy,* and the rest of the laws of nature) are good (that is to say, *moral virtues*), and their contrary vices, evil.

Now the science of virtue and vice is moral philosophy; and therefore the true doctrine of the laws of nature is the true moral philosophy. But the writers of moral philosophy, though they acknowledge the same virtues and vices, yet not seeing wherein consisted their goodness, nor that they come to be praised as the means of peaceable, sociable, and comfortable living, place them in a mediocrity of passions (as if not the cause, but the degree of daring, made fortitude; or not the cause, but the quantity of a gift, made liberality).

[41]   These dictates of reason men use to call by the name of laws, but improperly; for they are but conclusions or theorems concerning what conduceth to the conservation and defence of themselves, whereas law, properly, is the word of him that by right hath command over others. But yet if we consider the same theorems, as delivered in the word of God, that by right commandeth all things; then are they properly called laws.

Chapter XVI
Of Persons, Authors, *and Things Personated*

[1]   A person is he *whose words or actions are considered either as his own, or as representing the words or actions of another man, or of any other thing to whom they are attributed, whether truly or by fiction.*

[2]   When they are considered as his own, then is he called a *natural person*; and when they are considered as representing the words and actions of another, then is he a *feigned* or *artificial person*.

[3]   The word Person is Latin, instead whereof the Greeks have *prosopon*, which signifies the *face*, as *persona* in Latin signifies the *disguise* or *outward appearance* of a man, counterfeited on the stage, and sometimes more particularly that part of it which disguiseth the face (as a mask or vizard); and from the stage hath been translated to any representer of speech and action, as well in tribunals as theatres. So that a *person* is the same that an *actor* is, both on the stage and in common conversation; and to *personate* is to *act*, or *represent*, himself or another; and he that acteth another is said to bear his person, or act in his name (in which sense *Cicero* useth it where he says *Unus sustineo tres personas: mei, adversarii, et judicis,* I bear three persons: my own, my adversary's, and the judge's), and is called in divers occasions diversly (as a *representer*, or *representative*, a *lieutenant*, a *vicar*, an *attorney*, a *deputy*, a *procurator*, an *actor*, and the like).

[4]   Of persons artificial, some have their words and actions *owned* by those whom they represent. And then the person is the *actor*, and he that owneth his words and actions is the AUTHOR, in which case the actor acteth by authority. For that which in speaking of goods and possessions is called an *owner* (and in Latin *dominus*, in Greek *kurios*), speaking of actions is called author. And as the right of possession is called dominion, so the right of doing any action is called AUTHORITY. So that by authority is always understood a right of doing any act; and *done by authority*, done by commission or licence from him whose right it is.

[5]   From hence it followeth that when the actor maketh a covenant by authority, he bindeth thereby the author, no less than if he had made it himself, and no less subjecteth him to all the consequences of the same. And therefore all that hath been said formerly [(*chap.* 14)] of the nature of covenants between man and man in their natural capacity is true also when they are made by their actors, representers, or procurators, that have authority from them so far forth as is in their commission, but no farther.

[6]   And therefore, he that maketh a covenant with the actor, or representer, not knowing the authority he hath, doth it at his own peril.

For no man is obliged by a covenant whereof he is not author, nor consequently by a covenant made against or beside the authority he gave.

[7]   When the actor doth anything against the law of nature by command of the author, if he be obliged by former covenant to obey him, not he, but the author breaketh the law of nature; for though the action be against the law of nature, yet it is not his; but contrarily, to refuse to do it is against the law of nature that forbiddeth breach of covenant.

[8]   And he that maketh a covenant with the author by mediation of the actor, not knowing what authority he hath, but only takes his word, in case such authority be not made manifest unto him upon demand, is no longer obliged; for the covenant made with the author is not valid without his counter-assurance. But if he that so covenanteth knew beforehand he was to expect no other assurance than the actor's word, then is the covenant valid, because the actor in this case maketh himself the author. And therefore, as when the authority is evident the covenant obligeth the author, not the actor, so when the authority is feigned it obligeth the actor only, there being no author but himself.

[9]   There are few things that are incapable of being represented by fiction. Inanimate things (as a church, an hospital, a bridge) may be personated by a rector, master, or overseer. But things inanimate cannot be authors, nor therefore give authority to their actors; yet the actors may have authority to procure their maintenance given them by those that are owners or governors of those things. And therefore, such things cannot be personated before there be some state of civil government.

[10]   Likewise, children, fools, and madmen that have no use of reason may be personated by guardians or curators, but can be no authors (during that time) of any action done by them, longer than (when they shall recover the use of reason) they shall judge the same reasonable. Yet during the folly, he that hath right of governing them may give authority to the guardian. But this again has no place but in a state civil, because before such estate, there is no dominion of persons.

[11]   An idol, or mere figment of the brain, may be personated (as were the gods of the heathen, which by such officers as the state appointed were personated, and held possessions, and other goods, and rights, which men from time to time dedicated and consecrated unto them). But idols cannot be authors; for an idol is nothing. The authority proceeded from the state; and therefore, before introduction of civil government the gods of the heathen could not be personated.

[12]   The true God may be personated. As he was, first by *Moses*, who governed the Israelites (that were not his, but God's people) not in his own name (with *hoc dicit Moses* [thus says Moses]), but in God's name

(with *hoc dicit Dominus* [thus says the Lord]). Secondly, by the Son of man, his own Son, our blessed Saviour *Jesus Christ*, that came to reduce the Jews, and induce all nations into the kingdom of his father, not as of himself, but as sent from his father. And thirdly, by the Holy Ghost, or Comforter, speaking and working in the Apostles; which Holy Ghost was a Comforter that came not of himself, but was sent and proceeded from them both.

[13]   A multitude of men are made *one* person, when they are by one man, or one person, represented so that it be done with the consent of every one of that multitude in particular. For it is the *unity* of the representer, not the *unity* of the represented, that maketh the person *one*. And it is the representer that beareth the person, and but one person, and *unity* cannot otherwise be understood in multitude.

[14]   And because the multitude naturally is not *one*, but *many*, they cannot be understood for one, but many, authors of everything their representative saith or doth in their name, every man giving their common representer authority from himself in particular, and owning all the actions the representer doth, in case they give him authority without stint; otherwise, when they limit him in what, and how far, he shall represent them, none of them owneth more than they gave him commission to act.

[15]   And if the representative consist of many men, the voice of the greater number must be considered as the voice of them all. For if the lesser number pronounce (for example) in the affirmative, and the greater in the negative, there will be negatives more than enough to destroy the affirmatives; and thereby the excess of negatives, standing uncontradicted, are the only voice the representative hath.

[16]   And a representative of even number, especially when the number is not great, whereby the contradictory voices are oftentimes equal, is therefore oftentimes mute and incapable of action. Yet in some cases contradictory voices equal in number may determine a question (as, in condemning or absolving, equality of votes, even in that they condemn not, do absolve; but not on the contrary condemn, in that they absolve not). For when a cause is heard, not to condemn is to absolve; but on the contrary, to say that not absolving is condemning, is not true. The like it is in a deliberation of executing presently, or deferring till another time; for when the voices are equal, the not decreeing execution is a decree of dilation.

[17]   Or if the number be odd, as three (or more) men (or assemblies) whereof every one has, by a negative voice, authority to take away the effect of all the affirmative voices of the rest, this number is no representative; because, by the diversity of opinions and interests of men, it

becomes oftentimes, and in cases of the greatest consequence, a mute person, and unapt, as for many things else, so for the government of a multitude, especially in time of war.

[18]   Of authors there be two sorts. The first simply so called, which I have before defined to be him that owneth the action of another simply. The second is he that owneth an action or covenant of another conditionally (that is to say, he undertaketh to do it, if the other doth it not at, or before, a certain time). And these authors conditional are generally called SURETIES (in Latin *fidejussores* and *sponsores*; and particularly for debt, *praedes*; and for appearance before a judge or magistrate, *vades*).

Part II

Classical Sources: Contractualism

2

From *The Social Contract*

Jean-Jacques Rousseau

Book I

[1] I want to inquire whether in the civil order there can be some legit- [*351*]
imate and sure rule of administration, taking men as they are, and the
laws as they can be: In this inquiry I shall try always to combine what
right permits with what interest prescribes, so that justice and utility may
not be disjoined.

[2] I begin without proving the importance of my subject. I shall be
asked whether I am a prince or a lawgiver that I write on Politics? I reply
that I am not, and that that is why I write on Politics. If I were a prince
or a legislator, I would not waste my time saying what needs doing; I
would do it, or keep silent.

[3] Born a citizen of a free State, and a member of the sovereign, the
right to vote in it is enough to impose on me the duty to learn about public
affairs, regardless of how weak might be the influence of my voice on
them. Happy, whenever I meditate about Governments, always to find in
my inquiries new reasons for loving that of my country!

Chapter One
Subject of this First Book

[1] Man is born free, and everywhere he is in chains. One believes
himself the others' master, and yet is more a slave than they. How did this

Jean-Jacques Rousseau, *The Social Contract and Other Later Political Writings*, Victor
Gourevitch, ed. (Cambridge: Cambridge University Press, 1997), pp. 41–68.

Page numbers (set in italic in square brackets) in the margin, and inserted in
the text, refer to Vol. III of Jean-Jacques Rousseau, *Oeuvres complètes* [OC], ed. B.
Gagnebin and M. Raymond (Paris: Pléiade, 1959–95), which is the standard edition of
Rousseau's works.

change come about? I do not know. What can make it legitimate? I believe I can solve this question.

[2]   If I considered only force, and the effect that follows from it, [352] I would say; as long as a People is compelled to obey and does obey, it does well; as soon as it can shake off the yoke and does shake it off, it does even better; for in recovering its freedom by the same right as the right by which it was robbed of it, either the people is well founded to take it back, or it was deprived of it without foundation. But the social order is a sacred right, which provides the basis for all the others. Yet this right does not come from nature; it is therefore founded on conventions. The problem is to know what these conventions are. Before coming to that, I must establish what I have just set forth.

Chapter Two
Of the First Societies

[1]   The most ancient of all societies and the only natural one is that of the family. Even so children remain bound to the father only as long as they need him for their preservation. As soon as that need ceases, the natural bond dissolves. The children, exempt from the obedience they owe the father, the father exempt from the cares he owed the children, all equally return to independence. If they remain united, they are no longer so naturally but voluntarily, and even the family maintains itself only by convention.

[2]   This common freedom is a consequence of man's nature. His first law is to attend to his own preservation, his first cares are those he owes himself, and since, as soon as he has reached the age of reason, he is sole judge of the means proper to preserve himself, he becomes his own master.

[3]   The family is, then, if you will, the first model of political societies; the chief is the image of the father, the people are the image of the children, and all, being born equal and free, alienate their freedom only for the sake of their utility. The only difference is that in the family the father's love for his children repays him for the cares he bestows on them, and that in the State the pleasure of commanding takes the place of the chief's lack of love for his peoples.

[4]   Grotius denies that all human power is established for [353] the sake of the governed: he gives slavery as an example. His most frequent mode of argument is always to establish right by fact.* One could use a more consistent method, but not one more favorable to Tyrants.

* "Learned investigations of public right are often nothing but the history of ancient abuses, and it was a misplaced single-mindedness to have taken the trouble to study them too closely." Ms *Treatise on the Interests of France in Relation to Her Neighbors; by* M. L[e] M[arquis] d'A[rgenson]. This is precisely what Grotius did.

[5]   So that, according to Grotius, it is an open question whether humankind belongs to a hundred men, or whether those hundred men belong to humankind, and throughout his book he appears to incline to the first opinion: that is also Hobbes's sentiment. Here, then, is humankind, divided into herds of cattle, each with its chief who tends it to devour it.

[6]   As a shepherd is of a nature superior to his flock's, so too are the shepherds of men, who are their chiefs, of a nature superior to their peoples'. This is how, according to Philo, the Emperor Caligula reasoned; concluding rather well from this analogy that kings were Gods, or that peoples were beasts.

[7]   Caligula's reasoning amounts to that of Hobbes and of Grotius. Aristotle before all of them had also said that men are not naturally equal, but that some were born for slavery and others for domination.

[8]   Aristotle was right, but he mistook the effect for the cause. Any man born in slavery is born for slavery, nothing could be more certain. Slaves lose everything in their chains, even the desire to be rid of them; they love their servitude, as the companions of Ulysses loved their brutishness.* Hence, if there are slaves by nature, it is because there were slaves contrary to nature. Force made the first slaves, their cowardice perpetuated them.

[9]   I have said nothing about King Adam, or about emperor Noah, father of three great monarchs who among themselves divided the uni[354]verse, as did the children of Saturn, whom some believed they recognized in them. I hope my moderation will be appreciated; for since I am a direct descendant from one of these Princes, and perhaps from the elder branch, for all I know, I might, upon verification of titles, find I am the legitimate King of humankind. Be that as it may, it cannot be denied that Adam was Sovereign of the world as Robinson was of his island, as long as he was its sole inhabitant; and what made this empire convenient was that the monarch, secure on his throne, had neither rebellions, nor wars, nor conspirators to fear.

Chapter Three
The Right of the Stronger

[1]   The stronger is never strong enough to be forever master, unless he transforms his force into right, and obedience into duty. Hence the right of the stronger; a right which is apparently understood ironically, and in principle really established: But will no one ever explain this word to us? Force is a physical power; I fail to see what morality can result from its

---

* See a small treatise by Plutarch entitled: *That Beasts Use Reason.*

effects. To yield to force is an act of necessity, not of will; at most it is an act of prudence. In what sense can it become a duty?

[2]   Let us assume this alleged right for a moment. I say that it can only result in an unintelligible muddle. For once force makes right, the effect changes together with the cause; every force that overcomes the first, inherits its right. Once one can disobey with impunity, one can do so legitimately, and since the stronger is always right, one need only make sure to be the stronger. But what is a right that perishes when force ceases? If one has to obey by force, one need not obey by duty, and if one is no longer forced to obey, one is no longer obliged to do so. Clearly, then, this word "right" adds nothing to force; it means nothing at all here.

[3]   Obey the powers that be. If this means yield to force, the precept is good but superfluous, I warrant that it [355] will never be violated. All power comes from God, I admit it; but so does all illness. Does this mean it is forbidden to call the doctor? A brigand takes me by surprise at the edge of a woods: am I not only forced to hand over my purse, but also obliged in conscience to hand it over even if I could withhold it? For the pistol he holds is, after all, also a power.

[4]   Let us agree, then, that force does not make right, and that one is only obliged to obey legitimate powers. Thus my original question keeps coming back.

Chapter Four
Of Slavery

[1]   Since no man has a natural authority over his fellow-man, and since force produces no right, conventions remain as the basis of all legitimate authority among men.

[2]   If, says Grotius, an individual can alienate his freedom, and enslave himself to a master, why could not a whole people alienate its freedom and subject itself to a king? There are quite a few ambiguous words here which call for explanation, but let us confine ourselves to the word *alienate*. To alienate is to give or to sell. Now, a man who enslaves himself to another does not give himself, he sells himself, at the very least for his subsistence: but a people, what does it sell itself for? A king, far from furnishing his subjects' subsistence, takes his own entirely from them, and according to Rabelais a king does not live modestly. Do the subjects then give their persons on condition that their goods will be taken as well? I do not see what they have left to preserve.

[3]   The despot, it will be said, guarantees civil tranquility for his subjects. All right; but what does it profit them if the wars his ambition brings

on them, if his insatiable greed, the harassment by his administration cause them more distress than their own dissension would have done? What does it profit them if this very tranquility is one of their miseries? Life is also tranquil in dungeons; is that enough to feel well in them? The Greeks imprisoned in the Cyclops's cave lived there [356] tranquilly, while awaiting their turn to be devoured.

[4]   To say a man gives himself gratuitously is to say something absurd and inconceivable; such an act is illegitimate and null, for the simple reason that whoever does so is not in his right mind. To say the same of a whole people is to assume a people of madmen; madness does not make right.

[5]   Even if everyone could alienate himself, he could not alienate his children; they are born men and free; their freedom belongs to them, no one but they themselves has the right to dispose of it. Before they have reached the age of reason, their father may in their name stipulate conditions for their preservation, for their well-being; but he cannot give them away irrevocably and unconditionally; for such a gift is contrary to the ends of nature and exceeds the rights of paternity. Hence, for an arbitrary government to be legitimate, the people would, in each generation, have to be master of accepting or rejecting it, but in that case the government would no longer be arbitrary.

[6]   To renounce one's freedom is to renounce one's quality as man, the rights of humanity, and even its duties. There can be no possible compensation for someone who renounces everything. Such a renunciation is incompatible with the nature of man, and to deprive one's will of all freedom is to deprive one's actions of all morality. Finally, a convention that stipulates absolute authority on one side, and unlimited obedience on the other, is vain and contradictory. Is it not clear that one is under no obligation toward a person from whom one has the right to demand everything, and does not this condition alone, without equivalent and without exchange, nullify the act? For what right can my slave have against me, since everything he has belongs to me, and his right being mine, this right of mine against myself is an utterly meaningless expression?

[7]   Grotius and the rest derive from war another origin of the alleged right of slavery. Since, according to them, the victor has the right to kill the vanquished, the latter can buy back his life at the cost of his freedom; a convention they regard as all the more legitimate because it proves profitable to both parties. But it is clear that this alleged right to kill the vanquished in no way results from the state of war. Men are not naturally enemies, if only because when they live in their primitive independence [357] the relation among them is not sufficiently stable to constitute either

a state of peace or a state of war. It is the relation between things and not between men that constitutes war, and since the state of war cannot arise from simple personal relations but only from property relations, private war or war between one man and another can exist neither in the state of nature, where there is no stable property, nor in the social state, where everything is under the authority of the laws.

[8]   Individual fights, duels, skirmishes, are acts that do not constitute a state; and as for the private wars authorized by the ordinances of King Louis IX of France and suspended by the peace of God, they are abuses of feudal government, an absurd system if ever there was one, contrary both to the principles of natural right and to all good polity.

[9]   War is then not a relationship between one man and another, but a relationship between one State and another, in which individuals are enemies only by accident, not as men, nor even as citizens,* but as soldiers; not as members of the fatherland, but as its defenders. Finally, any State can only have other States, and not men, as enemies, inasmuch as it is impossible to fix a true relation between things of different natures.

[10]   This principle even conforms to the established maxims of all ages and to the constant practice of all civilized peoples. Declarations of war are warnings not so much to the powers as to their subjects. The foreigner, whether he be a king, a private individual, or a people, who robs, kills, or detains subjects without declaring war on their prince, is not an enemy, he is a brigand. Even in the midst of war, a just prince may well seize everything in enemy territory that belongs to the public, but he respects the person and the goods of private individuals; he respects rights on which his own are founded. Since the aim of war is the destruction of the enemy State, one has the right to kill its defenders as long as they bear arms; but as soon as they lay down their arms and surrender they cease to be enemies or the enemy's instruments, and become simply men once

---

*   The Romans who understood and respected the right of war better than any nation in the world were so scrupulous in this regard that a citizen was not allowed to serve as a volunteer without having enlisted specifically against the enemy, and one designated as such by name. When a Legion in which the Younger Cato fought his first campaign under Popilius was reorganized, the Elder Cato wrote to Popilius that if he was willing to have his son continue to serve under him, he would have to have him take a new military oath because, the first oath having been vacated, he could no longer bear arms against the enemy. And the same Cato wrote to his son to be careful not to appear in battle without having taken this new oath. I know that the siege of Clusium and other individual facts can be urged against me, but I cite laws, practices. The Romans are the people who least frequently transgressed their laws, and they are the only ones to have had such fine ones. [1782 edn.]

more, and one no longer has a right over their life. It is sometimes possible to kill the State without killing a single one of its members: and [*358*] war confers no right that is not necessary to its end. These principles are not those of Grotius; they are not founded on the authority of poets, but follow from the nature of things, and are founded on reason.

[11]   As regards the right of conquest, it has no other foundation than the law of the stronger. If war does not give the victor the right to massacre vanquished peoples, then this right which he does not have cannot be the foundation of the right to enslave them. One has the right to kill the enemy only when one cannot make him a slave. Hence the right to make him a slave does not derive from the right to kill him: it is therefore an iniquitous exchange to make him buy his life, over which one has no right whatsoever, at the cost of his freedom. Is it not clear that by establishing the right of life and death by the right of slavery, and the right of slavery by the right of life and death, one falls into a vicious circle?

[12]   Even assuming this terrible right to kill all, I say that a slave made in war or a conquered people is not bound to anything at all toward their master, except to obey him as long as they are forced to do so. In taking an equivalent of his life, the victor did not spare it: instead of killing him unprofitably, he killed him usefully. So far, then, is he from having acquired over him any authority associated with his force, that they continue in a state of war as before; their relation itself is its effect, and the exercise of the right of war presupposes the absence of a peace treaty. They have made a convention; very well: but that convention, far from destroying the state of war, presupposes its continuation.

[13]   Thus, from whatever angle one looks at things, the right to slavery is null, not only because it is illegitimate, but because it is absurd and meaningless. These words *slavery* and *right* are contradictory; they are mutually exclusive. Either between one man and another, or between a man and a people, the following speech will always be equally absurd. *I make a convention with you which is entirely at your expense and entirely to my profit, which I shall observe as long as I please, and which you shall observe as long as I please.*

Chapter Five
That One Always Has to Go Back to a First Convention

[1]   Even if I were to grant everything I have thus far refuted, the [*359*] abettors of despotism would be no better off. There will always be a great difference between subjugating a multitude and ruling a society. When scattered men, regardless of their number, are successively enslaved to a

single man, I see in this nothing but a master and slaves, I do not see in it a people and its chief; it is, if you will, an aggregation, but not an association; there is here neither public good, nor body politic. That man, even if he had enslaved half the world, still remains nothing but a private individual; his interest, separate from that of the others, still remains nothing but a private interest. When this same man dies, his empire is left behind scattered and without a bond, like an oak dissolves and collapses into a heap of ashes on being consumed by fire.

[2]   A people, says Grotius, can give itself to a king. So that according to Grotius a people is a people before giving itself to a king. That very gift is a civil act, it presupposes a public deliberation. Hence before examining the act by which a people elects a king, it would be well to examine the act by which a people is a people. For this act, being necessarily prior to the other, is the true foundation of society.

[3]   Indeed, if there were no prior convention, then, unless the election were unanimous, why would the minority be obliged to submit to the choice of the majority, and why would a hundred who want a master have the right to vote on behalf of ten who do not want one? The law of majority rule is itself something established by convention, and presupposes unanimity at least once.

Chapter Six
Of the Social Pact

[360]   [1]   I assume men having reached the point where the obstacles that interfere with their preservation in the state of nature prevail by their resistance over the forces which each individual can muster to maintain himself in that state. Then that primitive state can no longer subsist, and humankind would perish if it did not change its way of being.

[2]   Now, since men cannot engender new forces, but only unite and direct those that exist, they are left with no other means of self-preservation than to form, by aggregation, a sum of forces that might prevail over those obstacles' resistance, to set them in motion by a single impetus, and make them act in concert.

[3]   This sum of forces can only arise from the cooperation of many: but since each man's force and freedom are his primary instruments of self-preservation, how can he commit them without harming himself, and without neglecting the cares he owes himself? This difficulty, in relation to my subject, can be stated in the following terms.

[4]   "To find a form of association that will defend and protect the person and goods of each associate with the full common force, and by

means of which each, uniting with all, nevertheless obey only himself and remain as free as before." This is the fundamental problem to which the social contract provides the solution.

[5]   The clauses of this contract are so completely determined by the nature of the act that the slightest modification would render them null and void; so that although they may never have been formally stated, they are everywhere the same, everywhere tacitly admitted and recognized; until, the social compact having been violated, everyone is thereupon restored to his original rights and resumes his natural freedom while losing the conventional freedom for which he renounced it.

[6]   These clauses, rightly understood, all come down to just one, namely the total alienation of each associate with all of his rights to the whole community: For, in the first place, since each gives himself entirely, the condition is [361] equal for all, and since the condition is equal for all, no one has any interest in making it burdensome to the rest.

[7]   Moreover, since the alienation is made without reservation, the union is as perfect as it can be, and no associate has anything further to claim: For if individuals were left some rights, then, since there would be no common superior who might adjudicate between them and the public, each, being judge in his own case on some issue, would soon claim to be so on all, the state of nature would subsist and the association necessarily become tyrannical or empty.

[8]   Finally, each, by giving himself to all, gives himself to no one, and since there is no associate over whom one does not acquire the same right as one grants him over oneself, one gains the equivalent of all one loses, and more force to preserve what one has.

[9]   If, then, one sets aside everything that is not of the essence of the social compact, one finds that it can be reduced to the following terms: *Each of us puts his person and his full power in common under the supreme direction of the general will; and in a body we receive each member as an indivisible part of the whole.*

[10]   At once, in place of the private person of each contracting party, this act of association produces a moral and collective body made up of as many members as the assembly has voices, and which receives by this same act its unity, its common *self*, its life and its will. The public person thus formed by the union of all the others formerly assumed the name *City** and now assumes [362] that of *Republic* or of *body politic*, which its

---

*   The true sense of this word is almost entirely effaced among the moderns; most take a city for a City, and a bourgeois for a Citizen. They do not know that houses make the city but Citizens make the City. This same error once cost the Carthaginians dear.

members call *State* when it is passive, *Sovereign* when active, *Power* when comparing it to similar bodies. As for the associates, they collectively assume the name *people* and individually call themselves *Citizens* as participants in the sovereign authority, and *Subjects* as subjected to the laws of the State. But these terms are often confused and mistaken for one another; it is enough to be able to distinguish them where they are used in their precise sense.

Chapter Seven
Of the Sovereign

[1] This formula shows that the act of association involves a reciprocal engagement between the public and private individuals, and that each individual, by contracting, so to speak, with himself, finds himself engaged in a two-fold relation: namely, as member of the Sovereign toward private individuals, and as a member of the State toward the Sovereign. But here the maxim of civil right, that no one is bound by engagements toward himself, does not apply; for there is a great difference between assuming an obligation toward oneself, and assuming a responsibility toward a whole of which one is a part.

[2] It should also be noted that the public deliberation which can obligate all subjects toward the Sovereign because of the two different relations in terms of which each subject is viewed cannot, for the opposite reason, obligate the Sovereign toward itself, and that it is therefore contrary to the nature of the body politic for the Sovereign to impose on itself a law which it cannot break. Since the Sovereign can consider itself only in terms of one and the same relation, it is then in the same situation as a private individual contracting with himself: which shows that there is not, nor can there be, any kind of fundamental law that is obligatory

---

I have not read that the subjects of any Prince were ever given the title *Cives*, not even the Macedonians in ancient times nor, in our days, the English, although they are closer to freedom than all the others. Only the French assume the name *Citizen* casually, because they have no genuine idea of it, as can be seen in their Dictionaries; otherwise they would be committing the crime of Lese-Majesty in usurping it: for them this name expresses a virtue and not a right. When Bodin wanted to speak of our Citizens and Bourgeois, he committed a bad blunder in taking the one for the other. M. d'Alembert made no mistake about it, and in his article *Geneva* he correctly distinguished the [362] four orders of men (even five, if simple foreigners are included) there are in our city, and only two of which make up the Republic. No other French author has, to my knowledge, understood the true meaning of the word *Citizen*.

for the body of the people, not even the social contract. This does not mean [363] that this body cannot perfectly well enter into engagements with others about anything that does not detract from this contract; for with regard to foreigners it becomes a simple being, an individual.

[3]   But the body politic or Sovereign, since it owes its being solely to the sanctity of the contract, can never obligate itself, even toward another, to anything that detracts from that original act, such as to alienate any part of itself or to subject itself to another Sovereign. To violate the act by which it exists would be to annihilate itself, and what is nothing produces nothing.

[4]   As soon as this multitude is thus united in one body, one cannot injure one of the members without attacking the body, and still less can one injure the body without the members being affected. Thus duty and interest alike obligate the contracting parties to help one another, and the same men must strive to combine in this two-fold relation all the advantages attendant on it.

[5]   Now the Sovereign, since it is formed entirely of the individuals who make it up, has not and cannot have any interests contrary to theirs: consequently the Sovereign power has no need of a guarantor toward the subjects, because it is impossible for the body to want to harm all of its members, and we shall see later that it cannot harm any one of them in particular. The Sovereign, by the mere fact that it is, is always everything it ought to be.

[6]   But this is not the case regarding the subjects' relations to the Sovereign, and notwithstanding the common interest, the Sovereign would have no guarantee of the subjects' engagements if it did not find means to ensure their fidelity.

[7]   Indeed each individual may, as a man, have a particular will contrary to or different from the general will he has as a Citizen. His particular interest may speak to him quite differently from the common interest; his absolute and naturally independent existence may lead him to look upon what he owes to the common cause as a gratuitous contribution, the loss of which will harm others less than its payment burdens him and, by considering the moral person that constitutes the State as a being of reason because it is not a man, he would enjoy the rights of a citizen without being willing to fulfill the duties of a subject; an injustice, the progress of which would cause the ruin of the body politic.

[364] [8]   Hence for the social compact not to be an empty formula, it tacitly includes the following engagement which alone can give force to

the rest, that whoever refuses to obey the general will shall be constrained to do so by the entire body: which means nothing other than that he shall be forced to be free; for this is the condition which, by giving each Citizen to the Fatherland, guarantees him against all personal dependence; the condition which is the device and makes for the operation of the political machine, and alone renders legitimate civil engagements which would otherwise be absurd, tyrannical, and liable to the most enormous abuses.

Chapter Eight
Of the Civil State

[1] This transition from the state of nature to the civil state produces a most remarkable change in man by substituting justice for instinct in his conduct, and endowing his actions with the morality they previously lacked. Only then, when the voice of duty succeeds physical impulsion and right succeeds appetite, does man, who until then had looked only to himself, see himself forced to act on other principles, and to consult his reason before listening to his inclinations. Although in this state he deprives himself of several advantages he has from nature, he gains such great advantages in return, his faculties are exercised and developed, his ideas enlarged, his sentiments ennobled, his entire soul is elevated to such an extent, that if the abuses of this new condition did not often degrade him to beneath the condition he has left, he should ceaselessly bless the happy moment which wrested him from it forever, and out of a stupid and bounded animal made an intelligent being and a man.

[2] Let us reduce this entire balance to terms easy to compare. What man loses by the social contract is his natural freedom and an unlimited right to everything that tempts him and he can reach; what he gains is civil freedom and property in everything he possesses. In order not to be mistaken about these compensations, one has [365] to distinguish clearly between natural freedom which has no other bounds than the individual's forces, and civil freedom which is limited by the general will, and between possession which is merely the effect of force or the right of the first occupant, and property which can only be founded on a positive title.

[3] To the preceding one might add to the credit of the civil state moral freedom, which alone makes man truly the master of himself; for the impulsion of mere appetite is slavery, and obedience to the law one has prescribed to oneself is freedom. But I have already said too much on this topic, and the philosophical meaning of the word *freedom* is not my subject here.

Chapter Nine
Of Real Property

[1]   Each member of the community gives himself to it at the moment of its formation, such as he then is, he himself with all his forces, of which the goods he possesses are a part. It is not that by this act possession changes in nature by changing hands, and becomes property in the hands of the Sovereign: But just as the City's forces are incomparably greater than a private individual's, so public possession in fact has greater force and is more irrevocable, without being any more legitimate, at least for foreigners. For with regard to its members, the State is master of all their goods by the social contract which serves as the basis of all rights within the State; but with regard to other Powers it is master of all of its members' goods only by the right of the first occupant which it derives from private individuals.

[2]   The right of the first occupant, although more real than the right of the stronger, becomes a true right only after the right of property has been established. Every man naturally has the right to everything he needs; but the positive act that makes him the proprietor of some good excludes him from all the rest. Having received his share, he must be bound by it, and he has no further right to the community [of goods]. That is why the right of the first occupant, so weak in the state of nature, is respected by everyone living in civil society. [366] In this right one respects not so much what is another's as what is not one's own.

[3]   In general, to authorize the right of the first occupant to any piece of land, the following conditions must apply. First, that this land not yet be inhabited by anyone; second, that one occupy only as much of it as one needs to subsist: In the third place, that one take possession of it not by a vain ceremony, but by labor and cultivation, the only sign of property which others ought to respect in the absence of legal titles.

[4]   Indeed, does not granting the right of the first occupant to need and to labor extend it as far as it can go? Can this right be left unbounded? Shall it suffice to set foot on a piece of common land forthwith to claim to be its master? Shall having the force to drive other men off it for a moment suffice to deprive them of the right ever to return? How can a man or a people seize an immense territory and deprive all mankind of it except by a punishable usurpation, since it deprives the rest of mankind of a place to live and of foods which nature gives to all in common? When Núñez Balboa, standing on the shore, took possession of the southern seas and of all of South America in the name of the crown of Castile, was that enough to dispossess all of its inhabitants and to exclude all the Princes

of the world? If it had been, then such ceremonies were repeated quite unnecessarily, and all the catholic King had to do was from his council-chamber all at once to take possession of the entire universe; except for afterwards subtracting from his empire what the other Princes already possessed before.

[5] It is intelligible how individuals' combined and contiguous pieces of ground become the public territory, and how the right of sovereignty, extending from subjects to the land they occupy, becomes at once real and personal; which places the possessors in a position of greater dependence, and turns their very forces into the guarantors of their fidelity. This advantage seems not to have been fully appreciated by ancient monarchs who, only calling themselves Kings of the Persians, of the Scythians, of the Macedonians, seem to have looked upon themselves as chiefs of men rather than as masters of the country. Present-day monarchs [367] more shrewdly call themselves Kings of France, of Spain, of England, etc. By thus holding the land, they are quite sure of holding its inhabitants.

[6] What is remarkable about this alienation is that the community, far from despoiling individuals of their goods by accepting them, only secures to them their legitimate possession, changes usurpation into a genuine right, and use into property. Thereupon the possessors, since they are considered to be the trustees of the public good, since their rights are respected by all the members of the State and preserved by all of its forces against foreigners, have, by a surrender that is advantageous to the public and even more so to themselves, so to speak acquired everything they have given. The paradox is easily explained by the distinction between the rights the Sovereign and the proprietor have to the same land, as will be seen below.

[7] It may also happen that men begin to unite before they possess anything and that, seizing a piece of land sufficient for all, they enjoy its use in common or divide it among themselves, either equally or accord-ing to proportions established by the Sovereign. Regardless of the manner of this acquisition, the right every individual has over his own land is always subordinate to the right the community has over everyone, without which there would be neither solidity in the social bond, nor real force in the exercise of Sovereignty.

[8] I shall close this chapter and this book with a comment that should serve as the basis of the entire social system; it is that the fun-damental pact, rather than destroying natural equality, on the contrary substitutes a moral and legitimate equality for whatever physical in-equality nature may have placed between men, and that while they may

be unequal in force or in genius, they all become equal by convention and by right.*

Book II

Chapter One
That Sovereignty is Inalienable

[1]   The first and the most important consequence of the principles estab- [OC
lished so far is that the general will alone can direct the forces of the State   111,
according to the end of its institution, which is the common good: for   368]
while the opposition of particular interests made the establishment of
societies necessary, it is the agreement of these same interests which made
it possible. What these different interests have in common is what forms
the social bond, and if there were not some point on which all interests
agree, no society could exist. Now it is solely in terms of this common
interest that society ought to be governed.

[2]   I say, then, that sovereignty, since it is nothing but the exercise of
the general will, can never be alienated, and that the sovereign, which is
nothing but a collective being, can only be represented by itself; power
can well be transferred, but not will.

[3]   Indeed, while it is not impossible that a particular will agree
with the general will on some point, it is in any event impossible for this
agreement to be lasting and constant; for the particular will tends, by its
nature, to partiality, and the general will to equality. It is even more impossible to have a guarantee of this agreement, even if it always obtained; it
would be an effect not of art, but of chance. The Sovereign may well say,
I currently will what a given man wills or at least what he says he wills; but
it cannot say: what this man is going to will tomorrow, I too shall will it;
since it is absurd for the will to [369] shackle itself for the future, and since
no will can consent to anything contrary to the good of the being that wills.
If, then, the people promises simply to obey, it dissolves itself by this very
act, it loses its quality of being a people; as soon as there is a master, there is
no more sovereign, and the body politic is destroyed forthwith.

[4]   This is not to say that the commands of the chiefs may not be taken
for general wills as long as the sovereign is free to oppose them and does

---

* Under bad governments this equality is only apparent and illusory; it serves only
to maintain the poor in his misery and the rich in his usurpation. In fact the laws are
always useful to those who possess something and harmful to those who have nothing:
Whence it follows that the social state is advantageous for men only insofar as all have
something and none has too much of anything.

not do so. In such a case the people's consent has to be presumed from universal silence. This will be explained more fully.

Chapter Two
That Sovereignty is Indivisible

[1]   For the same reason that sovereignty is inalienable, it is indivisible. For either the will is general* or it is not; it is either the will of the body of the people, or that of only a part. In the first case, the declaration of this will is an act of sovereignty and constitutes law; in the second case it is merely a particular will, or an act of magistracy; at most it is a decree.

[2]   But our politicians, unable to divide sovereignty in its principle, divide it in its object; they divide it into force and will, into legislative and executive power, into rights of taxation, justice and war, into domestic administration and the power to conduct foreign affairs: sometimes they mix up all these parts and sometimes they separate them; they turn the Sovereign into a being that is fantastical and formed of disparate pieces; it is as if they were putting together man out of several bodies one of which had eyes, another arms, another feet, and nothing else. Japanese conjurors are said to carve up a child before the spectators' eyes, then, throwing all of its members into the air one after the other, they make [370] the child fall back down alive and all reassembled. That is more or less what our politicians' tricks are like; having dismembered the social body by a sleight-of-hand worthy of the fairground, they put the pieces back together no one knows how.

[3]   This error comes from not having framed precise notions of sovereign authority, and from having taken what were mere emanations from this authority for parts of this authority itself. Thus, for example, the act of declaring war and that of making peace have been regarded as acts of sovereignty, which they are not; for neither of these acts is a law but only an application of the law, a particular act which decides a case, as will clearly be seen once the idea that attaches to the word *law* has been fixed.

[4]   By examining the other divisions in the same way, one would discover that whenever one believes one sees sovereignty divided, one is mistaken, that the rights which one takes for parts of this sovereignty are all subordinate to it, and always presuppose supreme wills which these rights simply implement.

[5]   It would be difficult to exaggerate how much this lack of precision has clouded the conclusions of writers on matters of political right

---

*   For a will to be general, it is not always necessary that it be unanimous, but it is necessary that all votes be counted; any formal exclusion destroys generality.

when they sought to adjudicate the respective rights of kings and peoples by the principles they had established. Anyone can see in chapters three and four of the first Book of Grotius how that learned man and his translator Barbeyrac get entangled and constrained by their sophisms, fearful of saying too much or not saying enough according to their views, and of offending the interests they had to reconcile. Grotius, a refugee in France, discontented with his fatherland, and wanting to pay court to Louis XIII to whom his book is dedicated, spares nothing to despoil peoples of all their rights, and to invest kings with them as artfully as possible. This would certainly also have been to the taste of Barbeyrac, who dedicated his translation to King George I of England. But unfortunately the expulsion of James II, which he calls an abdication, forced him to be on his guard, to equivocate, to be evasive, in order not to make a usurper of William. If these two writers had adopted the true principles, all their difficulties would have been solved, and they would always have been consistent; but they would have sadly told the truth and [371] paid court only to the people. Now, truth does not lead to fortune, and the people confers no ambassadorships, professorships or pensions.

Chapter Three
Whether the General Will Can Err

[1]   From the preceding it follows that the general will is always upright and always tends to the public utility: but it does not follow from it that the people's deliberations are always equally upright. One always wants one's good, but one does not always see it: one can never corrupt the people, but one can often cause it to be mistaken, and only when it is, does it appear to want what is bad.

[2]   There is often a considerable difference between the will of all and the general will: the latter looks only to the common interest, the former looks to private interest, and is nothing but a sum of particular wills; but if, from these same wills, one takes away the pluses and the minuses which cancel each other out,* what is left as the sum of the differences is the general will.

[3]   If, when an adequately informed people deliberates, the Citizens had no communication among themselves, the general will would always

---

* *Each interest,* says the M[arquis] d'A[rgenson], *has different principles. The agreement between two individual interests is formed by opposition to a third party's interest.* He might have added that the agreement between all interests is formed by opposition to each one's interest. If there were no different interests, the common interest would scarcely be sensible since it would never encounter obstacles: everything would run by itself, and politics would cease to be an art.

result from the large number of small differences, and the deliberation would always be good. But when factions arise, small associations at the expense of the large association, the will of each one of these associations becomes general in relation to its members and particular in relation to the State; there can then no longer be said to be as many voters as [372] there are men, but only as many as there are associations. The differences become less numerous and yield a less general result. Finally, when one of these associations is so large that it prevails over all the rest, the result you have is no longer a sum of small differences, but one single difference; then there is no longer a general will, and the opinion that prevails is nothing but a private opinion.

[4] It is important, then, that in order to have the general will expressed well, there be no partial society in the State, and every Citizen state only his own opinion.* Such was the single sublime institution of the great Lycurgus. That if there are partial societies, their number must be multiplied, and inequality among them prevented, as was done by Solon, Numa, Servius. These are the only precautions that will ensure that the general will is always enlightened, and that the people make no mistakes.

Chapter Four
Of the Limits of Sovereign Power

[1] If the State or the City is only a moral person whose life consists in the union of its members, and if the most important of its cares is the care for its self-preservation, then it has to have some universal and coercive force to move and arrange each part in the manner most conformable to the whole. Just as nature gives each man absolute power over his members, the social pact gives the body politic absolute power over all of its members, and it is this same power which, directed by the general will, bears, as I have said, the name of sovereignty.

[373] [2] But in addition to the public person, we must consider the private persons who make it up, and whose life and freedom are naturally independent of it. It is therefore important to distinguish clearly

---

* "In truth, says Machiavelli, some divisions harm Republics, and some benefit them; harmful are those that are accompanied by factions and parties; beneficial are those that do not give rise to factions and parties. Therefore, since the founder of a Republic cannot prevent enmities, he must make the best provision possible against factions." *Hist[ory] of Floren[ce]*, Bk. vii [ch. 1].

between the respective rights of the Citizens and of the Sovereign,* as well as between duties which the former have to fulfill as subjects, and the natural right which they must enjoy as men.

[3]   It is agreed that each man alienates by the social pact only that portion of his power, his goods, his freedom, which it is important for the community to be able to use, but it should also be agreed to that the Sovereign is alone judge of that importance.

[4]   All the services a Citizen can render the State, he owes to it as soon as the Sovereign requires them; but the Sovereign, for its part, cannot burden the subjects with any shackles that are useless to the community; it cannot even will to do so: for under the law of reason nothing is done without cause, any more than under the law of nature.

[5]   The commitments which bind us to the social body are obligatory only because they are mutual, and their nature is such that in fulfilling them one cannot work for others without also working for oneself. Why is the general will always upright, and why do all consistently will each one's happiness, if not because there is no one who does not appropriate the word *each* to himself, and think of himself as he votes for all? Which proves that the equality of right and the notion of justice which it produces follows from each one's preference for himself and hence from the nature of man; that the general will, to be truly such, must be so in its object as well as in its essence, that it must issue from all in order to apply to all, and that it loses its natural rectitude when it tends toward some individual and determinate object; for then, judging what is foreign to us, we have no true principle of equity to guide us.

[6]   Indeed, whenever what is at issue is a particular fact or right regarding a point not regulated by a general and prior convention, the affair grows contentious. [374] In such a suit, where interested private individuals are one of the parties, and the public the other, I do not see what law should be followed or what judge should pronounce judgment. It would be ridiculous, under these circumstances, to try to invoke an express decision of the general will, which can only be the decision of one of the parties, and is, therefore, as far as the other party is concerned, nothing but a foreign, particular will which on this occasion is inclined to injustice and subject to error. Thus, just as a particular will cannot represent the general will, so the general will changes in nature when it has a particular object, and it cannot, being general, pronounce judgment on a particular man or fact. For example, when the people of Athens appointed

---

*   Attentive readers, please do not rush to accuse me of contradiction. I have not been able to avoid it verbally, in view of the poverty of the language; but wait.

or cashiered its chiefs, bestowed honors on one, imposed penalties on another, and by a multitude of particular decrees indiscriminately performed all the acts of government, the people no longer had a general will properly so called; it no longer acted as a Sovereign but as a magistrate. This will appear contrary to the commonly held ideas, but I must be allowed the time to set forth my own.

[7]   In view of this, one has to understand that what generalizes the will is not so much the number of voices, as it is the common interest which unites them: for in this institution, everyone necessarily submits to the conditions which he imposes on others; an admirable agreement between interest and justice which confers on common deliberations a character of equity that is seen to vanish in the discussion of any particular affair, for want of a common interest which unites and identifies the rule of the judge with that of the party.

[8]   From whatever side one traces one's way back to the principle, one always reaches the same conclusion: namely, that the social pact establishes among the Citizens an equality such that all commit themselves under the same conditions and must all enjoy the same rights. Thus by the nature of the pact every act of sovereignty, that is to say every genuine act of the general will, either obligates or favors all Citizens equally, so that the Sovereign knows only the body of the nation and does not single out any one of those who make it up. What, then, is, properly, an act of sovereignty? It is not a convention of the superior with the inferior, but a convention of the body with each one of its members: [375] A convention which is legitimate because it is based on the social contract, equitable because it is common to all, and secure because the public force and the supreme power are its guarantors. So long as subjects are subjected only to conventions such as these, they obey no one, but only their own will; and to ask how far the respective rights of Sovereign and Citizens extend is to ask how far the Citizens can commit themselves to one another, each to all, and all to each.

[9]   From this it is apparent that the Sovereign power, absolute, sacred, and inviolable though it is, does not and cannot exceed the limits of the general conventions, and that everyone may fully dispose of such of his goods and freedom as are left him by these conventions: so that it is never right for the Sovereign to burden one subject more than another, because it then turns into a particular affair, and its power is no longer competent.

[10]   These distinctions once admitted, it is so [evidently] false that the social contract involves any renunciation on the part of individuals, that [rather] as a result of the contract their situation really proves to be preferable to what it had been before, and that instead of an alienation they have

only made an advantageous exchange of an uncertain and precarious way of being in favor of a more secure and better one, of natural independence in favor of freedom, of the power to harm others in favor of their own security, and of their force which others could overwhelm in favor of right made invincible by the social union. Their very life which they have dedicated to the State is constantly protected by it, and when they risk it for its defense, what are they doing but returning to it what they have received from it? What are they doing that they would not have done more frequently and at greater peril in the state of nature, when, waging inevitable fights, they would be defending the means of preserving their lives by risking them? All have to fight for the fatherland if need be, it is true, but then no one ever has to fight for himself. Isn't it nevertheless a gain to risk for the sake of what gives us security just a part of what we would have to risk for our own sakes if we were deprived of this security?

Chapter Five
Of the Right of Life and Death

[1]   It is asked how individuals who have no right to dispose of their own life can transfer to the Sovereign this same right which they do not have. The question seems difficult to resolve only because it is badly put. Everyone has the right to risk his life in order to save it. Has anyone ever said that a person who jumps out of a window to escape a fire is guilty of suicide? Has that crime even ever been imputed to a person who dies in a storm, although he was not unaware of the danger when he set out?

[2]   The social treaty has the preservation of the contracting parties as its end. Whoever wills the end, also wills the means, and these means are inseparable from certain risks and even certain losses. Whoever wants to preserve his life at the expense of others ought also to give it up for them when necessary. Now, the Citizen is no longer judge of the danger the law wills him to risk, and when the Prince has said to him, it is expedient to the State that you die, he ought to die; since it is only on this condition that he has lived in security until then, and his life is no longer only a bounty of nature, but a conditional gift of the State.

[3]   The death penalty imposed on criminals can be looked upon from more or less the same point of view: it is in order not to become the victim of an assassin that one consents to die if one becomes an assassin oneself. Under this treaty, far from disposing of one's own life, one only thinks of guaranteeing it, and it should not be presumed that at the time any of the contracting parties is planning to get himself hanged.

[4]   Besides, every evil-doer who attacks social right becomes a rebel and a traitor to the fatherland by his crimes, by violating its laws he ceases to be a member of it, and even enters into war with it. Then the preservation of the State is incompatible with his own, one of the two has to perish, and when the guilty man is put to death, it is less as a Citizen than as an enemy. The proceedings, the [377] judgment are the proofs and declaration that he has broken the social treaty, and consequently is no longer a member of the State. Now, since he recognized himself as one, at the very least by residence, he must be cut off from it either by exile as a violator of the treaty, or by death as a public enemy; for such an enemy is not a moral person, but a man, and in that case killing the vanquished is by right of war.

[5]   But, it will be said, the condemnation of a Criminal is a particular act. Granted; and indeed such a condemnation does not belong to the Sovereign's province; it is a right the Sovereign can confer without itself being able to exercise it. My ideas all fit together, but I cannot well present them all at once.

[6]   Besides, frequent harsh punishments are always a sign of weakness or laziness in the Government. There is not a single wicked man who could not be made good for something. One only has the right to put to death, even as an example, someone who cannot be preserved without danger.

[7]   As for the right to pardon, or to exempt a guilty man from the penalty prescribed by law and imposed by a judge, it belongs exclusively to the one which is above judge and law; that is to say, to the Sovereign: And even the Sovereign's right in this is not altogether clear, and the occasions to exercise it are very rare. In a well-governed State there are few punishments, not because many pardons are granted, but because there are few criminals: when the State is in decline the large number of crimes ensures their impunity. Under the Roman Republic neither the Senate nor the Consuls ever attempted to grant pardons; nor did the people itself grant any, although it sometimes revoked its own verdict. Frequent pardons proclaim that crimes will soon no longer need them, and anyone can see where that leads. But I feel my heart murmur and check my pen; let us leave these questions to be discussed by the just man who has never lapsed, and never himself been in need of pardon.

Chapter Six
Of Law

[1]   By the social pact we have given the body politic existence and life: the task now is to give it motion and will by legislation. For the initial

act by which this body assumes form and unity still leaves entirely un-
determined what it must do to preserve itself.

[2]   What is good and conformable to order is so by the nature of
things and independently of human conventions. All justice comes from
God, he alone is its source; but if we were capable of receiving it from so
high, we would need neither government nor laws. No doubt there is a
universal justice emanating from reason alone; but this justice, to be
admitted among us, has to be reciprocal. Considering things in human
terms, the laws of justice are vain among men for want of natural sanctions; they only bring good to the wicked and evil to the just when he
observes them toward everyone while no one observes them toward him.
Conventions and laws are therefore necessary to combine rights with
duties and to bring justice back to its object. In the state of nature, where
everything is common, I owe nothing to those to whom I have promised
nothing. I recognize as another's only what is of no use to myself. It is not
so in the civil state where all rights are fixed by law.

[3]   But what, then, finally, is a law? So long as one leaves it at attach-
ing only metaphysical ideas to this word, one will continue reasoning
without understanding one another, and even once it has been stated
what a law of nature is, one will not have been brought any closer to
knowing what a law of the State is.

[4]   I have already said that there is no general will about a particular
object. Indeed, this particular object is either within the State or outside
the State. If it is outside the State, a will that is foreign is not general in
relation to it; and if this object is inside the State, it is a part of it: Then
a relation is formed between the whole and its part that makes them into
two separate beings, of which the part is [379] one, and the whole, less
that part, the other. But the whole less a part is not the whole, and as long
as this relation persists there is no longer a whole but two unequal parts;
from which it follows that neither is the will of one of these parts general
in relation to the other.

[5]   But when the whole people enacts statutes for the whole people
it considers only itself, and if a relation is then formed, it is between the
entire object from one point of view and the entire object from another
point of view, with no division of the whole. Then the matter with regard
to which the statute is being enacted is general, as is the enacting will. It
is this act which I call law.

[6]   When I say that the object of the laws is always general, I mean
that the law considers the subjects in a body and their actions in the
abstract, never any man as an individual or a particular action. Thus the
law can very well state that there will be privileges, but it cannot confer

them on any one by name; the law can create several Classes of Citizens, it can even specify the qualifications that entitle to membership in these classes, but it cannot nominate this person or that for admission to them; it can establish a royal government and hereditary succession, but it cannot elect a king or name a royal family; in a word, any function that relates to an individual does not fall within the province of the legislative power.

[7]   On this idea one immediately sees that one need no longer ask whose province it is to make laws, since they are acts of the general will; nor whether the Prince is above the laws, since it is a member of the State; nor whether the law can be unjust, since no man can be unjust toward himself; nor how one is both free and subject to the laws, since they are merely records of our wills.

[8]   One also sees that since the law combines the universality of the will and that of the object, what any man, regardless of who he may be, orders on his own authority is not a law; what even the Sovereign orders regarding a particular object is not a law either, but a decree, nor is it an act of sovereignty but of magistracy.

[9]   I therefore call Republic any State ruled by laws, whatever may be the form of administration: for then the public interest alone governs, and the [*380*] public thing counts for something. Every legitimate Government is republican:* I shall explain in the sequel what Government is.

[10]   Laws are, properly speaking, nothing but the conditions of the civil association. The People subject to the laws ought to be their author; only those who are associating may regulate the conditions of the society; but how will they regulate them? Will it be by common agreement, by a sudden inspiration? Has the body politic an organ to state its wills? Who will give it the foresight necessary to form its acts and to publish them in advance, or how will it declare them in time of need? How will a blind multitude, which often does not know what it wills because it rarely knows what is good for it, carry out an undertaking as great, as difficult as a system of legislation? By itself the people always wills the good, but by itself it does not always see it. The general will is always upright, but the judgment which guides it is not always enlightened. It must be made to see objects as they are, sometimes as they should appear to it,

---

*   By this word I understand not only an Aristocracy or a Democracy, but in general any government guided by the general will, which is the law. To be legitimate, the Government must not be confused with the Sovereign, but be its minister: Then monarchy itself is a republic. This will become clearer in the following book [not included in this excerpt].

shown the good path which it is seeking, secured against seduction by particular wills, bring together places and times within its purview, weigh the appeal of present, perceptible advantages against the danger of remote and hidden evils. Individuals see the good they reject, the public wills the good it does not see. All are equally in need of guides: The first must be obligated to conform their wills to their reason; the other must be taught to know what it wills. Then public enlightenment results in the union of understanding and will in the social body, from this union results the smooth cooperation of the parts, and finally the greatest force of the whole. Hence arises the necessity of a Lawgiver.

From *Groundwork of the Metaphysics of Morals*

Immanuel Kant

The will is thought as a capacity to determine itself to acting in conformity with the *representation of certain laws*. And such a capacity can be found only in rational beings. Now, what serves the will as the objective ground of its self-determination is an end, and this, if it is given by reason alone, must hold equally for all rational beings. What, on the other hand, contains merely the ground of the possibility of an action the effect of which is an end is called a *means*. The subjective ground of desire is an *incentive*; the objective ground of volition is a *motive*; hence the distinction between subjective ends, which rest on incentives, and objective ends, which depend on motives, which hold for every rational being. Practical prin-

4:428 ciples are *formal* if they abstract from all subjective ends, whereas they are *material* if they have put these, and consequently certain incentives, at their basis. The ends that a rational being proposes at his discretion as *effects* of his actions (material ends) are all only relative; for only their mere relation to a specially constituted[1] faculty of desire on the part of the subject gives them their worth, which can therefore furnish no universal principles, no principles valid and necessary for all rational beings and also for every volition, that is, no practical laws. Hence all these relative ends are only the ground of hypothetical imperatives.

But suppose there were something the *existence of which in itself* has an absolute worth, something which as *an end in itself* could be a ground of determinate laws; then in it, and in it alone, would lie the ground of a possible categorical imperative, that is, of a practical law.

Immanuel Kant, *Groundwork of the Metaphysics of Morals*, Mary Gregor, trans. and ed. (Cambridge: Cambridge University Press, 1998), pp. 36–43.

Marginal notations are to volume and page of the standard German edition of Kant's works: Kant's *Gesammelte Schriften*, ed. Royal Prussian (later German) Academy of Sciences (Berlin: George Reimer, later Walter de Gruyter & Co.).

Now I say that the human being and in general every rational being *exists* as an end in itself, *not merely as a means* to be used by this or that will at its discretion; instead he must in all his actions, whether directed to himself or also to other rational beings, always be regarded *at the same time as an end*. All objects of the inclinations have only a conditional worth; for, if there were not inclinations and the needs based on them, their object would be without worth. But the inclinations themselves, as sources of needs, are so far from having an absolute worth, so as to make one wish to have them,[2] that it must instead be the universal wish of every rational being to be altogether free from them. Thus the worth of any object *to be acquired* by our action is always conditional. Beings the existence of which rests not on our will but on nature, if they are beings without reason, still have only a relative worth, as means, and are therefore called *things*,[3] whereas rational beings are called *persons* because their nature already marks them out as an end in itself, that is, as something that may not be used merely as a means, and hence so far limits all choice (and is an object of respect). These, therefore, are not merely subjective ends, the existence of which as an effect of our action has a worth *for us*, but rather *objective ends*, that is, beings[4] the existence of which is in itself an end, and indeed one such that no other end, to which they would serve *merely* as means, can be put in its place, since without it nothing of *absolute worth* would be found anywhere; but if all worth were conditional and therefore contingent, then no supreme practical principle for reason could be found anywhere.

If, then, there is to be a supreme practical principle and, with respect to the human will, a categorical imperative, it must be one such that, from the representation of what is necessarily an end for everyone because it is an *end in itself*, it constitutes an *objective* principle of the will and thus can serve as a universal practical law.[5] The ground of this principle is: *rational nature exists as an end in itself*. The human being necessarily represents his own existence in this way; so far it is thus a *subjective* principle of human actions. But every other rational being also represents his existence in this way consequent on[6] just the same rational ground that also holds for me;* thus it is at the same time an *objective* principle from which, as a supreme practical ground, it must be possible to derive all laws of the will. The practical imperative will therefore be the following: *So act that you use humanity, whether in your own person or in the person of any other, always at the same time as an end, never merely as a means. . . .*   4:429

---

* Here I put forward this proposition as a postulate. The grounds for it will be found in the last Section.

This principle of humanity, and in general of every rational nature, *as an end in itself* (which is the supreme limiting condition of the freedom of action of every human being) is not borrowed from experience; first because of its universality, since it applies to all rational beings as such and no experience is sufficient to determine anything about them; second because in it humanity is represented not as an end of human beings (subjectively), that is, not as an object that we of ourselves actually make our end, but as an objective end that, whatever ends we may have, ought as law to constitute the supreme limiting condition of all subjective ends, so that the principle must arise from pure reason. That is to say, the ground of all practical lawgiving lies (in accordance with the first principle) *objectively in the rule* and the form of universality which makes it fit to be a law (possibly[7] a law of nature); *subjectively*, however, it lies in the *end*; but the subject of all ends is every rational being as an end in itself (in accordance with the second principle); from this there follows now the third practical principle of the will, as supreme condition of its harmony with universal practical reason, the idea *of the will of every rational being as a will giving universal law.*

4:431

In accordance with this principle all maxims are repudiated that are inconsistent with the will's own giving of universal law. Hence the will is not merely subject to the law but subject to it in such a way that it must be viewed as also giving the law to itself[8] and just because of this as first subject to the law (of which it can regard itself as the author).[9]

Imperatives as they were represented above – namely in terms of the conformity of actions with universal law similar to a *natural order* or of the universal *supremacy as ends*[10] of rational beings in themselves – did exclude from their commanding authority any admixture of interest as incentive, just by their having been represented as categorical; but they were only *assumed*[11] to be categorical because we had to make such an assumption if we wanted to explain the concept of duty. But that there are practical propositions which command categorically could not itself be proved,[12] any more than it could be proved either here or anywhere else in this section; one thing, however, could still have been done: namely, to indicate in the imperative itself the renunciation of all interest, in volition from duty, by means of some determination the imperative contains, as the specific mark distinguishing[13] categorical from hypothetical imperatives; and this is done in the present third formula of the principle, namely the idea of the will of every rational being as a *will giving universal law.*

4:432

For when we think of a will of this kind, then although a will that *stands under law* may be bound to this law by means of some interest, a will that is itself the supreme lawgiver cannot possibly, as such, depend upon some interest; for, a will that is dependent in this way would itself need yet another law that would limit the interest of its self-love to the condition of a validity for universal law.

Thus the *principle* of every human will as *a will giving universal law through all its maxims,** provided it is otherwise correct, would be very *well suited* to be the categorical imperative by this: that just because of the idea of giving universal law *it is based on no interest* and therefore, among all possible imperatives, can alone be *unconditional*; or still better, by converting the proposition, if there is a categorical imperative (i.e., a law for every will of a rational being) it can only command that everything be done from the maxim of one's will as a will that could at the same time have as its object itself as giving universal law; for only then is the practical principle, and the imperative that the will obeys, unconditional, since it can have no interest as its basis.

If we look back upon all previous efforts that have ever been made to discover the principle of morality, we need not wonder now why all of them had to fail. It was seen that the human being is bound to laws by his duty, but it never occurred to them that he is subject *only to laws given by himself but still universal* and that he is bound only to act in conformity with his own will, which, however, in accordance with nature's end[14] is a will giving universal law. For, if one thought of him only as subject to a law (whatever it may be), this law had to carry with it some interest by way of attraction or constraint, since it did not as a law arise from *his* will; in order to conform with the law, his will had instead to be constrained by *something else* to act in a certain way.[15] By this quite necessary consequence, however, all the labor to find a supreme ground of duty was irretrievably lost. For, one never arrived at duty but instead at the necessity of an action from a certain interest. This might be one's own or another's interest. But then the imperative had to turn out always conditional and could not be fit for a moral command. I will therefore call this basic principle the principle of the **autonomy** of the will in contrast with every other, which I accordingly count as **heteronomy**.

4:433

The concept of every rational being as one who must regard himself as giving universal law through all the maxims of his will, so as to appraise himself and his actions from this point of view, leads to a very fruitful concept dependent upon it,[16] namely that of *a kingdom*[17] *of ends*.

---

* I may be excused from citing examples to illustrate this principle, since those that have already illustrated the categorical imperative and its formula can all serve for the same end here.

By a *kingdom* I understand a systematic union of various rational beings through common laws. Now since laws determine ends in terms of their universal validity, if we abstract from the personal differences of rational beings as well as from all the content of their private ends we shall be able to think of a whole of all ends in systematic connection (a whole both of rational beings as ends in themselves and of the ends of his own that each may set himself), that is, a kingdom of ends, which is possible in accordance with the above principles.

For, all rational beings stand under the *law* that each of them is to treat himself and all others *never merely as means* but always *at the same time as ends in themselves*. But from this there arises a systematic union of rational beings through common objective laws, that is, a kingdom, which can be called a kingdom of ends (admittedly only an ideal) because what these laws have as their purpose is just the relation of these beings to one another as ends and means.

A rational being belongs as a *member* to the kingdom of ends when he gives universal laws in it but is also himself subject to these laws. He belongs to it *as sovereign*[18] when, as lawgiving, he is not subject to the will of any other.

A rational being must always regard himself as lawgiving in a kingdom of ends possible through freedom of the will, whether as a member or as sovereign. He cannot, however, hold the position of sovereign merely by the maxims of his will but only in case he is a completely independent being, without needs and with unlimited resources[19] adequate to his will.

4:434

Morality consists, then, in the reference of all action to the lawgiving by which alone a kingdom of ends is possible. This lawgiving must, however, be found in every rational being himself and be able to arise from his will, the principle of which is, accordingly: to do no action on any other maxim than one such that it would be consistent with it to be a universal law, and hence to act only *so that the will could regard itself as at the same time giving universal law through its maxim*. Now, if maxims are not already of their nature in agreement with this objective principle of rational beings as givers of universal law, the necessity of an action in accordance with this principle is called practical necessitation, that is, *duty*. Duty does not apply to the sovereign in the kingdom of ends, but it does apply to every member of it and indeed to all in equal measure.

The practical necessity of acting in accordance with this principle, that is, duty, does not rest at all on feelings, impulses, and inclinations but merely on the relation of rational beings to one another, in which the will of a rational being must always be regarded as at the same time *law-giving*, since otherwise it could not be thought as an *end in itself*. Reason accordingly refers every maxim of the will as giving universal law to every other will and also to every action toward oneself, and does so not for the sake of any other practical motive or any future advantage but from the idea of the *dignity* of a rational being, who obeys no law other than that which he himself at the same time gives.

In the kingdom of ends everything has either a *price* or a *dignity*.[20] What has a price can be replaced by something else as its *equivalent*; what on the other hand is raised above all price and therefore admits of no equivalent has a dignity.

What is related to general human inclinations and needs has a *market price*; that which, even without presupposing a need, conforms with a certain taste, that is, with a delight[21] in the mere purposeless[22] play of our mental powers, has a *fancy price*;[23] but that which constitutes the condition under which alone something can be an end in itself has not merely a relative worth, that is, a price, but an inner worth, that is, *dignity*. 4:435

Now, morality is the condition under which alone a rational being can be an end in itself, since only through this is it possible to be a lawgiving member in the kingdom of ends. Hence morality, and humanity insofar as it is capable of morality, is that which alone has dignity. Skill and diligence in work have a market price; wit, lively imagination and humor have a fancy price; on the other hand, fidelity in promises and benevolence from basic principles (not from instinct) have an inner worth. Nature, as well as art, contains nothing that, lacking these, it could put in their place; for their worth does not consist in the effects arising from them, in the advantage and use they provide, but in dispositions,[24] that is, in maxims of the will that in this way are ready to manifest themselves through actions, even if success does not favor them. Such actions also need no recommendation from any subjective disposition[25] or taste, so as to be looked upon with immediate favor and delight, nor do they need any immediate propensity or feeling for them; they present the will that practices them as the object of an immediate respect, and nothing but reason is required to *impose* them upon the will, not to *coax* them from it, which latter would in any case be a contradiction in the case of duties. This estimation therefore lets the worth of such a cast of mind be cognized as dignity and puts it infinitely above all price, with which it cannot be brought into comparison or competition at all without, as it were, assaulting its holiness.[26]

And what is it, then, that justifies a morally good disposition, or virtue, in making such high claims? It is nothing less than the *share* it affords a rational being *in the giving of universal laws,* by which it makes him fit to be a member of a possible kingdom of ends, which he was already destined to be by his own nature as an end in itself and, for that very reason, as lawgiving in the kingdom of ends – as free with respect to all laws of nature, obeying only those which he himself gives and in accordance with which his maxims can belong to a giving of universal law (to which at the

4:436   same time he subjects himself). For, nothing can have a worth other than that which the law determines for it. But the lawgiving itself, which determines all worth, must for that very reason have a dignity, that is, an unconditional, incomparable worth; and the word *respect* alone provides a becoming expression for the estimate of it that a rational being must give. *Autonomy* is therefore the ground of the dignity of human nature and of every rational nature.

Notes

1   *geartetes.*

2   *um sie selbst zu wünschen.*

3   *Sachen.*

4   *Dinge.* Although both *Sache* and *Ding* would usually be translated as "thing," *Sache* has the technical sense of something usable that does not have free choice, i.e., "*Sache ist ein Ding*" to which nothing can be imputed (*The Metaphysics of Morals* 6:223).

5   *ausmacht, mithin zum allgemeinen praktischen Gesetz dienen kann.* It is not clear, grammatically, whether the subject of "can serve" is "end in itself" or "objective principle."

6   *zufolge.*

7   *allenfalls.*

8   Or "as itself lawgiving," *als selbstgesetzgebend.*

9   *Urheber.*

10   *Zweckvorzuges.*

11   *angenommen.*

12   *bewiesen werden.*

13   *Unterscheidungszeichen.*

14   *dem Naturzwecke nach.*

15   *sondern dieser gesetzmässig von etwas anderm genötigt wurde, auf gewisse Weise zu handeln.*

16   Or "attached to it," *ihm anhangenden.*

17   *Reich,* which could also be translated "commonwealth."

18   *als Oberhaupt.*

19   *Vermögen.*

20   *Würde.*

21   *Wohlgefallen.*
22   *zwecklosen.*
23   *Affectionspreis.*
24   *Gesinnungen.*
25   *Disposition.*
26   *Heiligkeit.*

Part III

Contemporary Expressions: Contractarianism

4

Why Contractarianism?

David Gauthier

I

As the will to truth thus gains self-consciousness – there can be no doubt of that – morality will gradually *perish* now: this is the great spectacle in a hundred acts reserved for the next two centuries in Europe – the most terrible, most questionable, and perhaps also the most hopeful of all spectacles.

Nietzsche[1]

Morality faces a foundational crisis. Contractarianism offers the only plausible resolution of this crisis. These two propositions state my theme. What follows is elaboration.

Nietzsche may have been the first, but he has not been alone, in recognizing the crisis to which I refer. Consider these recent statements. "The hypothesis which I wish to advance is that in the actual world which we inhabit the language of morality is in . . . [a] state of grave disorder . . . we have – very largely, if not entirely – lost our comprehension, both theoretical and practical, of morality" (Alasdair MacIntyre).[2] "The resources of most modern moral philosophy are not well adjusted to the modern world" (Bernard Williams).[3] "There are no objective values. . . . [But] the main tradition of European moral philosophy includes the contrary claim" (J. L. Mackie).[4] "Moral hypotheses do not help explain why people observe what they observe. So ethics is problematic and nihilism must be taken seriously. . . . An extreme version of nihilism holds that morality is simply an illusion. . . . In this version, we should abandon morality, just

David Gauthier, "Why Contractarianism," *Contractarianism and Rational Choice*, Peter Vallentyne, ed. (Cambridge: Cambridge University Press, 1991), pp. 15–30.

as an atheist abandons religion after he has decided that religious facts
cannot help explain observations" (Gilbert Harman).[5]

I choose these statements to point to features of the crisis that morality faces. They suggest that moral language fits a world view that we have
abandoned – a view of the world as purposively ordered. Without this
view, we no longer truly understand the moral claims we continue to
make. They suggest that there is a lack of fit between what morality
presupposes – objective values that help explain our behavior, and the
psychological states – desires and beliefs – that, given our present world
view, actually provide the best explanation. This lack of fit threatens to
undermine the very idea of a morality as more than an anthropological
curiosity. But how could this be? How could morality *perish*?

II

To proceed, I must offer a minimal characterization of the morality that
faces a foundational crisis. And this is the morality of justified constraint.
From the standpoint of the agent, moral considerations present themselves as constraining his choices and actions, in ways independent of
his desires, aims, and interests. Later, I shall add to this characterization, but for the moment it will suffice. For it reveals clearly what is in
question – the ground of constraint. This ground seems absent from our
present world view. And so we ask, what reason can a person have for
recognizing and accepting a constraint that is independent of his desires
and interests? He may agree that such a constraint would be *morally*
justified; he would have a reason for accepting it *if* he had a reason for
accepting morality. But what justifies paying attention to morality, rather
than dismissing it as an appendage of outworn beliefs? We ask, and
seem to find no answer. But before proceeding, we should consider three
objections.

The first is to query the idea of constraint. Why should morality be seen
as constraining our choices and actions? Why should we not rather say
that the moral person chooses most freely, because she chooses in the light
of a true conception of herself, rather than in the light of the false conceptions that so often predominate? Why should we not link morality
with self-understanding? Plato and Hume might be enlisted to support
this view, but Hume would be at best a partial ally, for his representation
of "virtue in all her genuine and most engaging charms, . . . talk[ing] not
of useless austerities and rigors, suffering and self-denial," but rather
making "her votaries . . . , during every instant of their existence, if pos-

sible, cheerful and happy," is rather overcast by his admission that "in the case of justice, . . . a man, taking things in a certain light, may often seem to be a loser by his integrity."[6] Plato, to be sure, goes further, insisting that only the just man has a healthy soul, but heroic as Socrates' defense of justice may be, we are all too apt to judge that Glaucon and Adeimantus have been charmed rather than reasoned into agreement, and that the unjust man has not been shown necessarily to be the loser.[7] I do not, in any event, intend to pursue this direction of thought. Morality, as we, heirs to the Christian and Kantian traditions, conceive it, constrains the pursuits to which even our reflective desires would lead us. And this is not simply or entirely a constraint on self-interest; the affections that morality curbs include the social ones of favoritism and partiality, to say nothing of cruelty.

The second objection to the view that moral constraint is insufficiently grounded is to query the claim that it operates independently of, rather than through, our desires, interests, and affections. Morality, some may say, concerns the well-being of all persons, or perhaps of all sentient creatures.[8] And one may then argue, either with Hume, that morality arises in and from our sympathetic identification with our fellows, or that it lies directly in well-being, and that our affections tend to be disposed favorably toward it. But, of course, not all of our affections. And so our sympathetic feelings come into characteristic opposition to other feelings, in relation to which they function as a constraint.

This is a very crude characterization, but it will suffice for the present argument. This view grants that morality, as we understand it, is without purely *rational* foundations, but reminds us that we are not therefore unconcerned about the well-being of our fellows. Morality is founded on the widespread, sympathetic, other-directed concerns that most of us have, and these concerns do curb self-interest, and also the favoritism and partiality with which we often treat others. Nevertheless, if morality depends for its practical relevance and motivational efficacy entirely on our sympathetic feelings, it has no title to the prescriptive grip with which it has been invested in the Christian and Kantian views to which I have referred, and which indeed Glaucon and Adeimantus demanded that Socrates defend to them in the case of justice. For to be reminded that some of the time we do care about our fellows and are willing to curb other desires in order to exhibit that care tells us nothing that can guide us in those cases in which, on the face of it, we do not care, or do not care enough – nothing that will defend the demands that morality makes on us in the hard cases. That not all situations in which concern for others combats self-concern are hard cases is true, but morality, as we ordinarily understand it, speaks to the hard cases, whereas its Humean or naturalistic replacement does not.

These remarks apply to the most sustained recent positive attempt to create a moral theory – that of John Rawls. For the attempt to describe our moral capacity, or more particularly, for Rawls, our sense of justice, in terms of principles, plausible in the light of our more general psychological theory, and coherent with "our considered judgments in reflective equilibrium,"[9] will not yield any answer to why, in those cases in which we have no, or insufficient, interest in being just, we should nevertheless follow the principles. John Harsanyi, whose moral theory is in some respects a utilitarian variant of Rawls' contractarian construction, recognizes this explicitly: "All we can prove by rational arguments is that anybody who wants to serve our common human interests in a rational manner must obey these commands."[10] But although morality may offer itself in the service of our common human interests, it does not offer itself only to those who want to serve them.

Morality is a constraint that, as Kant recognized, must not be supposed to depend solely on our feelings. And so we may not appeal to feelings to answer the question of its foundation. But the third objection is to dismiss this question directly, rejecting the very idea of a foundational crisis. Nothing justifies morality, for morality needs no justification. We find ourselves, in morality as elsewhere, in mediis rebus. We make, accept and reject, justify and criticize moral judgments. The concern of moral theory is to systematize that practice, and so to give us a deeper understanding of what moral justification is. But there are no extramoral foundations for moral justification, any more than there are extraepistemic foundations for epistemic judgments. In morals as in science, foundationalism is a bankrupt project.

Fortunately, I do not have to defend *normative* foundationalism. One problem with accepting moral justification as part of our ongoing practice is that, as I have suggested, we no longer accept the world view on which it depends. But perhaps a more immediately pressing problem is that we have, ready to hand, an alternative mode for justifying our choices and actions. In its more austere and, in my view, more defensible form, this is to show that choices and actions maximize the agent's expected utility, where utility is a measure of considered preference. In its less austere version, this is to show that choices and actions satisfy, not a subjectively defined requirement such as utility, but meet the agent's objective interests. Since I do not believe that we have objective interests, I shall ignore this latter. But it will not matter. For the idea is clear; we have a mode of justification that does not require the introduction of moral considerations.[11]

Let me call this alternative nonmoral mode of justification, neutrally, deliberative justification. Now moral and deliberative justification are directed at the same objects – our choices and actions. What if they conflict? And what do we say to the person who offers a deliberative justification of his choices and actions and refuses to offer any other? We can say, of course, that his behavior lacks *moral* justification, but this seems to lack any hold, unless he chooses to enter the moral framework. And such entry, he may insist, lacks any deliberative justification, at least for him.

If morality perishes, the justificatory enterprise, in relation to choice and action, does not perish with it. Rather, one mode of justification perishes, a mode that, it may seem, now hangs unsupported. But not only unsupported, for it is difficult to deny that deliberative justification is more clearly basic, that it cannot be avoided insofar as we are rational agents, so that if moral justification conflicts with it, morality seems not only unsupported but opposed by what is rationally more fundamental.

Deliberative justification relates to our deep sense of self. What distinguishes human beings from other animals, and provides the basis for rationality, is the capacity for semantic representation. You can, as your dog on the whole cannot, represent a state of affairs to yourself, and consider in particular whether or not it is the case, and whether or not you would want it to be the case. You can represent to yourself the contents of your beliefs, and your desires or preferences. But in representing them, you bring them into relation with one another. You represent to yourself that the Blue Jays will win the World Series, and that a National League team will win the World Series, and that the Blue Jays are not a National League team. And in recognizing a conflict among those beliefs, you find rationality thrust upon you. Note that the first two beliefs could be replaced by preferences, with the same effect.

Since in representing our preferences we become aware of conflict among them, the step from representation to choice becomes complicated. We must, somehow, bring our conflicting desires and preferences into some sort of coherence. And there is only one plausible candidate for a principle of coherence – a maximizing principle. We order our preferences, in relation to decision and action, so that we may choose in a way that maximizes our expectation of preference fulfillment. And in so doing, we show ourselves to be rational agents, engaged in deliberation and deliberative justification. There is simply nothing else for practical rationality to be.

The foundational crisis of morality thus cannot be avoided by pointing to the existence of a practice of justification within the moral framework, and denying that any extramoral foundation is relevant. For an extra-moral mode of justification is already present, existing not side by side with moral justification, but in a manner tied to the way in which we unify our beliefs and preferences and so acquire our deep sense of self. We need not suppose that this deliberative justification is itself to be understood foundationally. All that we need suppose is that moral justification does not plausibly survive conflict with it.

III

In explaining why we may not dismiss the idea of a foundational crisis in morality as resulting from a misplaced appeal to a philosophically dis-credited or suspect idea of foundationalism, I have begun to expose the character and dimensions of the crisis. I have claimed that morality faces an alternative, conflicting, deeper mode of justification, related to our deep sense of self, that applies to the entire realm of choice and action, and that evaluates each *action* in terms of the reflectively held concerns of its *agent*. The relevance of the agent's concerns to practical justification does not seem to me in doubt. The relevance of anything else, except insofar as it bears on the agent's concerns, does seem to me very much in doubt. If the agent's reflectively endorsed concerns, his preferences, desires, and aims, are, with his considered beliefs, constitutive of his self-conception, then I can see no remotely plausible way of arguing from their relevance to that of anything else that is not similarly related to his sense of self. And, indeed, I can see no way of introducing anything as relevant to practical justification except through the agent's self-conception. My assertion of this practical individualism is not a conclusive argument, but the burden of proof is surely on those who would maintain a contrary position. Let them provide the arguments – if they can.

Deliberative justification does not refute morality. Indeed, it does not offer morality the courtesy of a refutation. It ignores morality, and seem-ingly replaces it. It preempts the arena of justification, apparently leaving morality no room to gain purchase. Let me offer a controversial com-parison. Religion faces – indeed, has faced – a comparable foundational crisis. Religion demands the worship of a divine being who purposively orders the universe. But it has confronted an alternative mode of explan-ation. Although the emergence of a cosmological theory based on effi-cient, rather than teleological, causation provided warning of what was to come, the supplanting of teleology in biology by the success of evolution-ary theory in providing a mode of explanation that accounted in efficient-causal terms for the *appearance* of a purposive order among living beings, may seem to toll the death knell for religion as an intellectually respectable enterprise. But evolutionary biology and, more generally, modern science do not refute religion. Rather they ignore it, replacing its explanations by ontologically simpler ones. Religion, understood as affirming the justifiable worship of a divine being, may be unable to survive its foundational crisis. Can morality, understood as affirming justifiable constraints on choice independent of the agent's concerns, survive?

There would seem to be three ways for morality to escape religion's apparent fate. One would be to find, for moral facts or moral properties, an explanatory role that would entrench them prior to any consideration of justification.[12] One could then argue that any mode of justification that ignored moral considerations would be ontologically defective. I mention this possibility only to put it to one side. No doubt there are persons who accept moral constraints on their choices and actions, and it would not be possible to explain those choices and actions were we to ignore this. But our explanation of their behavior need not commit us to their view. Here the comparison with religion should be straightforward and uncontroversial. We could not explain many of the practices of the religious without reference to their beliefs. But to characterize what a religious person is doing as, say, an act of worship, does not commit us to supposing that an object of worship actually exists, though it does commit us to supposing that she believes such an object to exist. Similarly, to characterize what a moral agent is doing as, say, fulfilling a duty does not commit us to supposing that there are any duties, though it does commit us to supposing that he believes that there are duties. The skeptic who accepts neither can treat the apparent role of morality in explanation as similar to that of religion. Of course, I do not consider that the parallel can be ultimately sustained, since I agree with the religious skeptic but not with the moral skeptic. But to establish an explanatory role for morality, one must first demonstrate its justificatory credentials. One may not assume that it has a prior explanatory role.

The second way would be to reinterpret the idea of justification, showing that, more fully understood, deliberative justification is incomplete, and must be supplemented in a way that makes room for morality. There is a long tradition in moral philosophy, deriving primarily from Kant, that is committed to this enterprise. This is not the occasion to embark on a critique of what, in the hope again of achieving a neutral characterization, I shall call universalistic justification. But critique may be out of place. The success of deliberative justification may suffice. For theoretical claims about its incompleteness seem to fail before the simple

practical recognition that it works. Of course, on the face of it, deliberative justification does not work to provide a place for morality. But to
suppose that it must, if it is to be fully adequate or complete as a mode
of justification, would be to assume what is in question, whether moral
justification is defensible.

If, independent of one's actual desires, and aims, there were objective
values, and if, independent of one's actual purposes, one were part of
an objectively purposive order, then we might have reason to insist on
the inadequacy of the deliberative framework. An objectively purposive
order would introduce considerations relevant to practical justification
that did not depend on the agent's self-conception. But the supplanting
of teleology in our physical and biological explanations closes this possibility, as it closes the possibility of religious explanation.

I turn then to the third way of resolving morality's foundational crisis.
The first step is to embrace deliberative justification, and recognize that
morality's place must be found within, and not outside, its framework.
Now this will immediately raise two problems. First of all, it will seem
that the attempt to establish any constraint on choice and action, within
the framework of a deliberation that aims at the maximal fulfillment of
the agent's considered preferences, must prove impossible. But even if
this be doubted, it will seem that the attempt to establish a constraint
independent of the agent's preferences, within such a framework, verges on
lunacy. Nevertheless, this is precisely the task accepted by my third way.
And, unlike its predecessors, I believe that it can be successful; indeed, I
believe that my recent book, *Morals by Agreement*, shows how it can
succeed.[13]

I shall not rehearse at length an argument that is now familiar to at
least some readers, and, in any event, can be found in that book. But let
me sketch briefly those features of deliberative rationality that enable it
to constrain maximizing choice. The key idea is that in many situations,
if each person chooses what, given the choices of the others, would
maximize her expected utility, then the outcome will be mutually disadvantageous in comparison with some alternative – everyone could do
better.[14] Equilibrium, which obtains when each person's action is a best
response to the others' actions, is incompatible with (Pareto-)optimality,
which obtains when no one could do better without someone else doing
worse. Given the ubiquity of such situations, each person can see the
benefit, to herself, of participating with her fellows in practices requiring
each to refrain from the direct endeavor to maximize her own utility,
when such mutual restraint is mutually advantageous. No one, of course,
can have reason to accept any unilateral constraint on her maximizing

behavior; each benefits from, and only from, the constraint accepted by her fellows. But if one benefits more from a constraint on others than one loses by being constrained oneself, one may have reason to accept a practice requiring everyone, including oneself, to exhibit such a constraint. We may represent such a practice as capable of gaining unanimous agreement among rational persons who were choosing the terms on which they would interact with each other. And this agreement is the basis of morality.

Consider a simple example of a moral practice that would command rational agreement. Suppose each of us were to assist her fellows only when either she could expect to benefit herself from giving assistance, or she took a direct interest in their well-being. Then, in many situations, persons would not give assistance to others, even though the benefit to the recipient would greatly exceed the cost to the giver, because there would be no provision for the giver to share in the benefit. Everyone would then expect to do better were each to give assistance to her fellows, regardless of her own benefit or interest, whenever the cost of assisting was low and the benefit of receiving assistance considerable. Each would thereby accept a constraint on the direct pursuit of her own concerns, not unilaterally, but given a like acceptance by others. Reflection leads us to recognize that those who belong to groups whose members adhere to such a practice of mutual assistance enjoy benefits in interaction that are denied to others. We may then represent such a practice as rationally acceptable to everyone.

This rationale for agreed constraint makes no reference to the content of anyone's preferences. The argument depends simply on the *structure* of interaction, on the way in which each person's endeavor to fulfill her own preferences affects the fulfillment of everyone else. Thus, each person's reason to accept a mutually constraining practice is independent of her particular desires, aims and interests, although not, of course, of the fact that she has such concerns. The idea of a purely rational agent, moved to act by reason alone, is not, I think, an intelligible one. Morality is not to be understood as a constraint arising from reason alone on the fulfillment of nonrational preferences. Rather, a rational agent is one who acts to achieve the maximal fulfillment of her preferences, and morality is a constraint on the manner in which she acts, arising from the effects of interaction with other agents.

Hobbes's Foole now makes his familiar entry onto the scene, to insist that however rational it may be for a person to agree with her fellows to practices that hold out the promise of mutual advantage, yet it is rational to follow such practices only when so doing directly conduces to her maximal preference fulfillment.[15] But then such practices impose no real constraint. The effect of agreeing to or accepting them can only be to change the expected payoffs of her possible choices, making it rational for her to choose what in the absence of the practice would not be utility maximizing. The practices would offer only true prudence, not true morality.

The Foole is guilty of a twofold error. First, he fails to understand that real acceptance of such moral practices as assisting one's fellows, or keeping one's promises, or telling the truth is possible only among those who are disposed to comply with them. If my disposition to comply extends only so far as my interests or concerns at the time of performance, then you will be the real fool if you interact with me in ways that demand a more rigorous compliance. If, for example, it is rational to keep promises only when so doing is directly utility maximizing, then among persons whose rationality is common knowledge, only promises that require such limited compliance will be made. And opportunities for mutual advantage will be thereby forgone.

Consider this example of the way in which promises facilitate mutual benefit. Jones and Smith have adjacent farms. Although neighbors, and not hostile, they are also not friends, so that neither gets satisfaction from assisting the other. Nevertheless, they recognize that, if they harvest their crops together, each does better than if each harvests alone. Next week, Jones's crop will be ready for harvesting; a fortnight hence, Smith's crop will be ready. The harvest in, Jones is retiring, selling his farm, and moving to Florida, where he is unlikely to encounter Smith or other members of their community. Jones would like to promise Smith that, if Smith helps him harvest next week, he will help Smith harvest in a fortnight. But Jones and Smith both know that in a fortnight, helping Smith would be a pure cost to Jones. Even if Smith helps him, he has nothing to gain by returning the assistance, since neither care for Smith nor, in the circumstances, concern for his own reputation, moves him. Hence, if Jones and Smith know that Jones acts straightforwardly to maximize the fulfillment of his preferences, they know that he will not help Smith. Smith, therefore, will not help Jones even if Jones pretends to promise assistance in return. Nevertheless, Jones would do better could he make and keep such a promise – and so would Smith.

The Foole's second error, following on his first, should be clear; he fails to recognize that in plausible circumstances, persons who are genuinely disposed to a more rigorous compliance with moral practices than would follow from their interests at the time of performance can expect to do better than those who are not so disposed. For the former, constrained maximizers as I call them, will be welcome partners in mutually advantageous cooperation, in which each relies on the voluntary adherence of the others, from which the latter, straightforward maximizers, will be excluded. Constrained maximizers may thus expect more favorable opportunities than their fellows. Although in assisting their fellows, keeping their promises, and complying with other moral practices, they forgo preference fulfillment that they might obtain, yet they do better overall than those who always maximize expected utility, because of their superior opportunities.

In identifying morality with those constraints that would obtain agreement among rational persons who were choosing their terms of interaction, I am engaged in rational reconstruction. I do not suppose that we have actually agreed to existent moral practices and principles. Nor do I suppose that all existent moral practices would secure our agreement, were the question to be raised. Not all existent moral practices need be justifiable – need be ones with which we ought willingly to comply. Indeed, I do not even suppose that the practices with which we ought willingly to comply need be those that would secure our present agreement. I suppose that justifiable moral practices are those that would secure our agreement ex ante, in an appropriate premoral situation. They are those to which we should have agreed as constituting the terms of our future interaction, had we been, per impossible, in a position to decide those terms. Hypothetical agreement thus provides a test of the justifiability of our existent moral practices.

IV

Many questions could be raised about this account, but here I want to consider only one. I have claimed that moral practices are rational, even though they constrain each person's attempt to maximize her own utility, insofar as they would be the objects of unanimous ex ante agreement. But to refute the Foole, I must defend not only the rationality of agreement, but also that of compliance, and the defense of compliance threatens to preempt the case for agreement, so that my title should be "Why Constraint?" and not "Why Contractarianism?" It is rational to dispose oneself to accept certain constraints on direct maximization in choosing and acting, if and only if so disposing oneself maximizes one's expected utility. What then is the relevance of agreement, and especially of hypothetical agreement? Why should it be rational to dispose oneself to accept only those constraints that would be the object of mutual agreement in an appropriate premoral situation, rather than those constraints that are found in our existent moral practices? Surely it is acceptance of the latter that makes a person welcome in interaction with his fellows. For compliance with existing morality will be what they expect, and take into account in choosing partners with whom to cooperate.

I began with a challenge to morality – how can it be rational for us to accept its constraints? It may now seem that what I have shown is that it is indeed rational for us to accept constraints, but to accept them whether or not they might be plausibly considered moral. Morality, it may seem, has nothing to do with my argument; what I have shown is that it is rational to be disposed to comply with whatever constraints are generally accepted and expected, regardless of their nature. But this is not my view.

To show the relevance of agreement to the justification of constraints, let us assume an ongoing society in which individuals more or less acknowledge and comply with a given set of practices that constrain their choices in relation to what they would be did they take only their desires, aims, and interests directly into account. Suppose that a disposition to conform to these existing practices is prima facie advantageous, since persons who are not so disposed may expect to be excluded from desirable opportunities by their fellows. However, the practices themselves have, or at least need have, no basis in agreement. And they need satisfy no intuitive standard of fairness or impartiality, characteristics that we may suppose relevant to the identification of the practices with those of a genuine morality. Although we may speak of the practices as constituting the morality of the society in question, we need not consider them morally justified or acceptable. They are simply practices constraining individual behavior in a way that each finds rational to accept.

Suppose now that our persons, as rational maximizers of individual utility, come to reflect on the practices constituting their morality. They will, of course, assess the practices in relation to their own utility, but with the awareness that their fellows will be doing the same. And one question that must arise is: Why these practices? For they will recognize that the set of actual moral practices is not the only possible set of constraining practices that would yield mutually advantageous, optimal outcomes. They will recognize the possibility of alternative moral orders. At this point it will not be enough to say that, as a matter of fact, each person can expect to benefit from a disposition to comply with existing practices. For persons will also ask themselves: Can I benefit more, not from simply abandoning any morality, and recognizing no constraint, but from a partial rejection of existing constraints in favor of an alternative set? Once this question is asked, the situation is transformed; the existing moral order must be assessed, not only against simple noncompliance, but also against what we may call alternative compliance.

To make this assessment, each will compare her prospects under the existing practices with those she would anticipate from a set that, in the existing circumstances, she would expect to result from bargaining with her fellows. If her prospects would be improved by such negotiation, then she will have a real, although not necessarily sufficient, incentive to demand a change in the established moral order. More generally, if there are persons whose prospects would be improved by renegotiation, then the existing order will be recognizably unstable. No doubt those whose prospects would be worsened by renegotiation will have a clear incentive to resist, to appeal to the status quo. But their appeal will be a weak one, especially among persons who are not taken in by spurious ideological considerations, but focus on individual utility maximization. Thus, although in the real world, we begin with an existing set of moral practices as constraints on our maximizing behavior, yet we are led by reflection to the idea of an amended set that would obtain the agreement of everyone, and this amended set has, and will be recognized to have, a stability lacking in existing morality.

The reflective capacity of rational agents leads them from the given to the agreed, from existing practices and principles requiring constraint to those that would receive each person's assent. The same reflective capacity, I claim, leads from those practices that would be agreed to, in existing social circumstances, to those that would receive ex ante agreement, premoral and presocial. As the status quo proves unstable when it comes into conflict with what would be agreed to, so what would be agreed to proves unstable when it comes into conflict with what would have been agreed to in an appropriate presocial context. For as existing practices must seem arbitrary insofar as they do not correspond to what a rational person would agree to, so what such a person would agree to in existing circumstances must seem arbitrary in relation to what she would accept in a presocial condition.

What a rational person would agree to in existing circumstances depends in large part on her negotiating position vis-à-vis her fellows. But her negotiating position is significantly affected by the existing social institutions, and so by the currently accepted moral practices embodied in those institutions. Thus, although agreement may well yield practices differing from those embodied in existing social institutions, yet it will be influenced by those practices, which are not themselves the product of rational agreement. And this must call the rationality of the agreed practices into question. The arbitrariness of existing practices must infect any agreement whose terms are significantly affected by them. Although rational agreement is in itself a source of stability, yet this stability is undermined by the arbitrariness of the circumstances in which it takes place. To escape this arbitrariness, rational persons will revert from actual to hypothetical agreement, considering what practices they would have agreed to from an initial position not structured by existing institutions and the practices they embody.

The content of a hypothetical agreement is determined by an appeal to the equal rationality of persons. Rational persons will voluntarily accept an agreement only insofar as they perceive it to be equally advantageous to each. To be sure, each would be happy to accept an agreement more advantageous to herself than to her fellows, but since no one will accept an agreement perceived to be less advantageous, agents whose rationality is a matter of common knowledge will recognize the futility of aiming at or holding out for more, and minimize their bargaining costs by coordinating at the point of equal advantage. Now the extent of advantage is determined in a twofold way. First, there is advantage internal to an agreement. In this respect, the expectation of equal advantage is assured by procedural fairness. The step from existing moral practices to those resulting from actual agreement takes rational persons to a procedurally fair situation, in which each perceives the agreed practices to be ones that it is equally rational for all to accept, given the circumstances in which agreement is reached. But those circumstances themselves may be called into question insofar as they are perceived to be arbitrary – the result, in part, of compliance with constraining practices that do not themselves ensure the expectation of equal advantage, and so do not reflect the equal rationality of the complying parties. To neutralize this arbitrary element, moral practices to be fully acceptable must be conceived as constituting a possible outcome of a hypothetical agreement under circumstances that are unaffected by social institutions that themselves lack full acceptability. Equal rationality demands consideration of external circumstances as well as internal procedures.

But what is the practical import of this argument? It would be absurd to claim that mere acquaintance with it, or even acceptance of it, will lead to the replacement of existing moral practices by those that would secure presocial agreement. It would be irrational for anyone to give up the benefits of the existing moral order simply because he comes to realize that it affords him more than he could expect from pure rational agreement with his fellows. And it would be irrational for anyone to accept a long-term utility loss by refusing to comply with the existing moral order, simply because she comes to realize that such compliance affords her less than she could expect from pure rational agreement. Nevertheless, these realizations do transform, or perhaps bring to the surface, the character of the relationships between persons that are maintained by the existing constraints, so that some of these relationships come to be recognized as coercive. These realizations constitute the elimination of false consciousness, and they result from a process of rational reflection that brings persons into what, in my theory, is the parallel of Jürgen Habermas's ideal speech situation.[16] Without an argument to defend themselves in open dialogue with their fellows, those who are more than equally advantaged can hope to maintain their privileged position only if they can coerce their fellows into accepting it. And this, of course, may be possible. But coercion is not agreement, and it lacks any inherent stability.

Stability plays a key role in linking compliance to agreement. Aware of the benefits to be gained from constraining practices, rational persons will seek those that invite stable compliance. Now compliance is stable if it arises from agreement among persons each of whom considers both that the terms of agreement are sufficiently favorable to herself that it is rational for her to accept them, and that they are not so favorable to others that it would be rational for them to accept terms less favorable to them and more favorable to herself. An agreement affording equally favorable terms to all thus invites, as no other can, stable compliance.

V

In defending the claim that moral practices, to obtain the stable voluntary compliance of rational individuals, must be the objects of an appropriate hypothetical agreement, I have added to the initial minimal characterization of morality. Not only does morality constrain our choices and actions, but it does so in an impartial way, reflecting the equal rationality of the persons subject to constraint. Although it is no part of my argument to show that the requirements of contractarian morality will satisfy the Rawlsian test of cohering with our considered judgments in reflective equilibrium, yet it would be misleading to treat rationally agreed constraints on direct utility maximization as constituting a morality at all, rather than as replacing morality, were there no fit between their content and our pretheoretical moral views. The fit lies, I suggest, in the impartiality required for hypothetical agreement.

The foundational crisis of morality is thus resolved by exhibiting the rationality of our compliance with mutual, rationally agreed constraints on the pursuit of our desires, aims, and interests. Although bereft of a basis in objective values or an objectively purposive order, and confronted by a more fundamental mode of justification, morality survives by incorporating itself into that mode. Moral considerations have the same status, and the same role in explaining behavior, as the other reasons acknowledged by a rational deliberator. We are left with a unified account of justification, in which an agent's choices and actions are evaluated in relation to his preferences – to the concerns that are constitutive of his sense of self. But since morality binds the agent independently of the particular content of his preferences, it has the prescriptive grip with which the Christian and Kantian views have invested it.

In incorporating morality into deliberative justification, we recognize a new dimension to the agent's self-conception. For morality requires that a person have the capacity to commit himself, to enter into agreement with his fellows secure in the awareness that he can and will carry out his part of the agreement without regard to many of those considerations that normally and justifiably would enter into his future deliberations. And this is more than the capacity to bring one's desires and interests together with one's beliefs into a single coherent whole. Although this latter unifying capacity must extend its attention to past and future, the unification it achieves may itself be restricted to that extended present within which a person judges and decides. But in committing oneself to future action in accordance with one's agreement, one must fix at least a subset of one's desires and beliefs to hold in that future. The self that agrees and the self that complies must be one. "Man himself must first of all have become *calculable, regular, necessary,* even in his own image of himself, if he is to be able to stand security for *his own future,* which is what one who promises does!"[17]

In developing *"the right to make promises,"*[18] we human beings have found a contractarian bulwark against the perishing of morality.

Notes

Two paragraphs of Section II and most of Section IV are taken from "Morality, Rational Choice, and Semantic Representation – A Reply to My Critics," in E. F. Paul, F. D. Miller, Jr., and J. Paul (eds.), *The New Social Contract: Essays on Gauthier* (Oxford: Blackwell, 1988), pp. 173–4, 179–80, 184–5, 188–9 (this volume appears also as *Social Philosophy and Policy* 5 [1988], same pagination).

1   *On the Genealogy of Morals,* trans. by Walter Kaufmann and R. J. Hollingdale (New York: Random House, 1967), third essay, sec. 27, p. 161.
2   *After Virtue* (Notre Dame, IN: University of Notre Dame Press, 1981), p. 2.

3 *Ethics and the Limits of Philosophy* (Cambridge, MA: Harvard University Press, 1985), p. 197.

4 *Ethics: Inventing Right and Wrong* (Harmondsworth: Penguin, 1977), pp. 15, 30.

5 *The Nature of Morality* (New York: Oxford University Press, 1977), p. 11.

6 David Hume, *An Enquiry Concerning the Principles of Morals*, 1751, sec. IX, pt. II.

7 See Plato, *Republic*, esp. books II and IV.

8 Some would extend morality to the nonsentient, but sympathetic as I am to the rights of trolley cars and steam locomotives, I propose to leave this view quite out of consideration.

9 John Rawls, *A Theory of Justice* (Cambridge, MA: Harvard University Press, 1971), p. 51.

10 John C. Harsanyi, "Morality and the Theory of Rational Behaviour," in *Utilitarianism and Beyond*, edited by Amartya Sen and Bernard Williams (Cambridge: Cambridge University Press, 1982), p. 62.

11 To be sure, if we think of morality as expressed in certain of our affections and/or interests, it will incorporate moral considerations to the extent that they actually are present in our preferences. But this would be to embrace the naturalism that I have put to one side as inadequate.

12 This would meet the challenge to morality found in my previous quotation from Gilbert Harman.

13 See David Gauthier, *Morals by Agreement* (Oxford: Oxford University Press, 1986), especially chaps. V and VI.

14 The now-classic example of this type of situation is the Prisoner's Dilemma; see *Morals by Agreement*, pp. 79–80. More generally, such situations may be said, in economists' parlance, to exhibit market failure. See, for example, "Market Contractarianism" in Jules Coleman, *Markets, Morals, and the Law* (Cambridge: Cambridge University Press, 1988), chap. 10.

15 See Hobbes, *Leviathan*, London, 1651, chap. 15.

16 See Raymond Geuss, *The Idea of a Critical Theory: Habermas and the Frankfurt School* (Cambridge: Cambridge University Press, 1981), p. 65ff.

17 Nietzsche, *On the Genealogy of Morals*, trans. by Walter Kaufmann and R. J. Hollingdale (New York: Random House, 1967), second essay, sec. 1, p. 58.

18 Ibid., p. 57.

5

From *Morals by Agreement*

David Gauthier

VI
Compliance: Maximization Constrained

1.1 . . . The just person is fit for society because he has internalized the idea of mutual benefit, so that in choosing his course of action he gives primary consideration to the prospect of realizing the co-operative outcome. If he is able to bring about, or may reasonably expect to bring about, an outcome that is both (nearly) fair and (nearly) optimal, then he chooses to do so; only if he may not reasonably expect this does he choose to maximize his own utility.

In order to relate our account of the co-operative person to the conditions on rational interaction stated in [an earlier chapter], let us define a fair optimizing strategy (or choice, or response) as one that, given the expected strategies of the others, may be expected to yield an outcome that is nearly fair and optimal – an outcome with utility pay-offs close to those of the co-operative outcome . . . We speak of the response as nearly fair and optimal because in many situations a person will not expect others to do precisely what would be required by minimax relative concession, so that he may not be able to choose a strategy with an expected outcome that is completely fair or fully optimal. But we suppose that he will still be disposed to co-operative rather than to non-co-operative interaction.

A just person then accepts this reading of condition A [Each person's choice must be a rational response to the choices she expects the others to make]: A′: Each person's choice must be a fair optimizing response to the choice he expects the others to make, provided such a response is

David Gauthier, *Morals by Agreement* (Oxford: Clarendon Press, 1986), pp. 157–89.

available to him; otherwise, his choice must be a utility-maximizing response. A just person is disposed to interact with others on the basis of condition A'.

A just person must however be aware that not all (otherwise) rational persons accept this reading of the original condition A. In forming expectations about the choices of others, he need not suppose that their choices will satisfy A'. Thus as conditions of strategic interaction, we cannot dispense with the original conditions A, B, and C; 'rational response' remains (at least until our theory has gained universal acceptance) open to several interpretations.

1.2   Hobbes begins his moral theory with a purely permissive conception of the right of nature, stating what one may do, not what one must be let do, or what must be done for one. The permission is rational, for as Hobbes says, 'Neither by the word *right* is anything else signified, than that liberty which every man hath to make use of his natural faculties according to right reason.'[1] And Hobbes claims that in the natural condition of humankind this liberty is unlimited, so that 'every man has a Right to every thing; even to one anothers body.'[2] In so treating the right of nature, Hobbes expresses a straightforwardly maximizing view of rational action, subject to the material condition, central to his psychology, that each seeks above all his own preservation. For Hobbes each person has the initial right to do whatever he can to preserve himself, but there is no obligation on others, either to let him do or to do for him what is necessary to his preservation.

The condition in which this unlimited right is exercised by all persons is, Hobbes claims, one in which 'there can be no security to any man, (how strong or wise soever he be,) of living out the time, which Nature ordinarily alloweth men to live.'[3] Persons who seek their own preservation find themselves locked in mortal combat. But if reason brings human beings to this condition of war, it can also lead them out of it. Hobbes says, 'Reason suggesteth convenient Articles of Peace, upon which men may be drawn to agreement. These Articles . . . are called the Lawes of Nature.'[4] Laws of nature are precepts, 'found out by Reason, by which a man is forbidden to do, that, which is destructive of his life, or taketh away the means of preserving the same; and to omit, that, by which he thinketh it may be best preserved.'[5]

Since war is inimical to preservation, the fundamental or first law of nature is, 'That every man, ought to endeavour Peace, as farre as he has hope of obtaining it', to which Hobbes adds, 'and when he cannot obtain it, that he may seek, and use, all helps, and advantages of Warre.'[6] From this Hobbes immediately derives a second law, setting out, as the fundamental means to peace, 'That a man be willing, when others are so too, as farre-forth, as for Peace, and defence of himselfe he shall think it necessary, to lay down this right to all things; and be contented with so much liberty against other men, as he would allow other men against himselfe.'[7] Since the unlimited right of nature gives rise to war, renouncing some part of this right is necessary for peace. The renunciation must of course be mutual; each person expects to benefit, not from his own act of renunciation, but from that of his fellows, and so no one has reason to renounce his rights unilaterally. What Hobbes envisages is a rational bargain in which each accepts certain constraints on his freedom of action so that all may avoid the costs of the natural condition of war.

The defence of this second law is perfectly straightforward. Hobbes needs to say only that 'as long as every man holdeth this Right, of doing any thing he liketh; so long are all men in the condition of Warre.'[8] And the mutuality required by the law is defended in an equally simple way: 'if other men will not lay down their Right, as well as he; then there is no Reason for any one, to devest himselfe of his: For that were to expose himselfe to Prey, (which no man is bound to) rather than to dispose himselfe to Peace.'[9] It is directly advantageous for each to agree with his fellows to a mutual renunciation or laying down of right, and so a mutual acceptance of constraint. Hobbes conceives such constraint as obligation, arising only through agreement, for there is 'no Obligation on any man, which ariseth not from some Act of his own; for all men equally, are by Nature Free.'[10] Hobbes's theory, as our own, introduces morals by agreement.

Hobbes recognizes that it is one thing to make an agreement or covenant, quite another to keep it. He does not suppose that the second law of nature, enjoining us to agree, also enjoins us to compliance. Thus he introduces a third law of nature, 'That men performe their Covenants made', which he considers to be the 'Originall of JUSTICE'.[11] A just person is one who keeps the agreements he has rationally made.

Hobbes's defence of this third law lacks the straightforwardness of his defence of the second. As he recognizes, without it 'Covenants are in vain, and but Empty words; and the Right of all men to all things remaining, wee are still in the condition of Warre.'[12] But this does not show that conformity to it yields any direct benefit. Each person maximizes his expected utility in making a covenant, since each gains from the mutual renunciation it involves. But each does not maximize his expected utility in keeping a covenant, in so far as it requires him to refrain from exercising some part of his previous liberty. And this opens the door to the objection of the Foole.

We shall let him speak for himself.

> The Foole hath sayd in his heart, there is no such thing as Justice; and sometimes also with his tongue; seriously alleaging, that every mans conservation, and contentment, being committed to his own care, there could be no reason, why every man might not do what he thought conduced thereunto: and therefore also to make, or not make; keep, or not keep Covenants, was not against Reason, when it conduced to ones benefit. He does not therein deny, that there be Covenants; and that they are sometimes broken, sometimes kept; and that such breach of them may be called Injustice, and the observance of them Justice: but he questioneth, whether Injustice ... may not sometimes stand with that Reason, which dictateth to every man his own good. . . .[13]

The Foole does not seriously challenge the second law of nature, for Hobbes assumes that each person will make only those covenants that he expects to be advantageous, and such behaviour the Foole does not question. What the Foole challenges is the third law, the law requiring compliance, or adherence to one's covenants, for let it be ever so advantageous to make an agreement, may it not then be even more advantageous to violate the agreement made? And if advantageous, then is it not rational? The Foole challenges the heart of the connection between reason and morals that both Hobbes and we seek to establish – the rationality of accepting a moral constraint on the direct pursuit of one's greatest utility.

1.3   In replying to the Foole, Hobbes claims that the question is, given sufficient security of performance by one party, 'whether it be against reason, that is, against the benefit of the other to performe, or not'.[14] On the most natural interpretation, Hobbes is asking whether keeping one's covenant is a rational, that is utility-maximizing, response to covenant-keeping by one's fellows. If this is indeed Hobbes's view, then he is endeavouring to refute the Foole by appealing, in effect, to condition A for strategically rational choice, taking a rational response to be simply a utility-maximizing response. We may not be very hopeful about Hobbes's prospect of success.

Hobbes's first argument reminds the Foole that the rationality of choice depends on expectations, not actual results. It need not detain us. His second argument joins issue with the Foole at a deeper level.

> He . . . that breaketh his Covenant, and consequently declareth that he
> thinks he may with reason do so, cannot be received into any Society,
> that unite themselves for Peace and Defence, but by the errour of them
> that receive him; nor when he is received, be retayned in it, without
> seeing the danger of their errour; which errours a man cannot reason-
> ably reckon upon as the means of his security.[15]

A person disposed to violate his covenants cannot be admitted as a party
to co-operative arrangements by those who are both rational and aware
of his disposition, and so such a person cannot rationally expect to reap
the benefits available to co-operators. Even if his particular breaches of
covenant would benefit him, yet the disposition that leads him to such
breaches does not.

In effect Hobbes moves the question from whether it be against reason,
understood as utility-maximization, to keep one's agreement (given sufficient security of others keeping their agreements), to whether it be
against reason to be disposed to keep one's agreement. The disposition to
decide whether or not to adhere to one's covenants or agreements by
appealing to directly utility-maximizing considerations, is itself disadvantageous, if known, or sufficiently suspected, because it excludes one
from participating, with those who suspect one's disposition, in those co-
operative arrangements in which the benefits to be realized require each
to forgo utility-maximization – or in Hobbes's terminology, require
each to lay down some portion of his original, unlimited right of nature.
The disposition to keep one's agreement, given sufficient security, without
appealing to directly utility-maximizing considerations, makes one an
eligible partner in beneficial co-operation, and so is itself beneficial. This
will prove to be the key to our demonstration that a fully rational utility-
maximizer disposes himself to compliance with his rationally undertaken
covenants or agreements.

But for Hobbes to take full advantage of this response to the Foole,
he must revise his conception of rationality, breaking the direct connection between reason and benefit with which he began his reply.
Hobbes needs to say that it is rational to perform one's covenant even
when performance is not directly to one's benefit, provided that it is to
one's benefit to be disposed to perform. But this he never says. And as
long as the Foole is allowed to relate reason directly to benefit in performance, rather than to benefit in the disposition to perform, he can
escape refutation.

Hobbes does suggest a revision in his conception of rationality in his
discussion with Bishop Bramhall. Agreeing with Bramhall that 'moral
goodness is the conformity of an action with right reason', he does not

claim that what is morally good is conducive to one's benefit, but instead holds that

> All the real good . . . is that which is not repugnant to the law . . . for the law is all the right reason we have, and . . . is the infallible rule of moral goodness. The reason whereof is this, that because neither mine nor the Bishop's reason is . . . fit to be a rule of our moral actions, we have therefore set up over ourselves a sovereign governor, and agreed that his laws shall . . . dictate to us what is really good.[16]

To the Foole's contention that injustice may 'sometimes stand with that Reason, which dictateth to every man his own good',[17] Hobbes can reply that injustice may not stand with that reason that is constituted by the law of the sovereign. Just as it is unprofitable for each man to retain his entire natural right, so it is unprofitable for each man to retain his natural reason as guide to his actions. But Hobbes does not suppose that each man internalizes the right reason of the sovereign. His egoistic psychology allows the internalization of no standard other than that of direct concern with individual preservation and contentment. And so it is only in so far as the sovereign is able to enforce the law that compliance with it is rationally binding on the individual. But this is to propose a political, not a moral, solution to the problem posed by the Foole.

If the market acts as an invisible hand, directing the efforts of each person intending only his own benefit to a social optimum, the sovereign acts as a very visible foot, directing, by well-placed kicks, the efforts of each to the same social end. Each device performs the same task, ensuring the coincidence of an equilibrium in which each person maximizes his expected utility given the actions of his fellows, with an optimum in which each person gains the maximum utility compatible with the utilities of his fellows. Each device affects the conditions under which interaction occurs, leaving every individual free to maximize his utility given those conditions. Of course, the sovereign appears as a constraint on each person's freedom whereas the market does not, but this is the difference between visibility and invisibility; the sovereign visibly shapes the conditions that reconcile each person's interest with those of his fellows, whereas the market so shapes these conditions simply in virtue of its structure.

The sovereign makes morality, understood as a constraint on each person's endeavour to maximize his own utility, as unnecessary as does the market. Our moral enquiry has been motivated by the problems created for utility-maximizers by externalities. Adam Smith reminds us of the conditions in which externalities are absent, so that the market ensures that each person's free, maximizing behaviour results in an optimal outcome. Thomas Hobbes introduces the sovereign, who constrains each person's options so that maximizing behaviour results in a seemingly optimal outcome even when externalities are present. We may retain the idea of justice as expressing the requirement of impartiality for principles that regulate social interaction, but it no longer expresses a constraint on individual maximization. It would seem that between them, economics and politics resolve our problem with no need for morality.

But Hobbes's sovereign lacks the appeal of the market, and for good reason. The invisible hand is a costless solution to the problems of natural interaction, but the visible foot is a very costly solution. Those subject to the Hobbesian sovereign do not, in fact, attain an optimal outcome; each pays a portion of the costs needed to enforce adherence to agreements, and these costs render the outcome sub-optimal. Even if we suppose that power does not corrupt, so that the sovereign is the perfect instrument of his subjects, acting only in their interests, yet each would expect to do better if all would adhere voluntarily to their agreements, so that enforcement and its costs would be unnecessary. We pay a heavy price, if we are indeed creatures who rationally accept no internal constraint on the pursuit of our own utility, and who consequently are able to escape from the state of nature, in those circumstances in which externalities are unavoidably present, only by political, and not by moral, devices. Could we but voluntarily comply with our rationally undertaken agreements, we should save ourselves this price.

We do not suppose that voluntary compliance would eliminate the need for social institutions and practices, and their costs. But it would eliminate the need for some of those institutions whose concern is with enforcement. Authoritative decision-making cannot be eliminated, but our ideal would be a society in which the coercive enforcement of such decisions would be unnecessary. More realistically, we suppose that such enforcement is needed to create and maintain those conditions under which individuals may rationally expect the degree of compliance from their fellows needed to elicit their own voluntary compliance. Internal, moral constraints operate to ensure compliance under conditions of security established by external, political constraints. But before we can expect this view to be accepted we must show, what the Foole denies, that it is rational to dispose oneself to co-operate, and so to accept internal, moral constraints. Hobbes's argument that those not so disposed may not rationally be received into society, is the foundation on which we shall build.

2.1   The Foole, and those who share his conception of practical reason, must suppose that there are potentialities for co-operation to which each person would rationally agree, were he to expect the agreement to be carried out, but that remain unactualized, since each rationally expects that someone, perhaps himself, perhaps another, would not adhere to the agreement. [In an earlier chapter] we argued that co-operation is rational if each co-operator may expect a utility nearly equal to what he would be assigned by the principle of minimax relative concession. The Foole does not dispute the necessity of this condition, but denies its sufficiency. He insists that for it to be rational to comply with an agreement to co-operate, the utility an individual may expect from co-operation must also be no less than what he would expect were he to violate his agreement. And he then argues that for it to be rational to agree to co-operate, then, although one need not consider it rational to comply oneself, one must believe it rational for the others to comply. Given that everyone is rational, fully informed, and correct in his expectations, the Foole supposes that co-operation is actualized only if each person expects a utility from co-operation no less than his non-compliance utility. The benefits that could be realized through co-operative arrangements that do not afford each person at least his non-compliance utility remain forever beyond the reach of rational human beings – forever denied us because our very rationality would lead us to violate the agreements necessary to realize these benefits. Such agreements will not be made.

The Foole rejects what would seem to be the ordinary view that, given neither unforeseen circumstances nor misrepresentation of terms, it is rational to comply with an agreement if it is rational to make it. He insists that holders of this view have failed to think out the full implications of the maximizing conception of practical rationality. In choosing one takes one's stand in the present, and looks to the expected utility that will result from each possible action. What has happened may affect this utility; that one has agreed may affect the utility one expects from doing, or not doing, what would keep the agreement. But what has happened provides in itself no reason for choice. That one had reason for making an agreement can give one reason for keeping it only by affecting the utility of compliance. To think otherwise is to reject utility-maximization.

Let us begin our answer to the Foole by recalling the distinction introduced in [an earlier chapter] between an individual strategy and a joint strategy.[18] An individual strategy is a lottery over the possible actions of a single actor. A joint strategy is a lottery over possible outcomes. Co-operators have joint strategies available to them.

We may think of participation in a co-operative activity, such as a hunt, in which each huntsman has his particular role co-ordinated with that of the others, as the implementation of a single joint strategy. We may also extend the notion to include participation in a practice, such as the making and keeping of promises, where each person's behaviour is predicated on the conformity of others to the practice.

An individual is not able to ensure that he acts on a joint strategy, since whether he does depends, not only on what he intends, but on what those with whom he interacts intend. But we may say that an individual bases his action on a joint strategy in so far as he intentionally chooses what the strategy requires of him. Normally, of course, one bases one's action on a joint strategy only if one expects those with whom one interacts to do so as well, so that one expects actually to act on that strategy. But we need not import such an expectation into the conception of basing one's action on a joint strategy.

A person co-operates with his fellows only if he bases his actions on a joint strategy; to agree to co-operate is to agree to employ a joint rather than an individual strategy. The Foole insists that it is rational to co-operate only if the utility one expects from acting on the co-operative joint strategy is at least equal to the utility one would expect were one to act instead on one's best individual strategy. This defeats the end of co-operation, which is in effect to substitute a joint strategy for individual strategies in situations in which this substitution is to everyone's benefit.

A joint strategy is fully rational only if it yields an optimal outcome, or in other words, only if it affords each person who acts on it the maximum utility compatible in the situation with the utility afforded each other person who acts on the strategy. Thus we may say that a person acting on a rational joint strategy maximizes his utility, subject to the constraint set by the utilities it affords to every other person. An individual strategy is rational if and only if it maximizes one's utility given the *strategies* adopted by the other persons; a joint strategy is rational only if (but not if and only if) it maximizes one's utility given the *utilities* afforded to the other persons.

Let us say that a *straightforward* maximizer is a person who seeks to maximize his utility given the strategies of those with whom he interacts. A *constrained* maximizer, on the other hand, is a person who seeks in some situations to maximize her utility, given not the strategies but the utilities of those with whom she interacts. The Foole accepts the rationality of straightforward maximization. We, in defending condition A' for strategic rationality (stated in 1.1), accept the rationality of constrained maximization.

A constrained maximizer has a conditional disposition to base her actions on a joint strategy, without considering whether some individual strategy would yield her greater expected utility. But not all constraint could be rational; we must specify the characteristics of the conditional disposition. We shall therefore identify a constrained maximizer thus: (i) someone who is conditionally disposed to base her actions on a joint strategy or practice should the utility she expects were everyone so to base his action be no less than what she would expect were everyone to employ individual strategies, and approach what she would expect from the co-operative outcome determined by minimax relative concession; (ii) someone who actually acts on this conditional disposition should her expected utility be greater than what she would expect were everyone to employ individual strategies. Or in other words, a constrained maximizer is ready to co-operate in ways that, if followed by all, would yield outcomes that she would find beneficial and not unfair, and she does co-operate should she expect an actual practice or activity to be beneficial. In determining the latter she must take into account the possibility that some persons will fail, or refuse, to act co-operatively. Henceforth, unless we specifically state otherwise, we shall understand by a constrained maximizer one with this particular disposition.

There are three points in our characterization of constrained maximization that should be noted. The first is that a constrained maximizer is conditionally disposed to act, not only on the unique joint strategy that would be prescribed by a rational bargain, but on any joint strategy that affords her a utility approaching what she would expect from fully rational co-operation. The range of acceptable joint strategies is, and must be left, unspecified. The idea is that in real interaction it is reasonable to accept co-operative arrangements that fall short of the ideal of full rationality and fairness, provided they do not fall too far short. At some point, of course, one decides to ignore a joint strategy, even if acting on it would afford one an expected utility greater than one would expect were everyone to employ an individual strategy, because one hopes thereby to obtain agreement on, or acquiescence in, another joint strategy which in being fairer is also more favourable to oneself. At precisely what point one decides this we make no attempt to say. We simply defend a conception of constrained maximization that does not require that all acceptable joint strategies be ideal.

Constrained maximization thus links the idea of morals by agreement to actual moral practice. We suppose that some moral principles may be understood as representing joint strategies prescribed to each person as part of the ongoing co-operative arrangements that constitute society.

These principles require each person to refrain from the direct pursuit of her maximum utility, in order to achieve mutually advantageous and reasonably fair outcomes. Actual moral principles are not in general those to which we should have agreed in a fully rational bargain, but it is reasonable to adhere to them in so far as they offer a reasonable approximation to ideal principles. We may defend actual moral principles by reference to ideal co-operative arrangements, and the closer the principles fit, the stronger the defence. We do not of course suppose that our actual moral principles derive historically from a bargain, but in so far as the constraints they impose are acceptable to a rational constrained maximizer, we may fit them into the framework of a morality rationalized by the idea of agreement.

The second point is that a constrained maximizer does not base her actions on a joint strategy whenever a nearly fair and optimal outcome would result were everyone to do likewise. Her disposition to co-operate is conditional on her expectation that she will benefit in comparison with the utility she could expect were no one to co-operate. Thus she must estimate the likelihood that others involved in the prospective practice or interaction will act co-operatively, and calculate, not the utility she would expect were all to co-operate, but the utility she would expect if she co-operates, given her estimate of the degree to which others will co-operate. Only if this exceeds what she would expect from universal non-co-operation, does her conditional disposition to constraint actually manifest itself in a decision to base her actions on the co-operative joint strategy.

Thus, faced with persons whom she believes to be straightforward maximizers, a constrained maximizer does not play into their hands by basing her actions on the joint strategy she would like everyone to accept, but rather, to avoid being exploited, she behaves as a straightforward maximizer, acting on the individual strategy that maximizes her utility given the strategies she expects the others to employ. A constrained maximizer makes reasonably certain that she is among like-disposed persons before she actually constrains her direct pursuit of maximum utility.

But note that a constrained maximizer may find herself required to act in such a way that she would have been better off had she not entered into co-operation. She may be engaged in a co-operative activity that, given the willingness of her fellows to do their part, she expects to be fair and beneficial, but that, should chance so befall, requires her to act so that she incurs some loss greater than had she never engaged herself in the endeavour. Here she would still be disposed to comply, acting in a way that results in real disadvantage to herself, because given her *ex ante* beliefs about the dispositions of her fellows and the prospects of benefit, participation in the activity affords her greater expected utility than non-participation.

And this brings us to the third point, that constrained maximization is not straightforward maximization in its most effective disguise. The constrained maximizer is not merely the person who, taking a larger view than her fellows, serves her overall interest by sacrificing the immediate benefits of ignoring joint strategies and violating co-operative arrangements in order to obtain the long-run benefits of being trusted by others.[19] Such a person exhibits no real constraint. The constrained maximizer does not reason more effectively about how to maximize her utility, but reasons in a different way. We may see this most clearly by considering how each faces the decision whether to base her action on a joint strategy. The constrained maximizer considers (i) whether the outcome, should everyone do so, be nearly fair and optimal, and (ii) whether the outcome she realistically expects should she do so affords her greater utility than universal non-co-operation. If both of these conditions are satisfied she bases her action on the joint strategy. The straightforward maximizer considers simply whether the outcome he realistically expects should he base his action on the joint strategy affords him greater utility than the outcome he would expect were he to act on any alternative strategy – taking into account, of course, long-term as well as short-term effects. Only if this condition is satisfied does he base his action on the joint strategy.

Consider a purely isolated interaction, in which both parties know that how each chooses will have no bearing on how each fares in other interactions. Suppose that the situation has the familiar Prisoner's Dilemma structure; each benefits from mutual co-operation in relation to mutual non-co-operation, but each benefits from non-co-operation whatever the other does. In such a situation, a straightforward maximizer chooses not to co-operate. A constrained maximizer chooses to co-operate if, given her estimate of whether or not her partner will choose to co-operate, her own expected utility is greater than the utility she would expect from the non-co-operative outcome.

Constrained maximizers can thus obtain co-operative benefits that are unavailable to straightforward maximizers, however far-sighted the latter may be. But straightforward maximizers can, on occasion, exploit unwary constrained maximizers. Each supposes her disposition to be rational. But who is right?

2.2   To demonstrate the rationality of suitably constrained maximization we solve a problem of rational choice. We consider what a rational individual would choose, given the alternatives of adopting straight-forward maximization, and of adopting constrained maximization, as his disposition for strategic behaviour. Although this choice is about interaction, to make it is not to engage in interaction. Taking others' dispositions as fixed, the individual reasons parametrically to his own best disposition. Thus he compares the expected utility of disposing himself to maximize utility given others' expected strategy choices, with the utility of disposing himself to co-operate with others in bringing about nearly fair and optimal outcomes.

To choose between these dispositions, a person needs to consider only those situations in which they would yield different behaviour. If both would be expressed in a maximizing individual strategy, or if both would lead one to base action on the joint strategy one expects from others, then their utility expectations are identical. But if the disposition to constraint would be expressed in basing action on a joint strategy, whereas the disposition to maximize straightforwardly would be expressed in defecting from the joint strategy, then their utility expectations differ. Only situations giving rise to such differences need be considered. These situations must satisfy two conditions. First, they must afford the prospect of mutually beneficial and fair co-operation, since otherwise constraint would be pointless. And second, they must afford some prospect for individually beneficial defection, since otherwise no constraint would be needed to realize the mutual benefits.

We suppose, then, an individual, considering what disposition to adopt, for situations in which his expected utility is u should each person act on an individual strategy, u' should all act on a co-operative joint strategy, and u'' should he act on an individual strategy and the others base their actions on a co-operative joint strategy, and u is less than u' (so that he benefits from co-operation as required by the first condition) and u' in turn is less than u'' (so that he benefits from defection as required by the second condition).

Consider these two arguments which this person might put to himself:

Argument (1): Suppose I adopt straightforward maximization. Then if I expect the others to base their actions on a joint strategy, I defect to my best individual strategy, and expect a utility, u''. If I expect the others to act on individual strategies, then so do I, and expect a utility, u. If the probability that others will base their actions on a joint strategy is p, then my overall expected utility is $[pu'' + (1 - p)u]$.

Suppose I adopt constrained maximization. Then if I expect the others to base their actions on a joint strategy, so do I, and expect a utility u'. If I expect the others to act on individual strategies, then so do I, and expect a utility, u. Thus my overall expected utility is $[pu' + (1 - p)u]$.

Since u'' is greater than u', $[pu'' + (1 - p)u]$ is greater than $[pu' + (1 - p)u]$, for any value of p other than 0 (and for $p = 0$, the two are equal). Therefore, to maximize my overall expectation of utility, I should adopt straightforward maximization.

Argument (2): Suppose I adopt straightforward maximization. Then I must expect the others to employ maximizing individual strategies in interacting with me; so do I, and expect a utility, u.

Suppose I adopt constrained maximization. Then if the others are conditionally disposed to constrained maximization, I may expect them to base their actions on a co-operative joint strategy in interacting with me; so do I, and expect a utility u'. If they are not so disposed, I employ a maximizing strategy and expect u as before. If the probability that others are disposed to constrained maximization is p, then my overall expected utility is $[pu' + (1 - p)u]$.

Since u' is greater than u, $[pu' + (1 - p)u]$ is greater than u for any value of p other than 0 (and for $p = 0$, the two are equal). Therefore, to maximize my overall expectation of utility, I should adopt constrained maximization.

Since these arguments yield opposed conclusions, they cannot both be sound. The first has the form of a dominance argument. In any situation in which others act non-co-operatively, one may expect the same utility whether one is disposed to straightforward or to constrained maximization. In any situation in which others act co-operatively, one may expect a greater utility if one is disposed to straightforward maximization. Therefore one should adopt straightforward maximization. But this argument would be valid only if the probability of others acting co-operatively were, as the argument assumes, independent of one's own disposition. And this is not the case. Since persons disposed to co-operation only act co-operatively with those whom they suppose to be similarly disposed, a straightforward maximizer does not have the opportunities to benefit which present themselves to the constrained maximizer. Thus argument (1) fails.

Argument (2) takes into account what argument (1) ignores – the difference between the way in which constrained maximizers interact with those similarly disposed, and the way in which they interact with straightforward maximizers. Only those disposed to keep their agreements are rationally acceptable as parties to agreements. Constrained maximizers are able to make beneficial agreements with their fellows that the straightforward cannot, not because the latter would be unwilling to agree, but because they would not be admitted as parties to agreement given their disposition to violation. Straightforward maximizers are disposed to take advantage of their fellows should the opportunity arise; knowing this, their fellows would prevent such opportunity arising. With the same opportunities, straightforward maximizers would necessarily obtain greater benefits. A dominance argument establishes this. But because they differ in their dispositions, straightforward and constrained maximizers differ also in their opportunities, to the benefit of the latter.

But argument (2) unfortunately contains an undefended assumption. A person's expectations about how others will interact with him depend strictly on his own choice of disposition only if that choice is known by the others. What we have shown is that, if the straightforward maximizer and the constrained maximizer appear in their true colours, then the constrained maximizer must do better. But need each so appear? The Foole may agree, under the pressure of our argument and its parallel in the second argument we ascribed to Hobbes, that the question to be asked is not whether it is or is not rational to keep (particular) covenants, but whether it is or is not rational to be (generally) disposed to the keeping of covenants, and he may recognize that he cannot win by pleading the cause of straightforward maximization in a direct way. But may he not win by linking straightforward maximization to the appearance of constraint? Is not the Foole's ultimate argument that the truly prudent person, the fully rational utility-maximizer, must seek to appear trustworthy, an upholder of his agreements? For then he will not be excluded from the co-operative arrangements of his fellows, but will be welcomed as a partner, while he awaits opportunities to benefit at their expense – and, preferably, without their knowledge, so that he may retain the guise of constraint and trustworthiness.

There is a short way to defeat this manœuvre. Since our argument is to be applied to ideally rational persons, we may simply add another idealizing assumption, and take our persons to be *transparent*.[20] Each is directly aware of the disposition of his fellows, and so aware whether he is interacting with straightforward or constrained maximizers. Deception is impossible; the Foole must appear as he is.

But to assume transparency may seem to rob our argument of much of its interest. We want to relate our idealizing assumptions to the real world. If constrained maximization defeats straightforward maximization only if all persons are transparent, then we shall have failed to show that under actual, or realistically possible, conditions, moral constraints are rational. We shall have refuted the Foole but at the price of robbing our refutation of all practical import.

However, transparency proves to be a stronger assumption than our argument requires. We may appeal instead to a more realistic *translucency*, supposing that persons are neither transparent nor opaque, so that their disposition to co-operate or not may be ascertained by others, not with certainty, but as more than mere guesswork. Opaque beings would be condemned to seek political solutions for those problems of natural interaction that could not be met by the market. But we shall show that for beings as translucent as we may reasonably consider ourselves to be, moral solutions are rationally available.

2.3 If persons are translucent, then constrained maximizers (CMs) will sometimes fail to recognize each other, and will then interact non-co-operatively even if co-operation would have been mutually beneficial. CMs will sometimes fail to identify straightforward maximizers (SMs) and will then act co-operatively; if the SMs correctly identify the CMs they will be able to take advantage of them. Translucent CMs must expect to do less well in interaction than would transparent CMs; translucent SMs must expect to do better than would transparent SMs. Although it would be rational to choose to be a CM were one transparent, it need not be rational if one is only translucent. Let us examine the conditions under which the decision to dispose oneself to constrained maximization is rational for translucent persons, and ask if these are (or may be) the conditions in which we find ourselves.

As in the preceding subsection, we need consider only situations in which CMs and SMs may fare differently. These are situations that afford both the prospect of mutually beneficial co-operation (in relation to non-co-operation) and individually beneficial defection (in relation to co-operation). Let us simplify by supposing that the non-co-operative outcome results unless (i) those interacting are CMs who achieve mutual recognition, in which case the co-operative outcome results, or (ii) those interacting include CMs who fail to recognize SMs but are themselves recognized, in which case the outcome affords the SMs the benefits of individual defection and the CMs the costs of having advantage taken of mistakenly basing their actions on a co-operative strategy. We ignore the inadvertent taking of advantage when CMs mistake their fellows for SMs.

There are then four possible pay-offs – non-co-operation, co-operation, defection, and exploitation (as we may call the outcome for the person whose supposed partner defects from the joint strategy on which he bases his action). For the typical situation, we assign defection the value 1, co-operation u'' (less than 1), non-co-operation u' (less than u''), and exploitation 0 (less than u'). We now introduce three probabilities. The first, p, is the probability that CMs will achieve mutual recognition and so successfully co-operate. The second, q, is the probability that CMs will fail to recognize SMs but will themselves be recognized, so that defection and exploitation will result. The third, r, is the probability that a randomly selected member of the population is a CM. (We assume that everyone is a CM or an SM, so the probability that a randomly selected person is an SM is $(1 - r)$.) The values of p, q, and r must of course fall between 0 and 1.

Let us now calculate expected utilities for CMs and SMs in situations affording both the prospect of mutually beneficial co-operation and individually beneficial defection. A CM expects the utility u' unless (i) she succeeds in co-operating with other CMs or (ii) she is exploited by an SM. The probability of (i) is the combined probability that she interacts with a CM, r, and that they achieve mutual recognition, p, or rp. In this case she gains $(u'' - u')$ over her non-co-operative expectation u'. Thus the effect of (i) is to increase her utility expectation by a value $[rp(u'' - u')]$. The probability of (ii) is the combined probability that she interacts with an SM, $1 - r$, and that she fails to recognize him but is recognized, q, or $(1 - r)q$. In this case she receives 0, so she loses her non-co-operative expectation u'. Thus the effect of (ii) is to reduce her utility expectation by a value $[(1 - r)qu']$. Taking both (i) and (ii) into account, a CM expects the utility $\{u' + [rp(u'' - u')] - (1 - r)qu'\}$.

An SM expects the utility u' unless he exploits a CM. The probability of this is the combined probability that he interacts with a CM, r, and that he recognizes her but is not recognized by her, q; or rq. In this case he gains $(1 - u')$ over his non-co-operative expectation u'. Thus the effect is to increase his utility expectation by a value $[rq(1 - u')]$. An SM thus expects the utility $\{u' + [rq(1 - u')]\}$.

It is rational to dispose oneself to constrained maximization if and only if the utility expected by a CM is greater than the utility expected by an SM, which obtains if and only if p/q is *greater* than $\{(1 - u')/(u'' - u') + [(1 - r)u']/[r(u'' - u')]\}$.

The first term of this expression, $[(1 - u')/(u'' - u')]$, relates the gain from defection to the gain through co-operation. The value of defection is of course greater than that of co-operation, so this term is greater than 1. The second term, $\{[(1 - r)u']/[r(u'' - u')]\}$, depends for its value on r. If $r = 0$ (i.e. if there are no CMs in the population), then its value is infinite.

As r increases, the value of the expression decreases, until if $r = 1$ (i.e. if there are only CMs in the population) its value is 0.

We may now draw two important conclusions. First, it is rational to dispose oneself to constrained maximization only if the ratio of p to q, i.e. the ratio between the probability that an interaction involving CMs will result in co-operation and the probability that an interaction involving CMs and SMs will involve exploitation and defection, is greater than the ratio between the gain from defection and the gain through co-operation. If everyone in the population is a CM, then we may replace 'only if' by 'if and only if' in this statement, but in general it is only a necessary condition of the rationality of the disposition to constrained maximization.

Second, as the proportion of CMs in the population increases (so that the value of r increases), the value of the ratio of p to q that is required for it to be rational to dispose oneself to constrained maximization decreases. The more constrained maximizers there are, the greater the risks a constrained maximizer may rationally accept of failed co-operation and exploitation. However, these risks, and particularly the latter, must remain relatively small.

We may illustrate these conclusions by introducing typical numerical values for co-operation and non-co-operation, and then considering different values for r. One may suppose that on the whole, there is no reason that the typical gain from defection over co-operation would be either greater or smaller than the typical gain from co-operation over non-co-operation, and in turn no reason that the latter gain would be greater or smaller than the typical loss from non-co-operation to exploitation. And so, since defection has the value 1 and exploitation 0, let us assign co-operation the value $2/3$ and non-co-operation $1/3$.

The gain from defection, $(1 - u')$, thus is $2/3$; the gain through co-operation, $(u'' - u')$, is $1/3$. Since p/q must exceed $\{(1 - u')/(u'' - u') + [(1 - r)u']/[r(u'' - u')]\}$ for constrained maximization to be rational, in our typical case the probability p that CMs successfully co-operate must be more than twice the probability q that CMs are exploited by SMs, however great the probability r that a randomly selected person is a CM. If three persons out of four are CMs, so that $r = 3/4$, then p/q must be greater than $7/3$; if one person out of two is a CM, then p/q must be greater than 3; if one person in four is a CM, then p/q must be greater than 5. In general, p/q must be greater than $2 + (1 - r)/r$, or $(r + 1)/r$.

Suppose a population evenly divided between constrained and straightforward maximizers. If the constrained maximizers are able to co-operate successfully in two-thirds of their encounters, and to avoid being exploited by straightforward maximizers in four-fifths of their encounters, then constrained maximizers may expect to do better than their fellows. Of course, the even distribution will not be stable; it will be rational for the straightforward maximizers to change their disposition. These persons are sufficiently translucent for them to find morality rational.

2.4 A constrained maximizer is conditionally disposed to co-operate in ways that, followed by all, would yield nearly optimal and fair outcomes, and does co-operate in such ways when she may actually expect to benefit. In the two preceding subsections, we have argued that one is rationally so disposed if persons are transparent, or if persons are sufficiently translucent and enough are like-minded. But our argument has not appealed explicitly to the particular requirement that co-operative practices and activities be nearly optimal and fair. We have insisted that the co-operative outcome afford one a utility greater than non-co-operation, but this is much weaker than the insistence that it approach the outcome required by minimax relative concession.

But note that the larger the gain from co-operation, $(u'' - u')$, the smaller the minimum value of p/q that makes the disposition to constrained maximization rational. We may take p/q to be a measure of translucency; the more translucent constrained maximizers are, the better they are at achieving co-operation among themselves (increasing p) and avoiding exploitation by straightforward maximizers (decreasing q). Thus as practices and activities fall short of optimality, the expected value of co-operation, u'', decreases, and so the degree of translucency required to make co-operation rational increases. And as practices and activities fall short of fairness, the expected value of co-operation for those with less than fair shares decreases, and so the degree of translucency to make co-operation rational for them increases. Thus our argument does appeal implicitly to the requirement that co-operation yield nearly fair and optimal outcomes.

But there is a further argument in support of our insistence that the conditional disposition to co-operate be restricted to practices and activities yielding nearly optimal and fair outcomes. And this argument turns, as does our general argument for constraint, on how one's dispositions affect the characteristics of the situations in which one may reasonably expect to find oneself. Let us call a person who is disposed to co-operate in ways that, followed by all, yield nearly optimal and fair outcomes, *narrowly compliant*. And let us call a person who is disposed to co-operate in ways that, followed by all, merely yield her some benefit in relation to universal non-co-operation, *broadly compliant*. We need not deny that a broadly compliant person would expect to benefit in some situations in which a narrowly compliant person could not. But in many other situations a broadly compliant person must expect to lose by her disposition. For in so far as she is known to be broadly compliant, others will have every reason to maximize their utilities at her expense, by offering 'co-operation' on terms that offer her but little more than she could expect from non-co-operation. Since a broadly compliant person is disposed to seize whatever benefit a joint strategy may afford her, she finds herself with opportunities for but little benefit.

Since the narrowly compliant person is always prepared to accept co-operative arrangements based on the principle of minimax relative concession, she is prepared to be co-operative whenever co-operation can be mutually beneficial on terms equally rational and fair to all. In refusing other terms she does not diminish her prospects for co-operation with other rational persons, and she ensures that those not disposed to fair co-operation do not enjoy the benefits of any co-operation, thus making their unfairness costly to themselves, and so irrational.

[In the next chapter] we shall extend the conception of narrow compliance, so that it includes taking into account not only satisfaction of minimax relative concession, but also satisfaction of a standard of fairness for the initial bargaining position. We shall then find that for some circumstances, narrow compliance sets too high a standard. If the institutions of society fail to be both rational and impartial, then the narrowly compliant person may be unable to effect any significant reform of them, while depriving herself of what benefits an imperfect society nevertheless affords. Then – we must admit – rationality and impartiality can fail to coincide in individual choice.

But we suppose that among fully rational persons, institutions, practices, and agreements that do not satisfy the requirements of minimax relative concession must prove unstable. There would, of course, be some persons with an interest in maintaining the unfairness inherent in such structures. But among the members of a society each of whom is, and knows her fellows to be, rational and adequately informed, those who find themselves with less than they could expect from fair and optimal co-operation can, by disposing themselves to narrow compliance, effect the reform of their society so that it satisfies the requirements of justice. Reflection on how partiality sustains itself shows that, however important coercive measures may be, their effectiveness depends finally on an uncoerced support for norms that directly or indirectly sustain this partiality, a support which would be insufficiently forthcoming from clear-headed constrained maximizers of individual utility.

2.5 To conclude this long section, let us supplement our argument for the rationality of disposing ourselves to constrained maximization with three reflections on its implications – for conventional morality, for the treatment of straightforward maximizers, and for the cultivation of translucency.

First, we should not suppose that the argument upholds all of conventional morality, or all of those institutions and practices that purport to realize fair and optimal outcomes. If society is, in Rawls's words, 'a cooperative venture for mutual advantage', then it is rational to pay one's share of social costs – one's taxes. But it need not be rational to pay one's taxes, at least unless one is effectively coerced into payment, if one sees one's tax dollars used (as one may believe) to increase the chances of nuclear warfare and to encourage both corporate and individual parasitism. If tax evasion seems to many a rational practice, this does not show that it is irrational to comply with fair and optimal arrangements, but only, perhaps, that it is irrational to acquiesce willingly in being exploited.

Second, we should not suppose it is rational to dispose oneself to constrained maximization, if one does not also dispose oneself to exclude straightforward maximizers from the benefits realizable by co-operation. Hobbes notes that those who think they may with reason violate their covenants, may not be received into society except by the error of their fellows. If their fellows fall into that error, then they will soon find that it pays no one to keep covenants. Failing to exclude straightforward maximizers from the benefits of co-operative arrangements does not, and cannot, enable them to share in the long-run benefits of co-operation; instead, it ensures that the arrangements will prove ineffective, so that there are no benefits to share. And then there is nothing to be gained by constrained maximization; one might as well join the straightforward maximizers in their descent to the natural condition of humankind.

A third consideration relates more closely to the conceptions introduced in 2.3. Consider once again the probabilities p and q, the probability that CMs will achieve mutual recognition and co-operate, and the probability that CMs will fail to recognize SMs but will be recognized by them and so be exploited. It is obvious that CMs benefit from increasing p and decreasing q. And this is reflected in our calculation of expected utility for CMs; the value of $\{u' + [rp(u'' - u')] - (1 - r)qu'\}$ increases as p increases and as q decreases.

What determines the values of p and q? p depends on the ability of CMs to detect the sincerity of other CMs and to reveal their own sincerity to them. q depends on the ability of CMs to detect the insincerity of SMs and conceal their own sincerity from them, and the ability of SMs to detect the sincerity of CMs and conceal their own insincerity from them. Since any increase in the ability to reveal one's sincerity to other CMs is apt to be offset by a decrease in the ability to conceal one's sincerity from SMs, a CM is likely to rely primarily on her ability to detect the dispositions of others, rather than on her ability to reveal or conceal her own.

The ability to detect the dispositions of others must be well developed in a rational CM. Failure to develop this ability, or neglect of its exercise, will preclude one from benefiting from constrained maximization. And it can then appear that constraint is irrational. But what is actually irrational is the failure to cultivate or exercise the ability to detect others' sincerity or insincerity.

Both CMs and SMs must expect to benefit from increasing their ability to detect the dispositions of others. But if both endeavour to maximize their abilities (or the expected utility, net of costs, of so doing), then CMs may expect to improve their position in relation to SMs. For the benefits gained by SMs, by being better able to detect their potential victims, must be on the whole offset by the losses they suffer as the CMs become better able to detect them as potential exploiters. On the other hand, although the CMs may not enjoy any net gain in their interactions with SMs, the benefits they gain by being better able to detect other CMs as potential co-operators are not offset by corresponding losses, but rather increased as other CMs become better able to detect them in return.

Thus as persons rationally improve their ability to detect the dispositions of those with whom they interact, the value of p may be expected to increase, while the value of q remains relatively constant. But then p/q increases, and the greater it is, the less favourable need be other circumstances for it to be rational to dispose oneself to constrained maximization. Those who believe rationality and morality to be at loggerheads may have failed to recognize the importance of cultivating their ability to distinguish sincere co-operators from insincere ones.

David Hume points out that if 'it should be a virtuous man's fate to fall into the society of ruffians', then 'his particular regard to justice being no longer of use to his own safety or that of others, he must consult the dictates of self-preservation alone'.[21] If we fall into a society – or rather into a state of nature – of straightforward maximizers, then constrained maximization, which disposes us to justice, will indeed be of no use to us, and we must then consult only the direct dictates of our own utilities.

In a world of Fooles, it would not pay to be a constrained maximizer, and to comply with one's agreements. In such circumstances it would not be rational to be moral.

But if we find ourselves in the company of reasonably just persons, then we too have reason to dispose ourselves to justice. A community in which most individuals are disposed to comply with fair and optimal agreements and practices, and so to base their actions on joint co-operative strategies, will be self-sustaining. And such a world offers benefits to all which the Fooles can never enjoy.

Hume finds himself opposed by 'a sensible knave' who claimed that *'honesty is the best policy*, may be a good general rule, but is liable to many exceptions; and he . . . conducts himself with most wisdom, who observes the general rule, and takes advantage of all the exceptions.'[22] Hume confesses candidly that 'if a man think that this reasoning much requires an answer, it would be a little difficult to find any which will to him appear satisfactory and convincing'.[23] A little difficult, but not, if we are right, impossible. For the answer is found in treating honesty, not as a policy, but as a disposition. Only the person truly disposed to honesty and justice may expect fully to realize their benefits, for only such a person may rationally be admitted to those mutually beneficial arrangements – whether actual agreements or implicitly agreed practices – that rest on honesty and justice, on voluntary compliance. But such a person is not able, given her disposition, to take advantage of the 'exceptions'; she rightly judges such conduct irrational. The Foole and the sensible knave, seeing the benefits to be gained from the exceptions, from the advantageous breaches in honesty and compliance, but not seeing beyond these benefits, do not acquire the disposition. Among knaves they are indeed held for sensible, but among us, if we be not corrupted by their smooth words, they are only fools.

3.1   In defending constrained maximization we have implicitly reinterpreted the utility-maximizing conception of practical rationality. The received interpretation, commonly accepted by economists and elaborated in Bayesian decision theory and the Von Neumann–Morgenstern theory of games, identifies rationality with utility-maximization at the level of particular choices. A choice is rational if and only if it maximizes the actor's expected utility. We identify rationality with utility-maximization at the level of dispositions to choose. A disposition is rational if and only if an actor holding it can expect his choices to yield no less utility than the choices he would make were he to hold any alternative disposition. We shall consider whether particular choices are rational if and only if they express a rational disposition to choose.

It might seem that a maximizing disposition to choose would express itself in maximizing choices. But we have shown that this is not so. The essential point in our argument is that one's disposition to choose affects the situations in which one may expect to find oneself. A straightforward maximizer, who is disposed to make maximizing choices, must expect to be excluded from co-operative arrangements which he would find advantageous. A constrained maximizer may expect to be included in such arrangements. She benefits from her disposition, not in the choices she makes, but in her opportunities to choose.

We have defended the rationality of constrained maximization as a disposition to choose by showing that it would be rationally chosen. Now this argument is not circular; constrained maximization is a disposition for strategic choice that would be parametrically chosen. But the idea of a choice among dispositions to choose is a heuristic device to express the underlying requirement, that a rational disposition to choose be utility-maximizing. In parametric contexts, the disposition to make straightforwardly maximizing choices is uncontroversially utility-maximizing. We may therefore employ the device of a parametric choice among dispositions to choose to show that in strategic contexts, the disposition to make constrained choices, rather than straightforwardly maximizing choices, is utility-maximizing. We must however emphasize that it is not the choice itself, but the maximizing character of the disposition in virtue of which it is choiceworthy, that is the key to our argument.

But there is a further significance in our appeal to a choice among dispositions to choose. For we suppose that the capacity to make such choices is itself an essential part of human rationality. We could imagine beings so wired that only straightforward maximization would be a psychologically possible mode of choice in strategic contexts. Hobbes may have thought that human beings were so wired, that we were straightforwardly-maximizing machines. But if he thought this, then he was surely mistaken. At the core of our rational capacity is the ability to engage in self-critical reflection. The fully rational being is able to reflect on his standard of deliberation, and to change that standard in the light of reflection. Thus we suppose it possible for persons, who may initially assume that it is rational to extend straightforward maximization from parametric to strategic contexts, to reflect on the implications of this extension, and to reject it in favour of constrained maximization. Such persons would be making the very choice, of a disposition to choose, that we have been discussing in this chapter.

And in making that choice, they would be expressing their nature not only as rational beings, but also as moral beings. If the disposition to make straightforwardly maximizing choices were wired in to us, we could not constrain our actions in the way required for morality. Moral philosophers have rightly been unwilling to accept the received interpretation of the relation between practical rationality and utility-maximization because they have recognized that it left no place for a rational constraint on directly utility-maximizing behaviour, and so no place for morality as ordinarily understood. But they have then turned to a neo-Kantian account of rationality which has led them to dismiss the idea that those considerations that constitute a person's reasons for acting must bear some particular relationship to the person.[24] They have failed to relate our nature as moral beings to our everyday concern with the fulfilment of our individual preferences. But we have shown how morality issues from that concern. When we correctly understand how utility-maximization is identified with practical rationality, we see that morality is an essential part of maximization.

3.2   An objector might grant that it may be rational to dispose oneself to constrained maximization, but deny that the choices one is then disposed to make are rational.[25] The objector claims that we have merely exhibited another instance of the rationality of not behaving rationally. And before we can accuse the objector of paradox, he brings further instances before us.

Consider, he says, the costs of decision-making. Maximizing may be the most reliable procedure, but it need not be the most cost-effective. In many circumstances, the rational person will not maximize but satisfice – set a threshold level of fulfilment and choose the first course of action of those coming to mind that one expects to meet this level. Indeed, our objector may suggest, human beings, like other higher animals, are natural satisficers. What distinguishes us is that we are not hard-wired, so that we can choose differently, but the costs are such that it is not generally advantageous to exercise our option, even though we know that most of our choices are not maximizing.

Consider also, he says, the tendency to wishful thinking. If we set ourselves to calculate the best or maximizing course of action, we are likely to confuse true expectations with hopes. Knowing this, we protect ourselves by choosing on the basis of fixed principles, and we adhere to these principles even when it appears to us that we could do better to ignore them, for we know that in such matters appearances often deceive. Indeed, our objector may suggest, much of morality may be understood, not as constraints on maximization to ensure fair mutual benefit, but as constraints on wish-fulfilling behaviour to ensure closer approximation to maximization.

Consider again, he says, the benefits of threat behaviour. I may induce you to perform an action advantageous to me if I can convince you that, should you not do so, I shall then perform an action very costly to you, even though it would not be my utility maximizing choice. Hijackers seize aircraft, and threaten the destruction of everyone aboard, themselves included, if they are not transported to Havana. Nations threaten nuclear retaliation should their enemies attack them. Although carrying out a threat would be costly, if it works the cost need not be borne, and the benefit, not otherwise obtainable, is forthcoming.

But, our objector continues, a threat can be effective only if credible. It may be that to maximize one's credibility, and one's prospect of advantage, one must dispose oneself to carry out one's threats if one's demands are not met. And so it may be rational to dispose oneself to threat enforcement. But then, by parity of reasoning with our claims about constrained maximization, we must suppose it to be rational actually to carry out one's threats. Surely we should suppose instead that, although it is clearly irrational to carry out a failed threat, yet it may be rational to dispose oneself to just this sort of irrationality. And so similarly we should suppose that although it is clearly irrational to constrain one's maximizing behaviour, yet it may be rational to dispose oneself to this irrationality.

We are unmoved. We agree that an actor who is subject to certain weaknesses or imperfections may find it rational to dispose himself to make choices that are not themselves rational. Such dispositions may be the most effective way of compensating for the weakness or imperfection. They constitute a second-best rationality, as it were. But although it may be rational for us to satisfice, it would not be rational for us to perform the action so chosen if, cost free, the maximizing action were to be revealed to us. And although it may be rational for us to adhere to principles as a guard against wish-fulfilment, it would not be rational for us to do so if, beyond all doubt, the maximizing action were to be revealed to us.

Contrast these with constrained maximization. The rationale for disposing oneself to constraint does not appeal to any weakness or imperfection in the reasoning of the actor; indeed, the rationale is most evident for perfect reasoners who cannot be deceived. The disposition to constrained maximization overcomes externalities; it is directed to the core problem arising from the structure of interaction. And the entire point of disposing oneself to constraint is to adhere to it in the face of one's knowledge that one is not choosing the maximizing action.

Imperfect actors find it rational to dispose themselves to make less than rational choices. No lesson can be drawn from this about the dispositions and choices of the perfect actor. If her dispositions to choose are rational, then surely her choices are also rational.

But what of the threat enforcer? Here we disagree with our objector; it may be rational for a perfect actor to dispose herself to threat enforcement, and if it is, then it is rational for her to carry out a failed threat. Equally, it may be rational for a perfect actor to dispose herself to threat resistance, and if it is, then it is rational for her to resist despite the cost to herself. Deterrence, we have argued elsewhere, may be a rational policy, and non-maximizing deterrent choices are then rational.[26]

In a community of rational persons, however, threat behaviour will be proscribed. Unlike co-operation, threat behaviour does not promote mutual advantage. A successful threat simply redistributes benefits in favour of the threatener; successful threat resistance maintains the status quo. Unsuccessful threat behaviour, resulting in costly acts of enforcement or resistance, is necessarily non-optimal; its very *raison d'être* is to make everyone worse off. Any person who is not exceptionally placed must then have the *ex ante* expectation that threat behaviour will be overall disadvantageous. Its proscription must be part of a fair and optimal agreement among rational persons; one of the constraints imposed by minimax relative concession is abstinence from the making of threats. Our argument thus shows threat behaviour to be both irrational and immoral.

Constrained maximizers will not dispose themselves to enforce or to resist threats among themselves. But there are circumstances, beyond the moral pale, in which a constrained maximizer might find it rational to dispose herself to threat enforcement. If she found herself fallen among straightforward maximizers, and especially if they were too stupid to become threat resisters, disposing herself to threat enforcement might be the best thing she could do. And for her, carrying out failed threats would be rational, though not utility-maximizing.

Our objector has not made good his case. The dispositions of a fully rational actor issue in rational choices. Our argument identifies practical rationality with utility-maximization at the level of dispositions to choose, and carries through the implications of that identification in assessing the rationality of particular choices.

3.3 To conclude this chapter, let us note an interesting parallel to our theory of constrained maximization – Robert Trivers's evolutionary theory of reciprocal altruism.[27] We have claimed that a population of constrained maximizers would be rationally stable; no one would have reason to dispose herself to straightforward maximization. Similarly, if we think of constrained and straightforward maximization as parallel to genetic tendencies to reciprocal altruism and egoism, a population of reciprocal altruists would be genetically stable; a mutant egoist would be at an evolutionary disadvantage. Since she would not reciprocate, she would find herself excluded from co-operative relationships.

Trivers argues that natural selection will favour the development of the capacity to detect merely simulated altruism. This of course corresponds to our claim that constrained maximizers, to be successful, must be able to detect straightforward maximizers whose offers to co-operation are insincere. Exploitative interactions between CMs and SMs must be avoided.

Trivers also argues that natural selection will favour the development of guilt, as a device motivating those who fail to reciprocate to change their ways in future.[28] In our argument, we have not appealed to any affective disposition; we do not want to weaken the position we must defeat, straightforward maximization, by supposing that persons are emotionally indisposed to follow it. But we may expect that in the process of socialization, efforts will be made to develop and cultivate each person's feelings so that, should she behave as an SM, she will experience guilt. We may expect our affective capacities to be shaped by social practices in support of co-operative interaction.

If a population of reciprocal altruists is genetically stable, surely a population of egoists is also stable. As we have seen, the argument for the rationality of constrained maximization turns on the proportion of CMs in the population. A small proportion of CMs might well suffer more from exploitation by undetected SMs than by co-operation among themselves unless their capacities for detecting the dispositions of others were extraordinarily effective. Similarly, a mutant reciprocal altruist would be at a disadvantage among egoists; her attempts at co-operation would be rebuffed and she would lose by her efforts in making them.

Does it then follow that we should expect both groups of reciprocal altruists and groups of egoists to exist stably in the world? Not necessarily. The benefits of co-operation ensure that, in any given set of circumstances, each member of a group of reciprocal altruists should do better than a corresponding member of a group of egoists. Each reciprocal altruist should have a reproductive advantage. Groups of reciprocal altruists should therefore increase relative to groups of egoists in environments in which the two come into contact. The altruists must prevail – not in direct combat between the two (although the co-operation possible among reciprocal altruists may bring victory there), but in the indirect combat for evolutionary survival in a world of limited resources.

In his discussion of Trivers's argument, Jon Elster notes two points of great importance which we may relate to our own account of constrained maximization. The first is, 'The altruism is the more efficient because it is *not* derived from calculated self-interest.'[29] This is exactly our point at the end of 2.1 – constrained maximization is not straightforward maximization in its most effective guise. The constrained maximizer genuinely ignores the call of utility-maximization in following the co-operative practices required by minimax relative concession. There is no simulation; if there were, the benefits of co-operation would not be fully realized.

The second is that Trivers's account 'does not purport to explain specific instances of altruistic behaviour, such as, say, the tendency to save a drowning person. Rescue attempts are explained by a general tendency to perform acts of altruism, and this tendency is then made the object of the evolutionary explanation.'[30] In precisely the same way, we do not purport to give a utility-maximizing justification for specific choices of adherence to a joint strategy. Rather we explain those choices by a general disposition to choose fair, optimizing actions whenever possible, and this tendency is then given a utility-maximizing justification.

We do not, of course, have the competence to discuss whether or not human beings are genetically disposed to utility-maximizing behaviour. But if human beings are so disposed, then we may conclude that the disposition to constrained maximization increases genetic fitness.

Notes

1   Hobbes, *De Cive*, ch. I, para. 7; in *Man and Citizen*, p. 115.
2   Hobbes, *Leviathan*, ch. 14, p. 64.
3   Ibid.
4   Ibid., ch. 13, p. 63.
5   Ibid., ch. 14, p. 64.
6   Ibid.
7   Ibid., ch. 14, pp. 64–5.
8   Ibid., ch. 14, p. 65.
9   Ibid.
10   Ibid., ch. 21, p. 111.
11   Ibid., ch. 15, p. 71.
12   Ibid.
13   Ibid., ch. 15, p. 72.
14   Ibid., ch. 15, p. 73.
15   Ibid.
16   Hobbes, *The Questions Concerning Liberty, Necessity, and Chance*, 1656, no. xiv; in Sir William Molesworth (ed.), *The English Works of Thomas Hobbes*, 11 vols. (London, 1839–45), vol. 5, pp. 193–4.
17   Hobbes, *Leviathan*, ch. 15, p. 72.

18 Our answer to the Foole builds on, but supersedes, my discussion in 'Reason and Maximization', *Canadian Journal of Philosophy* 4 (1975), pp. 424–33.

19 Thus constrained maximization is not parallel to such strategies as 'tit-for-tat' that have been advocated for so-called iterated Prisoner's Dilemmas. Constrained maximizers may co-operate even if neither expects her choice to affect future situations. Thus our treatment of co-operation does not make the appeal to reciprocity necessary to Robert Axelrod's account; see 'The Emergence of Co-operation among Egoists', *American Political Science Review* 75 (1981), pp. 306–18.

20 That the discussion in 'Reason and Maximization' assumes transparency was pointed out to me by Derek Parfit. See his discussion of 'the self-interest theory' in *Reasons and Persons* (Oxford, 1984), esp. pp. 18–19. See also the discussion of 'Reason and Maximization' in S. L. Darwall, *Impartial Reason* (Ithaca, NY, 1983), esp. pp. 197–8.

21 Hume, *Enquiry*, iii. i, p. 187.

22 Ibid., ix. ii, pp. 282–3.

23 Ibid., ix. ii, p. 283.

24 See, for example, T. Nagel, *The Possibility of Altruism* (Oxford, 1970), pp. 90–124.

25 The objector might be Derek Parfit; see *Reasons and Persons*, pp. 19–23. His book appeared too recently to permit discussion of his arguments here.

26 See 'Deterrence, Maximization, and Rationality', *Ethics* 94 (1984), pp. 474–95; also in D. MacLean (ed.). *The Security Gamble: Deterrence Dilemmas in the Nuclear Age* (Totowa, NJ, 1984), pp. 101–22.

27 See R. L. Trivers, 'The Evolution of Reciprocal Altruism', *Quarterly Review of Biology* 46 (1971), pp. 35–57.

28 Ibid., p. 50.

29 J. Elster, *Ulysses and the Sirens: Studies in rationality and irrationality* (Cambridge, 1979), p. 145.

30 Ibid., pp. 145–6.

6

Convention

Gilbert Harman

1 Moral Conventions

Hume says that some, but not all, aspects of morality rest on "convention." There is a convention in Hume's sense when each of a number of people adheres to certain principles so that each of the others will also adhere to these principles. I adhere to the principles in my dealings with the others because I benefit from their adherence to these principles in their dealings with me and because I think that they will stop adhering to these principles in their dealings with me unless I continue to adhere to the principles in my dealings with them. For example, two farmers have a convention of helping each other till their fields. Farmer A helps farmer B till his fields so that when it comes time to till farmer A's fields, farmer B will help farmer A. Each farmer benefits from this practice, which depends upon their expectation that the other will continue it.

Hume mentions other conventions of this sort, for example those that give rise to the institutions of money. Certain pieces of paper can be traded for goods only because they will be accepted in turn by others in exchange for their goods. The conventions of language provide another example, one which indicates that conventions may be extremely subtle and even impossible for an ordinary person to describe in any precise and explicit way.

Conventions are reached through a process of implicit bargaining and mutual adjustment. Two people rowing a boat will adjust their actions with respect to each other so that they pull at the same time. It does not matter what their rate is, as long as both row at the same rate. If one tries to row more quickly and the other tries to row more slowly, some sort of compromise will have to be reached.

Gilbert Harman, "Convention," *The Nature of Morality* (New York: Oxford University Press, 1977), pp. 103–14.

Among the most important conventions, according to Hume, are those having to do with property. It is useful to each person that there should be a system of security regarding possessions. This system is entirely conventional; and until it develops, there is no such thing as property. Another important convention is the one that makes possible explicit contracts and promises. The convention is that, by using a certain form of words (or other sign), a person binds himself to do what he says he will do. The obligation to keep your promises therefore itself derives from a prior convention, according to Hume.

Hume says that the original motive to observe conventions is "natural" rather than moral, by which he means that it is a self-interested motive. Initially, each person continues to adhere to the conventional principles in his dealings with others so that they will continue to do so in their dealings with him. Eventually habits develop. Action in accordance with those principles becomes relatively automatic; it would be hard to change. Obligations based on those principles come to seem natural and obvious. According to Hume, these "natural" obligations will strike us as moral as soon as we reflect sympathetically on the usefulness of the relevant conventions to human society. For, as you will recall, Hume accepts a kind of ideal observer theory. In his view, moral judgments express feelings based on sympathy.

Hume himself does not think that everything about morality is conventional, although he thinks that much is. He holds that sympathy can lead us to approve or disapprove of some things apart from prior conventions – for example, we will approve of kindness to others even in a state of nature – and, in Hume's view, this is moral approval. But he would probably agree that moral *obligations* and *duties* depend on convention; in any event, I will assume in what follows that this is part of Hume's theory.

A more extreme theory than Hume's would treat every aspect of morality as conventional. For example, when Hume believes that a weak sympathy for others is built into people, it might be supposed instead that sympathy itself derives from a convention whereby people tacitly agree to respect each other at least to the extent of trying to feel sympathy for others. But we do not need to decide between Hume's theory and this more extreme version.

Hume's tacit convention theory of morality is a more specific version of the social custom theory. It has a number of advantages. For one thing, it provides a more specific account of the way in which morality involves social utility: certain rules are conventionally adopted because each person benefits from everyone else acting in accordance with those rules.

We therefore expect rules to be adopted if they promote social utility in the sense that they are beneficial to all.

To take another example, as noted in [an earlier] chapter we do not normally assume that you are obligated to help someone when you know that he would not help you if the situation were reversed; we feel that to help such a person would be to do something that is above and beyond the call of duty, a generous act rather than something you are obligated to do. But this is just what we would expect given Hume's theory. There are reasons of self-interest for people to adopt a convention of *mutual* aid, but no obvious reasons of this sort to extend this convention to aid those who do not participate in the convention. So, given Hume's theory, we would not expect an obligation or duty to help the person who would not help you. On the other hand, sympathy would lead an observer to approve of your helping this person; so, given Hume's theory, it would be a good thing if you were to help him even though you are not obligated to do so.

We noted in [a] previous chapter our reluctance to blame cannibals for eating human flesh, despite our abhorrence of their doing so and our view that it would be wrong for any of us to do so while visiting a society that practiced cannibalism. Given Hume's theory we might explain our own aversion to the eating of human flesh in the following way. We have a tacit convention in our society that we will respect each other as people. We will, in Kant's phrase, "treat people as ends," as if they were sacred and possessed a special kind of dignity. Furthermore, there are various conventional forms in which we have come to express our respect and we have therefore come to see it as demeaning to human dignity if persons are not treated according to these conventions. For example, if someone dies, we think it appropriate to hold a funeral and bury the body or perhaps cremate it. Given our current conventions, we will not eat the body. To do that would strike us as an insult to the memory of the person who has died. It would indicate a lack of respect for persons as persons. Our respect for people and our conventional habits of expressing that respect lead us automatically to reject the idea that we could eat human flesh; indeed, we have come to find the very idea disgusting.

Our reactions to the cannibals are complicated, however, because two moralities are relevant, theirs and ours. In judging the situation, we can simply appeal to our own morality: "Eating people is wrong!" But in judging the cannibals themselves, we must take their morality into account. We cannot simply blame them for what they do, because their moral understanding is not the same as ours. They see nothing wrong with eating people; and there is no obvious reason why they should. This makes it difficult for us to judge that it is wrong *of them* to eat human flesh. We do not feel comfortable in judging the cannibals themselves to be wrong. It does not seem right to say that each of them ought morally not to eat human flesh or that each of them has a moral duty or obligation not to do so. At best we might say that it ought not to be the case that they eat human flesh; but as we have seen before that is not the same sort of judgment at all. From our own point of view we can judge their acts and their situation, even their society and morality; but we cannot, it seems, judge *them*.

This explanation is related to a point mentioned in [an earlier chapter]. We are inclined to suppose that a person ought morally not to have done a particular thing only if we can also assume that he had a reason not to do it. We could not suppose that the cannibals ought morally not to eat human flesh unless we also supposed that they have a reason not to eat human flesh. The trouble is that we are presently assuming that they have no such reason, because their morality is not the same as ours. Given this assumption, we can make certain moral or evaluative judgments about the cannibals; for example, we can call them "ignorant savages." But we cannot correctly say of them that they are morally wrong to eat human flesh or that they ought morally not to do it.

2 Judging Outsiders

Now, it is very difficult to get a clear grasp on such examples just because it is not always clear when someone has a reason to do something and when he does not. To take a very different sort of example, Hitler, who had millions of people killed, was an extraordinarily evil man. In some sense we can say that he ought not to have killed those people and that what he did was wrong. Yet the following remarks are weak and even in some way odd: "It was wrong of Hitler to have ordered the extermination of the Jews." "Hitler ought morally not to have ordered the extermination of the Jews."

One might suppose that it is the enormity of Hitler's crime against humanity that makes such remarks seem too weak. He killed so many people; it would have been wrong of him to have killed only one. To say simply that it was wrong of him to have ordered the extermination of the Jews suggests that it was *only* wrong – that it is wrong only in the way in which murder is wrong. And, given what Hitler did, that is as if one were to say that it was *naughty* of Hitler to have ordered the extermination of the Jews.

This explanation, however, is not completely satisfactory. First of all, there are things we can say about Hitler without the same sort of oddity. Although it would be odd to say that it was wrong of Hitler to have acted as he did, it is not equally odd to say that what Hitler did was wrong. Similarly, there is no oddness in the remark, "What Hitler did ought never to have happened." That is not odd in the way that it is odd to say, "Hitler ought morally not to have ordered the extermination of the Jews." But, if the enormity of his crime makes the one remark odd, why doesn't it make the other remark as odd?

Another reason for doubting that the enormity of the crime, by itself, is the reason for the oddness in certain of these judgments is that we can make these very judgments about someone who has committed an equally enormous crime, at least if enormity is measured in numbers of people killed. For example, Stalin was also a mass murderer who ordered the purges of the thirties knowing that millions of people would be killed. Yet it is possible to think that Stalin was really only trying to do the right thing, that he hated the prospect of the purges, that he was however also alarmed at the consequences of not ordering the purges because he was afraid that the revolution was in danger of collapse. He found himself faced with a terrible choice and he opted for what he took to be the lesser of two evils. I am not suggesting that this is the truth about Stalin; it probably is not. I mean only that this is a possible view of Stalin. Of course, even someone taking such a sympathetic view of Stalin can suppose that Stalin was terribly mistaken. To take this view of Stalin is certainly not to condone Stalin's actions. It can never be right to order the deaths of millions of people like that, no matter what you hope to gain. Indeed, taking this view of Stalin, it is natural to say that it was wrong of Stalin to have ordered the purges; Stalin was morally wrong to have done so. The interesting question, then, is why is it not odd to say this about Stalin in the way that it is odd to say the same thing about Hitler. It cannot be the vast numbers of people killed that makes a difference, since vast numbers were killed by both men. And certainly the judgment that it was wrong of Stalin to have ordered the purges is not the judgment that it was *naughty* of him to have done so. Why then does it seem that if you say that it was wrong of Hitler to have done what he did you are saying something as odd and ridiculous as if you had said that it was naughty of Hitler to have done that.

Part of the answer has to do with our conception of the attitudes that we think Hitler and Stalin took toward their crimes, with the moral principles we think of them accepting, with our views of what they considered to be reasons for action. Hitler's attitude was in this respect much more extreme than Stalin's. Hitler is farther from us than Stalin is (or as Stalin is imagined to be in the view of him that I have sketched). Hitler is beyond the pale in a way that Stalin was not. Hitler was not just immoral, he was amoral, he was evil. Stalin was terrible and also, perhaps, evil; but he was not wholly beyond the reaches of morality as I have imagined him. We cannot but think of Hitler as beyond the reaches of morality or at least that part of morality that we invoke in judging him to be an evil man.

In saying that it was wrong of Hitler to have ordered the extermination of the Jews we would be saying that Hitler had a reason (every reason in the world) not to do what he did. But what is horrible about someone who did what he did is that he could not have had such a reason. If he was willing to exterminate a whole people, there was no reason for him not to do so: that is just what is so terrible about him. That is why it sounds too weak to say that it was wrong of him to do what he did. It suggests that he had a reason not to act as he did and we feel that any man who could have done what Hitler did must be the sort of man who would not have had a reason not to do it. Such a man is evil rather than wrong.

This is why it is odd to say that it was wrong of Hitler to have acted as he did but it is not odd to say that Hitler's act was wrong. The judgment that Hitler's act was wrong and the judgment that it never ought to have happened do not imply that Hitler had a reason not to do what he did. The fact that we feel that Hitler was not the sort of person who could have had such a reason does not undermine judgments of his *acts* in the way that it undermines certain judgments about *him*.

All this is explicable in Hume's tacit convention theory. Hitler, like the cannibals, is outside our morality, although in a different direction. We can judge his acts with reference to our morality, but not Hitler himself, since that would imply that he was someone who acknowledged the moral standards we use to judge him. To say, "It was wrong of Hitler" or "Hitler ought morally not to have done it" would imply that Hitler accepted the relevant moral conventions. But his actions show that he does not accept those conventions. He is therefore beyond the pale and an enemy of humanity.

There are other examples that confirm the same point. Consider judgments that we might make about Martians who felt no concern for us. Suppose that these Martians would not be deterred from a given course of action simply by the reflection that that course of action would harm some human being. These Martians would not treat such a consideration as any sort of reason. For them, the consideration would simply not tell against that course of action at all. In that case, we cannot say that it would be morally wrong of the Martians to harm us.

This is to disagree with Kant, who would say that, since a Martian is a rational being, it has a reason not to harm any of us, because we too are rational beings. "The Martian would not agree to our harming it; so how can it agree to its harming us?" Kant believes that reflection of this sort can provide the Martian with motivation not to harm us. If Kant were right, there would be no need for moral conventions. We could make do with pure practical reason alone.

Now a defender of Hume's tacit convention theory will assume, plausibly, that Kant is mistaken about the powers of pure practical reason. When we first come across the Martians, they may well have no reason to be concerned about us at all, and, in that case, there are no moral constraints on them in their dealings with us. If they harm us, that is not a matter of morality or immorality, although it may well be a matter of war between the planets. If it turns out that there is no way for us to harm the Martians, so that they do not need to be concerned about us even for reasons of self-interest, then a morality that encompasses us and them may never develop.

On the other hand, if a conflict develops that is in neither their interest nor ours, we and they may try to arrive at conventions that would reduce or eliminate this sort of conflict. For example, we and they might adopt a convention of respect for each other as rational beings that would involve, among other things, trying to avoid actions that would harm other rational beings. In that case, there would be a morality encompassing us and them.

This is how a morality would arise from a state of nature, according to a tacit convention theory. Before any conventions were established, there would be no such thing as right and wrong; it would not make sense to judge what people morally ought or ought not to do. But once a group of people developed conventional patterns of action in order to avoid conflicts with each other, their actions could be judged with reference to those conventions. People who remained outside the relevant group and still in a state of nature could, however, not be so judged.

3   Conventional Aspects of Morality

One reason for thinking that morality has arisen like this, as the result of convention, is that certain elements in our actual moral views seem to reflect what would be the result of implicit bargaining and mutual adjustments between people of different powers and resources. For example, consider a point I have alluded to several times. In our morality, harming someone is thought to be much worse than helping someone. That is why we suppose that a doctor cannot cut up one patient in order to save five other patients by distributing the one patient's organs according to need. Now, this general principle about harming and not helping may seem irrational and unmotivated, but it makes sense if we suppose that our moral views derive from a tacit convention that arose among people of different wealth, status, and power. For, whereas everyone would benefit equally from a conventional practice of trying not to harm each other, some people would benefit considerably more than others from a convention to help those who needed help. The rich and powerful do not need much help and are often in the best position to give it; so, if a strong principle of mutual aid were adopted, they would gain little and lose a great deal, because they would end up doing most of the helping and would receive little in return. On the other hand, the poor and weak might refuse to agree to a principle of noninterference or noninjury unless they also reached some agreement on mutual aid. We would therefore expect a compromise, as in our example of the two rowers who arrive at a rate intermediate between the rates that each prefers to row at. In the present case, the expected compromise would involve a strong principle of noninjury and a much weaker principle of mutual aid – which is just what we now have. If our moral principles were not in this way a result of bargaining and adjustment, it would be hard to see why we would suppose that there is this moral difference between harming and not helping; and it would be hard to understand how our moral principles could be the result of bargaining and adjustment in this way unless they were derived from some sort of convention in Hume's sense. So, this aspect of our moral views is evidence in favor of Hume's tacit convention theory.

Now, it is important that Hume's theory is an *actual* convention theory. Duties and obligations are seen as deriving from actual, not hypothetical, conventions. Hume's theory is therefore to be distinguished from hypothetical agreement theories that say that the correct moral rules are those that people *would* agree to under certain conditons of equality. Hume's explanation of moral motivation requires his actual convention theory and does not work on any sort of hypothetical agreement theory. Hume says that we act morally first out of self-interest and then out of a habit of following certain conventional rules. We cannot in the same way explain why someone would be motivated to adhere to principles he *would have* agreed to adhere to in a position of equality.

Furthermore, the suggested explanation of the moral difference we recognize between harming and not helping depends on the assumption that our morality rests on an actual convention among people of different powers and resources. It is not easy to see how this aspect of our moral views could be explained by assuming that obligations depend on what we *would* agree to in a position of equality. For, in such a position, it seems likely that we would not agree to our present moral principles.

4   The Tacit Convention Theory and Kant's Theory

Finally, it should also be observed that the tacit convention theory follows important aspects of Kant's theory, even though it rejects one of Kant's key ideas. Kant argued that we must think of the principles of morality as principles that each of us legislates for himself and for others, whom we perceive as also legislating the same principles. It is this second part that distinguishes Kant's theory from Hare's. Hare says that each person thinks of the principles of morality as principles that he legislates for himself and for others, but Hare does not assume that a person must think of the others as legislating the same principles. And this led to a difficulty for Hare (I argued) when we considered making judgments about someone who does not share the relevant principles. The tacit convention theory, like Kant's theory, sees moral principles as principles for which the source is both internal and external. They are principles legislated by others and by yourself. They represent the principles of a general will. Kant was wrong in thinking that these principles are determined by reason alone and therefore wrong to assume that they were universal. Nevertheless he was right to emphasize their objectivity and interpersonal character. The private principles of one person, which that person does not take to be shared by others, do not represent a normal case of moral principles. At best, they represent a limiting case. Morality is essentially social.

The tacit convention theory of morality is therefore not a version of pure externalism. It is a combination: internalism plus externalism. The principles that apply to you, according to this theory, are not simply whatever principles are conventionally accepted by the surrounding group; you must accept the conventions too. Otherwise they could not give you reasons to do things, and judgment about what you ought morally to do or about what it would be right or wrong of you to do could not be made with reference to those conventions. An amoral person can exist in the midst of others who share a common morality. But such a person can no more be judged in terms of other people's principles than can Hitler or the cannibals. If a Martian who does not care about human life decides to live in our midst but does not see any reason to accept our conventions, we cannot say correctly that the Martian is morally obligated not to harm us (although we can judge that it would be a bad thing if the Martians were to harm us). Similarly, it would be a misuse of language to say of hardened professional criminals that it is morally wrong of them to steal from others or that they ought morally not to kill people. Since they do not share our conventions, they have no moral reasons to refrain from stealing from us or killing us. (On the other hand, we can judge them enemies of society and can say that they ought to be hunted down and put into prison.)

Moralities are social. The are defined by the conventions of groups. But you belong to more than one group, and different groups have different conventions. Which conventions determine your moral obligations? They all do. Since you belong to a number of different groups, you are subject to a number of different moralities – the morality of your family, perhaps your school, a professional morality (your "business ethics"), the morality of your neighborhood, the various moralities of various groups of friends, the morality of your country, and finally, perhaps, a limited morality you share with most of humanity. These moralities will sometimes be in conflict, and give rise to a tragic situation in which you are faced with a conflict of loyalties. In that case, there is no clear moral solution to your problem. You must choose the group which is most important to you and act on its conventions.

There is a limiting case of morality in which the relevant "group" contains only one person. In that case, a person will be able to say he has certain moral obligations deriving from his personal principles and will not judge others to be similarly obligated (by his principles). For example, a pacifist may think that he morally ought not to participate in wars, although he will not make the same judgment about other persons. He will not say that it is wrong of them to participate, although he will certainly think that it is bad for everyone that they engage in wars. And there are many other cases in which a person imposes moral obligations and duties on himself without supposing that other persons are similarly obligated.

This represents a limiting case of morality rather than a central case (even though it may be a common case) because we normally think of a morality as a set of principles that can be used to judge more than one person and because, as we saw in [an earlier chapter], we think of morality as imposing external constraints on someone. Without objective external constraints, there would be no such thing as morality, as we ordinarily understand it, even if people adhered to their own personal principles. If there were only individual moralities, only sets of personal principles and no group conventions, morality as we normally think of it would not yet exist.

Part IV

Contemporary Expressions: Contractualism

From *A Theory of Justice*

John Rawls

Chapter I Justice as Fairness

3 *The Main Idea of the Theory of Justice*

My aim is to present a conception of justice which generalizes and carries to a higher level of abstraction the familiar theory of the social contract as found, say, in Locke, Rousseau, and Kant.[1] In order to do this we are not to think of the original contract as one to enter a particular society or to set up a particular form of government. Rather, the guiding idea is that the principles of justice for the basic structure of society are the object of the original agreement. They are the principles that free and rational persons concerned to further their own interests would accept in an initial position of equality as defining the fundamental terms of their association. These principles are to regulate all further agreements; they specify the kinds of social cooperation that can be entered into and the forms of government that can be established. This way of regarding the principles of justice I shall call justice as fairness.

Thus we are to imagine that those who engage in social cooperation choose together, in one joint act, the principles which are to assign basic rights and duties and to determine the division of social benefits. Men are to decide in advance how they are to regulate their claims against one another and what is to be the foundation charter of their society. Just as each person must decide by rational reflection what constitutes his good, that is, the system of ends which it is rational for him to pursue, so a group of persons must decide once and for all what is to count among them as just and unjust. The choice which rational men would make in this

John Rawls, *A Theory of Justice* (Cambridge, MA: Harvard University Press, 1971), pp. 11–22, 60–5, 118–22, 136–42, 150–61, 251–7.

hypothetical situation of equal liberty, assuming for the present that this choice problem has a solution, determines the principles of justice.

In justice as fairness the original position of equality corresponds to the state of nature in the traditional theory of the social contract. This original position is not, of course, thought of as an actual historical state of affairs, much less as a primitive condition of culture. It is understood as a purely hypothetical situation characterized so as to lead to a certain conception of justice.[2] Among the essential features of this situation is that no one knows his place in society, his class position or social status, nor does any one know his fortune in the distribution of natural assets and abilities, his intelligence, strength, and the like. I shall even assume that the parties do not know their conceptions of the good or their special psychological propensities. The principles of justice are chosen behind a veil of ignorance. This ensures that no one is advantaged or disadvantaged in the choice of principles by the outcome of natural chance or the contingency of social circumstances. Since all are similarly situated and no one is able to design principles to favor his particular condition, the principles of justice are the result of a fair agreement or bargain. For given the circumstances of the original position, the symmetry of everyone's relations to each other, this initial situation is fair between individuals as moral persons, that is, as rational beings with their own ends and capable, I shall assume, of a sense of justice. The original position is, one might say, the appropriate initial status quo, and thus the fundamental agreements reached in it are fair. This explains the propriety of the name "justice as fairness": it conveys the idea that the principles of justice are agreed to in an initial situation that is fair. The name does not mean that the concepts of justice and fairness are the same, any more than the phrase "poetry as metaphor" means that the concepts of poetry and metaphor are the same.

Justice as fairness begins, as I have said, with one of the most general of all choices which persons might make together, namely, with the choice of the first principles of a conception of justice which is to regulate all subsequent criticism and reform of institutions. Then, having chosen a conception of justice, we can suppose that they are to choose a constitution and a legislature to enact laws, and so on, all in accordance with the principles of justice initially agreed upon. Our social situation is just if it is such that by this sequence of hypothetical agreements we would have contracted into the general system of rules which defines it. Moreover, assuming that the original position does determine a set of principles (that is, that a particular conception of justice would be chosen), it will then be true that whenever social institutions satisfy these principles those engaged in them can say to one another that they are cooperating on terms to which they would agree if they were free and equal persons whose relations with respect to one another were fair. They could all view their arrangements as meeting the stipulations which they would acknowledge in an initial situation that embodies widely accepted and reasonable constraints on the choice of principles. The general recognition of this fact would provide the basis for a public acceptance of the corresponding principles of justice. No society can, of course, be a scheme of cooperation which men enter voluntarily in a literal sense; each person finds himself placed at birth in some particular position in some particular society, and the nature of this position materially affects his life prospects. Yet a society satisfying the principles of justice as fairness comes as close as a society can to being a voluntary scheme, for it meets the principles which free and equal persons would assent to under circumstances that are fair. In this sense its members are autonomous and the obligations they recognize self-imposed.

One feature of justice as fairness is to think of the parties in the initial situation as rational and mutually disinterested. This does not mean that the parties are egoists, that is, individuals with only certain kinds of interests, say in wealth, prestige, and domination. But they are conceived as not taking an interest in one another's interests. They are to presume that even their spiritual aims may be opposed, in the way that the aims of those of different religions may be opposed. Moreover, the concept of rationality must be interpreted as far as possible in the narrow sense, standard in economic theory, of taking the most effective means to given ends. I shall modify this concept to some extent, [as I explain in a later chapter], but one must try to avoid introducing into it any controversial ethical elements. The initial situation must be characterized by stipulations that are widely accepted.

In working out the conception of justice as fairness one main task clearly is to determine which principles of justice would be chosen in the original position. To do this we must describe this situation in some detail and formulate with care the problem of choice which it presents. These matters I shall take up in the immediately succeeding chapters. It may be observed, however, that once the principles of justice are thought of as arising from an original agreement in a situation of equality, it is an open question whether the principle of utility would be acknowledged. Offhand it hardly seems likely that persons who view themselves as equals, entitled to press their claims upon one another, would agree to a principle which may require lesser life prospects for some simply for the sake of a greater sum of advantages enjoyed by others. Since each desires to protect his interests, his capacity to advance his conception of the good, no one has a reason to acquiesce in an enduring loss for himself in order to bring about a greater net balance of satisfaction. In the absence of strong and lasting benevolent impulses, a rational man would not accept a basic structure merely because it maximized the algebraic sum of advantages irrespective of its permanent effects on his own basic rights and interests. Thus it seems that the principle of utility is incompatible with the conception of social cooperation among equals for mutual advantage. It appears to be inconsistent with the idea of reciprocity implicit in the notion of a well-ordered society. Or, at any rate, so I shall argue.

I shall maintain instead that the persons in the initial situation would choose two rather different principles: the first requires equality in the assignment of basic rights and duties, while the second holds that social and economic inequalities, for example inequalities of wealth and authority, are just only if they result in compensating benefits for everyone, and in particular for the least advantaged members of society. These principles rule out justifying institutions on the grounds that the hardships of some are offset by a greater good in the aggregate. It may be expedient but it is not just that some should have less in order that others may prosper. But there is no injustice in the greater benefits earned by a few provided that the situation of persons not so fortunate is thereby improved. The intuitive idea is that since everyone's well-being depends upon a scheme of cooperation without which no one could have a satisfactory life, the division of advantages should be such as to draw forth the willing cooperation of everyone taking part in it, including those less well situated. Yet this can be expected only if reasonable terms are proposed. The two principles mentioned seem to be a fair agreement on the basis of which those better endowed, or more fortunate in their social position, neither of which we can be said to deserve, could expect the willing cooperation of others when some workable scheme is a necessary condition of the welfare of all.[3] Once we decide to look for a conception of justice that nullifies the accidents of natural endowment and the contingencies of social circumstance as counters in quest for political and economic advantage, we are led to these principles. They express the result of leaving aside those aspects of the social world that seem arbitrary from a moral point of view.

The problem of the choice of principles, however, is extremely difficult. I do not expect the answer I shall suggest to be convincing to everyone. It is, therefore, worth noting from the outset that justice as fairness, like other contract views, consists of two parts: (1) an interpretation of the initial situation and of the problem of choice posed there, and (2) a set of principles which, it is argued, would be agreed to. One may accept the first part of the theory (or some variant thereof), but not the other, and conversely. The concept of the initial contractual situation may seem reasonable although the particular principles proposed are rejected. To be sure, I want to maintain that the most appropriate conception of this situation does lead to principles of justice contrary to utilitarianism and perfectionism, and therefore that the contract doctrine provides an alternative to these views. Still, one may dispute this contention even though one grants that the contractarian method is a useful way of studying ethical theories and of setting forth their underlying assumptions.

Justice as fairness is an example of what I have called a contract theory. Now there may be an objection to the term "contract" and related expressions, but I think it will serve reasonably well. Many words have misleading connotations which at first are likely to confuse. The terms "utility" and "utilitarianism" are surely no exception. They too have unfortunate suggestions which hostile critics have been willing to exploit; yet they are clear enough for those prepared to study utilitarian doctrine. The same should be true of the term "contract" applied to moral theories. As I have mentioned, to understand it one has to keep in mind that it implies a certain level of abstraction. In particular, the content of the relevant agreement is not to enter a given society or to adopt a given form of government, but to accept certain moral principles. Moreover, the undertakings referred to are purely hypothetical: a contract view holds that certain principles would be accepted in a well-defined initial situation.

The merit of the contract terminology is that it conveys the idea that principles of justice may be conceived as principles that would be chosen by rational persons, and that in this way conceptions of justice may be explained and justified. The theory of justice is a part, perhaps the most significant part, of the theory of rational choice. Furthermore, principles of justice deal with conflicting claims upon the advantages won by social cooperation; they apply to the relations among several persons or groups. The word "contract" suggests this plurality as well as the condition that the appropriate division of advantages must be in accordance with principles acceptable to all parties. The condition of publicity for principles of justice is also connoted by the contract phraseology. Thus, if these principles are the outcome of an agreement, citizens have a knowledge of the principles that others follow. It is characteristic of contract theories to stress the public nature of political principles. Finally there is the long tradition of the contract doctrine. Expressing the tie with this line of thought helps to define ideas and accords with natural piety. There are then several advantages in the use of the term "contract." With due precautions taken, it should not be misleading.

A final remark. Justice as fairness is not a complete contract theory. For it is clear that the contractarian idea can be extended to the choice of more or less an entire ethical system, that is, to a system including principles for all the virtues and not only for justice. Now for the most part I shall consider only principles of justice and others closely related to them; I make no attempt to discuss the virtues in a systematic way. Obviously if justice as fairness succeeds reasonably well, a next step would be to study the more general view suggested by the name "rightness as fairness." But even this wider theory fails to embrace all moral relationships, since it would seem to include only our relations with other persons and to leave out of account how we are to conduct ourselves toward animals and the rest of nature. I do not contend that the contract notion offers a way to approach these questions which are certainly of the first importance; and I shall have to put them aside. We must recognize the limited scope of justice as fairness and of the general type of view that it exemplifies. How far its conclusions must be revised once these other matters are understood cannot be decided in advance.

4   *The Original Position and Justification*

I have said that the original position is the appropriate initial status quo which insures that the fundamental agreements reached in it are fair. This fact yields the name "justice as fairness." It is clear, then, that I want to say that one conception of justice is more reasonable than another, or justifiable with respect to it, if rational persons in the initial situation would choose its principles over those of the other for the role of justice. Conceptions of justice are to be ranked by their acceptability to persons so circumstanced. Understood in this way the question of justification is settled by working out a problem of deliberation: we have to ascertain which principles it would be rational to adopt given the contractual situation. This connects the theory of justice with the theory of rational choice.

If this view of the problem of justification is to succeed, we must, of course, describe in some detail the nature of this choice problem. A problem of rational decision has a definite answer only if we know the beliefs and interests of the parties, their relations with respect to one another, the alternatives between which they are to choose, the procedure whereby they make up their minds, and so on. As the circumstances are presented in different ways, correspondingly different principles are accepted. The concept of the original position, as I shall refer to it, is that of the most philosophically favored interpretation of this initial choice situation for the purposes of a theory of justice.

But how are we to decide what is the most favored interpretation? I assume, for one thing, that there is a broad measure of agreement that principles of justice should be chosen under certain conditions. To justify a particular description of the initial situation one shows that it incorporates these commonly shared presumptions. One argues from widely accepted but weak premises to more specific conclusions. Each of the presumptions should by itself be natural and plausible; some of them may seem innocuous or even trivial. The aim of the contract approach is to establish that taken together they impose significant bounds on acceptable principles of justice. The ideal outcome would be that these conditions determine a unique set of principles; but I shall be satisfied if they suffice to rank the main traditional conceptions of social justice.

One should not be misled, then, by the somewhat unusual conditions which characterize the original position. The idea here is simply to make vivid to ourselves the restrictions that it seems reasonable to impose on arguments for principles of justice, and therefore on these principles themselves. Thus it seems reasonable and generally acceptable that no one should be advantaged or disadvantaged by natural fortune or social circumstances in the choice of principles. It also seems widely agreed that it should be impossible to tailor principles to the circumstances of one's own case. We should insure further that particular inclinations and aspirations, and persons' conceptions of their good do not affect the principles adopted. The aim is to rule out those principles that it would be rational to propose for acceptance, however little the chance of success, only if one knew certain things that are irrelevant from the standpoint of justice. For example, if a man knew that he was wealthy, he might find it rational to advance the principle that various taxes for welfare measures be counted unjust; if he knew that he was poor, he would most likely propose the contrary principle. To represent the desired restrictions one imagines a situation in which everyone is deprived of this sort of information. One excludes the knowledge of those contingencies which sets men at odds and allows them to be guided by their prejudices. In this manner the veil of ignorance is arrived at in a natural way. This concept should cause no difficulty if we keep in mind the constraints on arguments that it is meant to express. At any time we can enter the original position, so to speak, simply by following a certain procedure, namely, by arguing for principles of justice in accordance with these restrictions.

It seems reasonable to suppose that the parties in the original position are equal. That is, all have the same rights in the procedure for choosing principles; each can make proposals, submit reasons for their acceptance, and so on. Obviously the purpose of these conditions is to represent equality between human beings as moral persons, as creatures having a conception of their good and capable of a sense of justice. The basis of equality is taken to be similarity in these two respects. Systems of ends are not ranked in value; and each man is presumed to have the requisite ability to understand and to act upon whatever principles are adopted. Together with the veil of ignorance, these conditions define the principles of justice as those which rational persons concerned to advance their interests would consent to as equals when none are known to be advantaged or disadvantaged by social and natural contingencies.

There is, however, another side to justifying a particular description of the original position. This is to see if the principles which would be chosen match our considered convictions of justice or extend them in an acceptable way. We can note whether applying these principles would lead us to make the same judgments about the basic structure of society which we now make intuitively and in which we have the greatest confidence; or whether, in cases where our present judgments are in doubt and given with hesitation, these principles offer a resolution which we can affirm on reflection. There are questions which we feel sure must be answered in a certain way. For example, we are confident that religious intolerance and racial discrimination are unjust. We think that we have examined these things with care and have reached what we believe is an impartial judgment not likely to be distorted by an excessive attention to our own interests. These convictions are provisional fixed points which we presume any conception of justice must fit. But we have much less assurance as to what is the correct distribution of wealth and authority. Here we may be looking for a way to remove our doubts. We can check an interpretation of the initial situation, then, by the capacity of its principles to accommodate our firmest convictions and to provide guidance where guidance is needed.

In searching for the most favored description of this situation we work from both ends. We begin by describing it so that it represents generally shared and preferably weak conditions. We then see if these conditions are strong enough to yield a significant set of principles. If not, we look for further premises equally reasonable. But if so, and these principles match our considered convictions of justice, then so far well and good. But presumably there will be discrepancies. In this case we have a choice. We can either modify the account of the initial situation or we can revise our existing judgments, for even the judgments we take provisionally as fixed points are liable to revision. By going back and forth, sometimes altering the conditions of the contractual circumstances, at others withdrawing our judgments and conforming them to principle, I assume that eventually we shall find a description of the initial situation that both expresses reasonable conditions and yields principles which match our considered judgments duly pruned and adjusted. This state of affairs I refer to as reflective equilibrium.[4] It is an equilibrium because at last our principles and judgments coincide; and it is reflective since we know to what principles our judgments conform and the premises of their derivation. At the moment everything is in order. But this equilibrium is not necessarily stable. It is liable to be upset by further examination of the conditions which should be imposed on the contractual situation and by particular cases which may lead us to revise our judgments. Yet for the time being we have done what we can to render coherent and to justify our convictions of social justice. We have reached a conception of the original position.

I shall not, of course, actually work through this process. Still, we may think of the interpretation of the original position that I shall present as the result of such a hypothetical course of reflection. It represents the attempt to accommodate within one scheme both reasonable philosophical conditions on principles as well as our considered judgments of justice. In arriving at the favored interpretation of the initial situation there is no point at which an appeal is made to self-evidence in the traditional sense either of general conceptions or particular convictions. I do not claim for the principles of justice proposed that they are necessary truths or derivable from such truths. A conception of justice cannot be deduced from self-evident premises or conditions on principles; instead, its justification is a matter of the mutual support of many considerations, of everything fitting together into one coherent view.

A final comment. We shall want to say that certain principles of justice are justified because they would be agreed to in an initial situation of equality. I have emphasized that this original position is purely hypothetical. It is natural to ask why, if this agreement is never actually entered into, we should take any interest in these principles, moral or otherwise. The answer is that the conditions embodied in the description of the original position are ones that we do in fact accept. Or if we do not, then perhaps we can be persuaded to do so by philosophical reflection. Each aspect of the contractual situation can be given supporting grounds. Thus what we shall do is to collect together into one conception a number of conditions on principles that we are ready upon due consideration to recognize as reasonable. These constraints express what we are prepared to regard as limits on fair terms of social cooperation. One way to look at the idea of the original position, therefore, is to see it as an expository device which sums up the meaning of these conditions and helps us to extract their consequences. On the other hand, this conception is also an intuitive notion that suggests its own elaboration, so that led on by it we are drawn to define more clearly the standpoint from which we can best interpret moral relationships. We need a conception that enables us to envision our objective from afar: the intuitive notion of the original position is to do this for us.[5]

Notes

1   As the text suggests, I shall regard Locke's *Second Treatise of Government*, Rousseau's *The Social Contract*, and Kant's ethical works beginning with *The Foundations of the Metaphysics of Morals* as definitive of the contract tradition. For all of its greatness, Hobbes's *Leviathan* raises special problems. A general historical survey is provided by J. W. Gough, *The Social Contract*, 2nd ed. (Oxford, The Clarendon Press, 1957), and Otto Gierke, *Natural Law and the Theory of Society*, trans. with an introduction by Ernest Barker (Cambridge, The University Press, 1934). A presentation of the contract view as primarily an ethical theory is to be found in G. R. Grice, *The Grounds of Moral Judgment* (Cambridge, The University Press, 1967). [See also § 19, note 3 of original publication.]

2   Kant is clear that the original agreement is hypothetical. See *The Metaphysics of Morals*, pt. I (*Rechtslehre*), especially § § 47, 52; and pt. II of the essay "Concerning the Common Saying: This May Be True in Theory but It Does Not Apply in Practice," in *Kant's Political Writings*, ed. Hans Reiss and trans. by H. B. Nisbet (Cambridge, The University Press, 1970), pp. 73–87. See Georges Vlachos, *La Pensée politique de Kant* (Paris, Presses Universitaires de France, 1962), pp. 326–35; and J. G. Murphy, *Kant: The Philosophy of Right* (London, Macmillan, 1970), pp. 109–12, 133–6, for a further discussion.

3   For the formulation of this intuitive idea I am indebted to Allan Gibbard.

4   The process of mutual adjustment of principles and considered judgments is not peculiar to moral philosophy. See Nelson Goodman, *Fact, Fiction, and Forecast* (Cambridge, Mass., Harvard University Press, 1955), pp. 65–8, for parallel remarks concerning the justification of the principles of deductive and inductive inference.

5   Henri Poincaré remarks: "Il nous faut une faculté qui nous fasse voir le but de loin, et, cette faculté, c'est l'intuition." *La Valeur de la science* (Paris, Flammarion, 1909), p. 27.

Chapter II   The Principles of Justice

11   Two Principles of Justice

I shall now state in a provisional form the two principles of justice that I believe would be chosen in the original position. In this section I wish to make only the most general comments, and therefore the first formulation of these principles is tentative. As we go on I shall run through several formulations and approximate step by step the final statement to be given much later. I believe that doing this allows the exposition to proceed in a natural way.

The first statement of the two principles reads as follows.

First: each person is to have an equal right to the most extensive basic liberty compatible with a similar liberty for others.

Second: social and economic inequalities are to be arranged so that they are both (a) reasonably expected to be to everyone's advantage, and (b) attached to positions and offices open to all.

There are two ambiguous phrases in the second principle, namely "everyone's advantage" and "open to all." Determining their sense more exactly will lead to a second formulation of the principle in § 13. The final version of the two principles is given in § 46; § 39 considers the rendering of the first principle.

By way of general comment, these principles primarily apply, as I have said, to the basic structure of society. They are to govern the assignment of rights and duties and to regulate the distribution of social and economic advantages. As their formulation suggests, these principles presuppose that the social structure can be divided into two more or less distinct parts, the first principle applying to the one, the second to the other. They distinguish between those aspects of the social system that define and secure the equal liberties of citizenship and those that specify and establish social and economic inequalities. The basic liberties of citizens are, roughly speaking, political liberty (the right to vote and to be eligible for public office) together with freedom of speech and assembly; liberty of conscience and freedom of thought; freedom of the person along with the right to hold (personal) property; and freedom from arbitrary arrest and seizure as defined by the concept of the rule of law. These liberties are all required to be equal by the first principle, since citizens of a just society are to have the same basic rights.

The second principle applies, in the first approximation, to the distribution of income and wealth and to the design of organizations that make use of differences in authority and responsibility, or chains of command. While the distribution of wealth and income need not be equal, it must be to everyone's advantage, and at the same time, positions of authority and offices of command must be accessible to all. One applies the second principle by holding positions open, and then, subject to this constraint, arranges social and economic inequalities so that everyone benefits.

These principles are to be arranged in a serial order with the first principle prior to the second. This ordering means that a departure from the institutions of equal liberty required by the first principle cannot be justified, or compensated for, by greater social and economic advantages. The distribution of wealth and income, and the hierarchies of authority, must be consistent with both the liberties of equal citizenship and equality of opportunity.

It is clear that these principles are rather specific in their content, and their acceptance rests on certain assumptions that I must eventually try to explain and justify. A theory of justice depends upon a theory of society in ways that will become evident as we proceed. For the present, it should be observed that the two principles (and this holds for all formulations) are a special case of a more general conception of justice that can be expressed as follows.

> All social values – liberty and opportunity, income and wealth, and the bases of self-respects – are to be distributed equally unless an unequal distribution of any, or all, of these values is to everyone's advantage.

Injustice, then, is simply inequalities that are not to the benefit of all. Of course, this conception is extremely vague and requires interpretation.

As a first step, suppose that the basic structure of society distributes certain primary goods, that is, things that every rational man is presumed to want. These goods normally have a use whatever a person's rational plan of life. For simplicity, assume that the chief primary goods at the disposition of society are rights and liberties, powers and opportunities, income and wealth. [Later on in Part Three of original publication the primary good of self-respect has a central place.] These are the social primary goods. Other primary goods such as health and vigor, intelligence and imagination, are natural goods; although their possession is influenced by the basic structure, they are not so directly under its control. Imagine, then, a hypothetical initial arrangement in which all the social primary goods are equally distributed: everyone has similar rights and duties, and income and wealth are evenly shared. This state of affairs provides a benchmark for judging improvements. If certain inequalities of wealth and organizational powers would make everyone better off than in this hypothetical starting situation, then they accord with the general conception.

Now it is possible, at least theoretically, that by giving up some of their fundamental liberties men are sufficiently compensated by the resulting social and economic gains. The general conception of justice imposes no restrictions on what sort of inequalities are permissible; it only requires that everyone's position be improved. We need not suppose anything so drastic as consenting to a condition of slavery. Imagine instead that men forego certain political rights when the economic returns are significant and their capacity to influence the course of policy by the exercise of these rights would be marginal in any case. It is this kind of exchange which the two principles as stated rule out; being arranged in serial order they do not permit exchanges between basic liberties and economic and social gains. The serial ordering of principles expresses an underlying preference among primary social goods. When this preference is rational so likewise is the choice of these principles in this order.

In developing justice as fairness I shall, for the most part, leave aside the general conception of justice and examine instead the special case of the two principles in serial order. The advantage of this procedure is that from the first the matter of priorities is recognized and an effort made to find principles to deal with it. One is led to attend throughout to the conditions under which the acknowledgment of the absolute weight of liberty with respect to social and economic advantages, as defined by the lexical order of the two principles, would be reasonable. Offhand, this ranking appears extreme and too special a case to be of much interest; but there is more justification for it than would appear at first sight. Or at any rate, so I shall maintain (§ 82). Furthermore, the distinction between fundamental rights and liberties and economic and social benefits marks a difference among primary social goods that one should try to exploit. It suggests an important division in the social system. Of course, the distinctions drawn and the ordering proposed are bound to be at best only approximations. There are surely circumstances in which they fail. But it is essential to depict clearly the main lines of a reasonable conception of justice; and under many conditions anyway, the two principles in serial order may serve well enough. When necessary we can fall back on the more general conception.

The fact that the two principles apply to institutions has certain consequences. Several points illustrate this. First of all, the rights and liberties referred to by these principles are those which are defined by the public rules of the basic structure. Whether men are free is determined by the rights and duties established by the major institutions of society. Liberty is a certain pattern of social forms. The first principle simply requires that certain sorts of rules, those defining basic liberties, apply to everyone equally and that they allow the most extensive liberty compatible with a like liberty for all. The only reason for circumscribing the rights defining liberty and making men's freedom less extensive than it might otherwise be is that these equal rights as institutionally defined would interfere with one another.

Another thing to bear in mind is that when principles mention persons, or require that everyone gain from an inequality, the reference is to representative persons holding the various social positions, or offices, or whatever, established by the basic structure. Thus in applying the second principle I assume that it is possible to assign an expectation of well-being to representative individuals holding these positions. This expectation indicates their life prospects as viewed from their social station. In general, the expectations of representative persons depend upon the distribution of rights and duties throughout the basic structure. When this changes, expectations change. I assume, then, that expectations are connected: by raising the prospects of the representative man in one position we presumably increase or decrease the prospects of representative men in other positions. Since it applies to institutional forms, the second principle (or rather the first part of it) refers to the expectations of representative individuals. As I shall discuss below, neither principle applies to distributions of particular goods to particular individuals who may be identified by their proper names. The situation where someone is considering how to allocate certain commodities to needy persons who are known to him is not within the scope of the principles. They are meant to regulate basic institutional arrangements. We must not assume that there is much similarity from the standpoint of justice between an administrative allotment of goods to specific persons and the appropriate design of society. Our common sense intuitions for the former may be a poor guide to the latter.

Now the second principle insists that each person benefit from permissible inequalities in the basic structure. This means that it must be reasonable for each relevant representative man defined by this structure, when he views it as a going concern, to prefer his prospects with the inequality to his prospects without it. One is not allowed to justify differences in income or organizational powers on the ground that the dis-advantages of those in one position are outweighed by the greater advantages of those in another. Much less can infringements of liberty be counterbalanced in this way. Applied to the basic structure, the principle of utility would have us maximize the sum of expectations of representative men (weighted by the number of persons they represent, on the classical view); and this would permit us to compensate for the losses of some by the gains of others. Instead, the two principles require that everyone benefit from economic and social inequalities. It is obvious, however, that there are indefinitely many ways in which all may be advantaged when the initial arrangement of equality is taken as a benchmark. How then are we to choose among these possibilities? The principles must be specified so that they yield a determinate conclusion. I now turn to this problem.

Chapter III   The Original Position

In this chapter I discuss the favored philosophical interpretation of the initial situation. I refer to this interpretation as the original position. I begin by sketching the nature of the argument for conceptions of justice and explaining how the alternatives are presented so that the parties are to choose from a definite list of traditional conceptions. Then I describe the conditions which characterize the initial situation under several head-ings: the circumstances of justice, the formal constraints of the concept of right, the veil of ignorance, and the rationality of the contracting parties. In each case I try to indicate why the features adopted for the favored interpretation are reasonable from a philosophical point of view. Next the natural lines of reasoning leading to the two principles of justice and to the principle of average utility are examined prior to a consideration of the relative advantages of these conceptions of justice. I argue that the two principles would be acknowledged and set out some of the main grounds to support this contention. In order to clarify the differences between the various conceptions of justice, the chapter concludes with another look at the classical principle of utility.

20   *The Nature of the Argument for Conceptions of Justice*

The intuitive idea of justice as fairness is to think of the first principles of justice as themselves the object of an original agreement in a suitably defined initial situation. These principles are those which rational persons concerned to advance their interests would accept in this position of equality to settle the basic terms of their association. It must be shown, then, that the two principles of justice are the solution for the problem of choice presented by the original position. In order to do this, one must establish that, given the circumstances of the parties, and their knowledge, beliefs, and interests, an agreement on these principles is the best way for each person to secure his ends in view of the alternatives available.

Now obviously no one can obtain everything he wants; the mere existence of other persons prevents this. The absolutely best for any man is that everyone else should join with him in furthering his conception of the good whatever it turns out to be. Or failing this, that all others are required to act justly but that he is authorized to exempt himself as he pleases. Since other persons will never agree to such terms of association these forms of egoism would be rejected. The two principles of justice, however, seem to be a reasonable proposal. In fact, I should like to show that these principles are everyone's best reply, so to speak, to the corresponding demands of the others. In this sense, the choice of this conception of justice is the unique solution to the problem set by the original position.

By arguing in this way one follows a procedure familiar in social theory. That is, a simplified situation is described in which rational individuals with certain ends and related to each other in certain ways are to choose among various courses of action in view of their knowledge of the circumstances. What these individuals will do is then derived by strictly deductive reasoning from these assumptions about their beliefs and interests, their situation and the options open to them. Their conduct is, in the phrase of Pareto, the resultant of tastes and obstacles.[1] In the theory of price, for example, the equilibrium of competitive markets is thought of as arising when many individuals each advancing his own interests give way to each other what they can best part with in return for what they most desire. Equilibrium is the result of agreements freely struck between willing traders. For each person it is the best situation that he can reach by free exchange consistent with the right and freedom of others to further their interests in the same way. It is for this reason that this state of affairs is an equilibrium, one that will persist in the absence of further changes in the circumstances. No one has any incentive to alter it. If a departure from this situation sets in motion tendencies which restore it, the equilibrium is stable.

Of course, the fact that a situation is one of equilibrium, even a stable one, does not entail that it is right or just. It only means that given men's estimate of their position, they act effectively to preserve it. Clearly a balance of hatred and hostility may be a stable equilibrium; each may think that any feasible change will be worse. The best that each can do for himself may be a condition of lesser injustice rather than of greater good. The moral assessment of equilibrium situations depends upon the background circumstances which determine them. It is at this point that the conception of the original position embodies features peculiar to moral theory. For while the theory of price, say, tries to account for the movements of the market by assumptions about the actual tendencies at work, the philosophically favored interpretation of the initial situation incorporates conditions which it is thought reasonable to impose on the choice of principles. By contrast with social theory, the aim is to characterize this situation so that the principles that would be chosen, whatever they turn out to be, are acceptable from a moral point of view. The original position is defined in such a way that it is a status quo in which any agreements reached are fair. It is a state of affairs in which the parties are equally represented as moral persons and the outcome is not conditioned by arbitrary contingencies or the relative balance of social forces. Thus justice as fairness is able to use the idea of pure procedural justice from the beginning.

It is clear, then, that the original position is a purely hypothetical situation. Nothing resembling it need ever take place, although we can by deliberately following the constraints it expresses simulate the reflections of the parties. The conception of the original position is not intended to explain human conduct except insofar as it tries to account for our moral judgments and helps to explain our having a sense of justice. Justice as fairness is a theory of our moral sentiments as manifested by our considered judgments in reflective equilibrium. These sentiments presumably affect our thought and action to some degree. So while the conception of the original position is part of the theory of conduct, it does not follow at all that there are actual situations that resemble it. What is necessary is that the principles that would be accepted play the requisite part in our moral reasoning and conduct.

One should note also that the acceptance of these principles is not conjectured as a psychological law or probability. Ideally anyway, I should like to show that their acknowledgment is the only choice consistent with the full description of the original position. The argument aims eventually to be strictly deductive. To be sure, the persons in the original position have a certain psychology, since various assumptions are made about their beliefs and interests. These assumptions appear along with other premises in the description of this initial situation. But clearly arguments from such premises can be fully deductive, as theories in politics and economics attest. We should strive for a kind of moral geometry with all the rigor which this name connotes. Unhappily the reasoning I shall give will fall far short of this, since it is highly intuitive throughout. Yet it is essential to have in mind the ideal one would like to achieve.

A final remark. There are, as I have said, many possible interpretations of the initial situation. This conception varies depending upon how the contracting parties are conceived, upon what their beliefs and interests are said to be, upon which alternatives are available to them, and so on. In this sense, there are many different contract theories. Justice as fairness is but one of these. But the question of justification is settled, as far as it can be, by showing that there is one interpretation of the initial situation which best expresses the conditions that are widely thought reasonable to impose on the choice of principles yet which, at the same time, leads to a conception that characterizes our considered judgments in reflective equilibrium. This most favored, or standard, interpretation I shall refer to as the original position. We may conjecture that for each traditional conception of justice there exists an interpretation of the initial situation in which its principles are the preferred solution. Thus, for example, there are interpretations that lead to the classical as well as the average principle of utility. These variations of the initial situation will be mentioned as we go along. The procedure of contract theories provides, then, a general analytic method for the comparative study of conceptions of justice. One tries to set out the different conditions embodied in the contractual situation in which their principles would be chosen. In this way one formulates the various underlying assumptions on which these conceptions seem to depend. But if one interpretation is philosophically most favored, and if its principles characterize our considered judgments, we have a procedure for justification as well. We cannot know at first whether such an interpretation exists, but at least we know what to look for.

24   *The Veil of Ignorance*

The idea of the original position is to set up a fair procedure so that any principles agreed to will be just. The aim is to use the notion of pure procedural justice as a basis of theory. Somehow we must nullify the effects of specific contingencies which put men at odds and tempt them to exploit social and natural circumstances to their own advantage. Now in order to do this I assume that the parties are situated behind a veil of ignorance. They do not know how the various alternatives will affect their own particular case and they are obliged to evaluate principles solely on the basis of general considerations.[2]

It is assumed, then, that the parties do not know certain kinds of particular facts. First of all, no one knows his place in society, his class position or social status; nor does he know his fortune in the distribution of natural assets and abilities, his intelligence and strength, and the like. Nor, again, does anyone know his conception of the good, the particulars of his rational plan of life, or even the special features of his psychology such as his aversion to risk or liability to optimism or pessimism. More than this, I assume that the parties do not know the particular circumstances of their own society. That is, they do not know its economic or political situation, or the level of civilization and culture it has been able to achieve. The persons in the original position have no information as to which generation they belong. These broader restrictions on knowledge are appropriate in part because questions of social justice arise between generations as well as within them, for example, the question of the appropriate rate of capital saving and of the conservation of natural resources and the environment of nature. There is also, theoretically anyway, the question of a reasonable genetic policy. In these cases too, in order to carry through the idea of the original position, the parties must not know the contingencies that set them in opposition. They must choose principles the consequences of which they are prepared to live with whatever generation they turn out to belong to.

As far as possible, then, the only particular facts which the parties know is that their society is subject to the circumstances of justice and whatever this implies. It is taken for granted, however, that they know the general facts about human society. They understand political affairs and the principles of economic theory; they know the basis of social organization and the laws of human psychology. Indeed, the parties are presumed to know whatever general facts affect the choice of the principles of justice. There are no limitations on general information, that is, on general laws and theories, since conceptions of justice must be adjusted to the characteristics of the systems of social cooperation which they are to regulate, and there is no reason to rule out these facts. It is, for example, a consideration against a conception of justice that, in view of the laws of moral psychology, men would not acquire a desire to act upon it even when the institutions of their society satisfied it. For in this case there would be difficulty in securing the stability of social cooperation. It is an important feature of a conception of justice that it should generate its own support. That is, its principles should be such that when they are embodied in the basic structure of society men tend to acquire the corresponding sense of justice. Given the principles of moral learning, men develop a desire to act in accordance with its principles. In this case a conception of justice is stable. This kind of general information is admissible in the original position.

The notion of the veil of ignorance raises several difficulties. Some may object that the exclusion of nearly all particular information makes it difficult to grasp what is meant by the original position. Thus it may be helpful to observe that one or more persons can at any time enter this position, or perhaps, better, simulate the deliberations of this hypothetical situation, simply by reasoning in accordance with the appropriate restrictions. In arguing for a conception of justice we must be sure that it is among the permitted alternatives and satisfies the stipulated formal constraints. No considerations can be advanced in its favor unless they would be rational ones for us to urge were we to lack the kind of knowledge that is excluded. The evaluation of principles must proceed in terms of the general consequences of their public recognition and universal application, it being assumed that they will be complied with by everyone. To say that a certain conception of justice would be chosen in the original position is equivalent to saying that rational deliberation satisfying certain conditions and restrictions would reach a certain conclusion. If necessary, the argument to this result could be set out more formally. I shall, however, speak throughout in terms of the notion of the original position. It is more economical and suggestive, and brings out certain essential features that otherwise one might easily overlook.

These remarks show that the original position is not to be thought of as a general assembly which includes at one moment everyone who will live at some time; or, much less, as an assembly of everyone who could live at some time. It is not a gathering of all actual or possible persons. To conceive of the original position in either of these ways is to stretch fantasy too far; the conception would cease to be a natural guide to intuition. In any case, it is important that the original position be interpreted so that one can at any time adopt its perspective. It must make no difference when one takes up this viewpoint, or who does so: the restrictions must be such that the same principles are always chosen. The veil of ignorance is a key condition in meeting this requirement. It insures not only that the information available is relevant, but that it is at all times the same.

It may be protested that the condition of the veil of ignorance is irrational. Surely, some may object, principles should be chosen in the light of all the knowledge available. There are various replies to this contention. Here I shall sketch those which emphasize the simplifications that need to be made if one is to have any theory at all. (Those based on the Kantian interpretation of the original position are given later, § 40.) To begin with, it is clear that since the differences among the parties are unknown to them, and everyone is equally rational and similarly situated, each is convinced by the same arguments. Therefore, we can view the choice in the original position from the standpoint of one person selected at random. If anyone after due reflection prefers a conception of justice to another, then they all do, and a unanimous agreement can be reached. We can, to make the circumstances more vivid, imagine that the parties are required to communicate with each other through a referee as intermediary, and that he is to announce which alternatives have been suggested and the reasons offered in their support. He forbids the attempt to form coalitions, and he informs the parties when they have come to an understanding. But such a referee is actually superfluous, assuming that the deliberations of the parties must be similar.

Thus there follows the very important consequence that the parties have no basis for bargaining in the usual sense. No one knows his situation in society nor his natural assets, and therefore no one is in a position to tailor principles to his advantage. We might imagine that one of the contractees threatens to hold out unless the others agree to principles favorable to him. But how does he know which principles are especially in his interests? The same holds for the formation of coalitions: if a group were to decide to band together to the disadvantage of the others, they would not know how to favor themselves in the choice of principles. Even if they could get everyone to agree to their proposal, they would have no assurance that it was to their advantage, since they cannot identify themselves either by name or description. The one case where this conclusion fails is that of saving. Since the persons in the original position know that they are contemporaries (taking the present time of entry interpretation), they can favor their generation by refusing to make any sacrifices at all for their successors; they simply acknowledge the principle that no one has a duty to save for posterity. Previous generations have saved or they have not; there is nothing the parties can now do to affect that. So in this instance the veil of ignorance fails to secure the desired result. Therefore I resolve the question of justice between generations in a different way by altering the motivation assumption. But with this adjustment no one is able to formulate principles especially designed to advance his own cause. Whatever his temporal position, each is forced to choose for everyone.[3]

The restrictions on particular information in the original position are, then, of fundamental importance. Without them we would not be able to work out any definite theory of justice at all. We would have to be content with a vague formula stating that justice is what would be agreed to without being able to say much, if anything, about the substance of the agreement itself. The formal constraints of the concept of right, those applying to principles directly, are not sufficient for our purpose. The veil of ignorance makes possible a unanimous choice of a particular conception of justice. Without these limitations on knowledge the bargaining problem of the original position would be hopelessly complicated. Even if theoretically a solution were to exist, we would not, at present anyway, be able to determine it.

The notion of the veil of ignorance is implicit, I think, in Kant's ethics (§ 40). Nevertheless the problem of defining the knowledge of the parties and of characterizing the alternatives open to them has often been passed over, even by contract theories. Sometimes the situation definitive of moral deliberation is presented in such an indeterminate way that one cannot ascertain how it will turn out. Thus Perry's doctrine is essentially contractarian: he holds that social and personal integration must proceed by entirely different principles, the latter by rational prudence, the former by the concurrence of persons of good will. He would appear to reject utilitarianism on much the same grounds suggested earlier: namely, that it improperly extends the principle of choice for one person to choices facing society. The right course of action is characterized as that which best advances social aims as these would be formulated by reflective agreement given that the parties have full knowledge of the circumstances and are moved by a benevolent concern for one another's interests. No effort is made, however, to specify in any precise way the possible outcomes of this sort of agreement. Indeed, without a far more elaborate account, no conclusions can be drawn.[4] I do not wish here to criticize others; rather, I want to explain the necessity for what may seem at times like so many irrelevant details.

Now the reasons for the veil of ignorance go beyond mere simplicity. We want to define the original position so that we get the desired solution. If a knowledge of particulars is allowed, then the outcome is biased by arbitrary contingencies. As already observed, to each according to his threat advantage is not a principle of justice. If the original position is to yield agreements that are just, the parties must be fairly situated and treated equally as moral persons. The arbitrariness of the world must be corrected for by adjusting the circumstances of the initial contractual situation. Moreover, if in choosing principles we required unanimity even when there is full information, only a few rather obvious cases could be decided. A conception of justice based on unanimity in these circumstances would indeed be weak and trivial. But once knowledge is excluded, the requirement of unanimity is not out of place and the fact that it can be satisfied is of great importance. It enables us to say of the preferred conception of justice that it represents a genuine reconciliation of interests.

A final comment. For the most part I shall suppose that the parties possess all general information. No general facts are closed to them. I do this mainly to avoid complications. Nevertheless a conception of justice is to be the public basis of the terms of social cooperation. Since common understanding necessitates certain bounds on the complexity of principles, there may likewise be limits on the use of theoretical knowledge in the original position. Now clearly it would be very difficult to classify and to grade for complexity the various sorts of general facts. I shall make no attempt to do this. We do however recognize an intricate theoretical construction when we meet one. Thus it seems reasonable to say that other things equal one conception of justice is to be preferred to another when it is founded upon markedly simpler general facts, and its choice does not depend upon elaborate calculations in the light of a vast array of theoretically defined possibilities. It is desirable that the grounds for a public conception of justice should be evident to everyone when circumstances permit. This consideration favors, I believe, the two principles of justice over the criterion of utility.

26   *The Reasoning Leading to the Two Principles of Justice*

In this and the next two sections [not excerpted here] I take up the choice between the two principles of justice and the principle of average utility. Determining the rational preference between these two options is perhaps the central problem in developing the conception of justice as fairness as a viable alternative to the utilitarian tradition. I shall begin in this section by presenting some intuitive remarks favoring the two principles. I shall also discuss briefly the qualitative structure of the argument that needs to be made if the case for these principles is to be conclusive.

It will be recalled that the general conception of justice as fairness requires that all primary social goods be distributed equally unless an unequal distribution would be to everyone's advantage. No restrictions are placed on exchanges of these goods and therefore a lesser liberty can be compensated for by greater social and economic benefits. Now looking at the situation from the standpoint of one person selected arbitrarily, there is no way for him to win special advantages for himself. Nor, on the other hand, are there grounds for his acquiescing in special disadvantages. Since it is not reasonable for him to expect more than an equal share in the division of social goods, and since it is not rational for him to agree to less, the sensible thing for him to do is to acknowledge as the first principle of justice one requiring an equal distribution. Indeed, this principle is so obvious that we would expect it to occur to anyone immediately.

Thus, the parties start with a principle establishing equal liberty for all, including equality of opportunity, as well as an equal distribution of income and wealth. But there is no reason why this acknowledgment should be final. If there are inequalities in the basic structure that work to make everyone better off in comparison with the benchmark of initial equality, why not permit them? The immediate gain which a greater equality might allow can be regarded as intelligently invested in view of its future return. If, for example, these inequalities set up various incentives which succeed in eliciting more productive efforts, a person in the original position may look upon them as necessary to cover the costs of training and to encourage effective performance. One might think that ideally individuals should want to serve one another. But since the parties are assumed not to take an interest in one another's interests, their acceptance of these inequalities is only the acceptance of the relations in which men stand in the circumstances of justice. They have no grounds for complaining of one another's motives. A person in the original position would, therefore, concede the justice of these inequalities. Indeed, it would be shortsighted of him not to do so. He would hesitate to agree to these regularities only if he would be dejected by the bare knowledge or perception that others were better situated; and I have assumed that the parties decide as if they are not moved by envy. In order to make the principle regulating inequalities determinate, one looks at the system from the standpoint of the least advantaged representative man. Inequalities are permissible when they maximize, or at least all contribute to, the long-term expectations of the least fortunate group in society.

Now this general conception imposes no constraints on what sorts of inequalities are allowed, whereas the special conception, by putting the two principles in serial order (with the necessary adjustments in meaning), forbids exchanges between basic liberties and economic and social benefits. I shall not try to justify this ordering here. From time to time in later chapters this problem will be considered. But roughly, the idea underlying this ordering is that if the parties assume that their basic liberties can be effectively exercised, they will not exchange a lesser liberty for an improvement in economic well-being. It is only when social conditions do not allow the effective establishment of these rights that one can concede their limitation; and these restrictions can be granted only to the extent that they are necessary to prepare the way for a free society. The denial of equal liberty can be defended only if it is necessary to raise the level of civilization so that in due course these freedoms can be enjoyed. Thus in adopting a serial order we are in effect making a special assumption in the original position, namely, that the parties know that the conditions of their society, whatever they are, admit the effective realization of the equal liberties. The serial ordering of the two principles of justice eventually comes to be reasonable if the general conception is consistently followed. This lexical ranking is the long-run tendency of the general view. For the most part I shall assume that the requisite circumstances for the serial order obtain.

It seems clear from these remarks that the two principles are at least a plausible conception of justice. The question, though, is how one is to argue for them more systematically. Now there are several things to do. One can work out their consequences for institutions and note their implications for fundamental social policy. In this way they are tested by a comparison with our considered judgments of justice. . . . But one can also try to find arguments in their favor that are decisive from the standpoint of the original position. In order to see how this might be done, it is useful as a heuristic device to think of the two principles as the maximin solution to the problem of social justice. There is an analogy between the two principles and the maximin rule for choice under uncertainty.[5] This is evident from the fact that the two principles are those a person would choose for the design of a society in which his enemy is to assign him his place. The maximin rule tells us to rank alternatives by their worst possible outcomes: we are to adopt the alternative the worst outcome of which is superior to the worst outcomes of the others. The persons in the original position do not, of course, assume that their initial place in society is decided by a malevolent opponent. As I note below, they should not reason from false premises. The veil of ignorance does not violate this idea, since an absence of information is not misinformation. But that the two principles of justice would be chosen if the parties were forced to protect themselves against such a contingency explains the sense in which this conception is the maximin solution. And this analogy suggests that if the original position has been described so that it is rational for the parties to adopt the conservative attitude expressed by this rule, a conclusive argument can indeed be constructed for these principles. Clearly the maximin rule is not, in general, a suitable guide for choices under uncertainty. But it is attractive in situations marked by certain special features. My aim, then, is to show that a good case can be made for the two principles based on the fact that the original position manifests these features to the fullest possible degree, carrying them to the limit, so to speak.

Consider the gain-and-loss table below. It represents the gains and losses for a situation which is not a game of strategy. There is no one playing against the person making the decision; instead he is faced with several possible circumstances which may or may not obtain. Which circumstances happen to exist does not depend upon what the person choosing decides or whether he announces his moves in advance. The numbers in the table are monetary values (in hundreds of dollars) in comparison with some initial situation. The gain (g) depends upon the individual's decision (d) and the circumstances (c). Thus $g = f(d, c)$. Assuming that there are three possible decisions and three possible circumstances, we might have this gain-and-loss table.

| | Circumstances | | |
Decisions	c_1	c_2	c_3
d_1	-7	8	12
d_2	-8	7	14
d_3	5	6	8

The maximin rule requires that we make the third decision. For in this case the worst that can happen is that one gains five hundred dollars, which is better than the worst for the other actions. If we adopt one of these we may lose either eight or seven hundred dollars. Thus, the choice of d_3 maximizes $f(d, c)$ for that value of c, which for a given d, minimizes f. The term "maximin" means the *maximum minimorum*; and the rule directs our attention to the worst that can happen under any proposed course of action, and to decide in the light of that.

Now there appear to be three chief features of situations that give plausibility to this unusual rule.[6] First, since the rule takes no account of the likelihoods of the possible circumstances, there must be some reason for sharply discounting estimates of these probabilities. Offhand, the most natural rule of choice would seem to be to compute the expectation of monetary gain for each decision and then to adopt the course of action with the highest prospect. (This expectation is defined as follows: let us suppose that g_{ij} represent the numbers in the gain-and-loss table, where i is the row index and j is the column index; and let p_j, $j = 1, 2, 3$, be the likelihoods of the circumstances, with $\Sigma p_j = 1$. Then the expectation for the ith decision is equal to $\Sigma \, p_j g_{ij}$.) Thus it must be, for example, that the situation is one in which a knowledge of likelihoods is impossible, or at best extremely insecure. In this case it is unreasonable not to be skeptical of probabilistic calculations unless there is no other way out, particularly if the decision is a fundamental one that needs to be justified to others.

The second feature that suggests the maximin rule is the following: the person choosing has a conception of the good such that he cares very little, if anything, for what he might gain above the minimum stipend that he can, in fact, be sure of by following the maximin rule. It is not worthwhile for him to take a chance for the sake of a further advantage, especially when it may turn out that he loses much that is important to him. This last provision brings in the third feature, namely, that the rejected alternatives have outcomes that one can hardly accept. The situation involves grave risks. Of course these features work most effectively in combination. The paradigm situation for following the maximin rule is when all three features are realized to the highest degree. This rule does not, then, generally apply, nor of course is it self-evident. Rather, it is a maxim, a rule of thumb, that comes into its own in special circumstances. Its application depends upon the qualitative structure of the possible gains and losses in relation to one's conception of the good, all this against a background in which it is reasonable to discount conjectural estimates of likelihoods.

It should be noted, as the comments on the gain-and-loss table say, that the entries in the table represent monetary values and not utilities. This difference is significant since for one thing computing expectations on the basis of such objective values is not the same thing as computing expected utility and may lead to different results. The essential point though is that in justice as fairness the parties do not know their conception of the good and cannot estimate their utility in the ordinary sense. In any case, we want to go behind de facto preferences generated by given conditions. Therefore expectations are based upon an index of primary goods and the parties make their choice accordingly. The entries in the example are in terms of money and not utility to indicate this aspect of the contract doctrine.

Now, as I have suggested, the original position has been defined so that it is a situation in which the maximin rule applies. In order to see this, let us review briefly the nature of this situation with these three special features in mind. To begin with, the veil of ignorance excludes all but the vaguest knowledge of likelihoods. The parties have no basis for determining the probable nature of their society, or their place in it. Thus they have strong reasons for being wary of probability calculations if any other course is open to them. They must also take into account the fact that their choice of principles should seem reasonable to others, in particular their descendants, whose rights will be deeply affected by it. There are further grounds for discounting that I shall mention as we go along. For the present it suffices to note that these considerations are strengthened by the fact that the parties know very little about the gain-and-loss table. Not only are they unable to conjecture the likelihoods of the various possible circumstances, they cannot say much about what the possible circumstances are, much less enumerate them and foresee the outcome of each alternative available. Those deciding are much more in the dark than the illustration by a numerical table suggests. It is for this reason that I have spoken of an analogy with the maximin rule.

Several kinds of arguments for the two principles of justice illustrate the second feature. Thus, if we can maintain that these principles provide a workable theory of social justice, and that they are compatible with reasonable demands of efficiency, then this conception guarantees a satisfactory minimum. There may be, on reflection, little reason for trying to do better. Thus much of the argument . . . is to show, by their application to the main questions of social justice, that the two principles are a satisfactory conception. These details have a philosophical purpose. Moreover, this line of thought is practically decisive if we can establish the priority of liberty, the lexical ordering of the two principles. For this priority implies that the persons in the original position have no desire to try for greater gains at the expense of the equal liberties. The minimum assured by the two principles in lexical order is not one that the parties wish to jeopardize for the sake of greater economic and social advantages. . . .

Finally, the third feature holds if we can assume that other conceptions of justice may lead to institutions that the parties would find intolerable. For example, it has sometimes been held that under some conditions the utility principle (in either form) justifies, if not slavery or serfdom, at any rate serious infractions of liberty for the sake of greater social benefits. We need not consider here the truth of this claim, or the likelihood that the requisite conditions obtain. For the moment, this contention is only to illustrate the way in which conceptions of justice may allow for outcomes which the parties may not be able to accept. And having the ready alternative of the two principles of justice which secure a satisfactory minimum, it seems unwise, if not irrational, for them to take a chance that these outcomes are not realized.

So much, then, for a brief sketch of the features of situations in which the maximin rule comes into its own and of the way in which the arguments for the two principles of justice can be subsumed under them. Thus if the list of traditional views represents the possible decisions, these principles would be selected by the rule. The original position clearly exhibits these special features to a very high degree in view of the fundamental character of the choice of a conception of justice. These remarks about the maximin rule are intended only to clarify the structure of the choice problem in the original position. They depict its qualitative anatomy. The arguments for the two principles will be presented more fully as we proceed. I want to conclude this section by taking up an objection which is likely to be made against the difference principle and which leads into an important question. The objection is that since we are to maximize (subject to the usual constraints) the long-term prospects of the least advantaged, it seems that the justice of large increases or decreases in the expectations of the more advantaged may depend upon small changes in the prospects of those worst off. To illustrate: the most extreme disparities in wealth and income are allowed provided that the expectations of the least fortunate are raised in the slightest degree. But at the same time similar inequalities favoring the more advantaged are forbidden when those in the worst position lose by the least amount. Yet it seems extraordinary that the justice of increasing the expectations of the better placed by a billion dollars, say, should turn on whether the prospects of the least favored increase or decrease by a penny. This objection is analogous to the following difficulty with the maximin rule. Consider the sequence of gain-and-loss tables:

$$
\begin{array}{cc}
0 & n \\
1/n & 1
\end{array}
$$

for all natural numbers n. Even if for some smallish number it is reasonable to select the second row, surely there is another point later in the sequence when it is irrational not to choose the first row contrary to the rule.

Part of the answer is that the difference principle is not intended to apply to such abstract possibilities. As I have said, the problem of social justice is not that of allocating *ad libitum* various amounts of something, whether it be money, or property, or whatever, among given individuals. Nor is there some substance of which expectations are made that can be shuffled from one representative man to another in all possible combinations. The possibilities which the objection envisages cannot arise in real cases; the feasible set is so restricted that they are excluded.[7] The reason for this is that the two principles are tied together as one conception of justice which applies to the basic structure of society as a whole. The operation of the principles of equal liberty and open positions prevents these contingencies from occurring. For as we raise the expectations of the more advantaged the situation of the worst off is continuously improved. Each such increase is in the latter's interest, up to a certain point anyway. For the greater expectations of the more favored presumably cover the costs of training and encourage better performance thereby contributing to the general advantage. While nothing guarantees that inequalities will not be significant, there is a persistent tendency for them to be leveled down by the increasing availability of educated talent and ever widening opportunities. The conditions established by the other principles insure that the disparities likely to result will be much less than the differences that men have often tolerated in the past.

We should also observe that the difference principle not only assumes the operation of other principles, but it presupposes as well a certain theory of social institutions. In particular . . . it relies on the idea that in a competitive economy (with or without private ownership) with an open class system excessive inequalities will not be the rule. Given the distribution of natural assets and the laws of motivation, great disparities will not long persist. Now the point to stress here is that there is no objection to resting the choice of first principles upon the general facts of economics and psychology. As we have seen, the parties in the original position are assumed to know the general facts about human society. Since this knowledge enters into the premises of their deliberations, their choice of principles is relative to these facts. What is essential, of course, is that these premises be true and sufficiently general. It is often objected, for example, that utilitarianism may allow for slavery and serfdom, and for other infractions of liberty. Whether these institutions are justified is made to depend upon whether actuarial calculations show that they yield a higher balance of happiness. To this the utilitarian replies that the nature of society is such that these calculations are normally against such denials of liberty. Utilitarians seek to account for the claims of liberty and equality by making certain standard assumptions, as I shall refer to them. Thus they suppose that persons have similar utility functions which satisfy the condition of diminishing marginal utility. It follows from these stipulations that, given a fixed amount of income say, the distribution should be equal, once we leave aside effects on future production. For so long as some have more than others, total utility can be increased by transfers to those who have less. The assignment of rights and liberties can be

regarded in much the same way. There is nothing wrong with this procedure provided the assumptions are sound.

Contract theory agrees, then, with utilitarianism in holding that the
fundamental principles of justice quite properly depend upon the natural
facts about men in society. This dependence is made explicit by the
description of the original position: the decision of the parties is taken in
the light of general knowledge. Moreover, the various elements of the
original position presuppose many things about the circumstances of
human life. Some philosophers have thought that ethical first principles
should be independent of all contingent assumptions, that they should
take for granted no truths except those of logic and others that follow
from these by an analysis of concepts. Moral conceptions should hold for
all possible worlds. Now this view makes moral philosophy the study
of the ethics of creation: an examination of the reflections an omnipotent
deity might entertain in determining which is the best of all possible
worlds. Even the general facts of nature are to be chosen. Certainly we
have a natural religious interest in the ethics of creation. But it would
appear to outrun human comprehension. From the point of view of contract theory it amounts to supposing that the persons in the original position know nothing at all about themselves or their world. How, then, can
they possibly make a decision? A problem of choice is well defined only
if the alternatives are suitably restricted by natural laws and other constraints, and those deciding already have certain inclinations to choose
among them. Without a definite structure of this kind the question posed
is indeterminate. For this reason we need have no hesitation in making
the choice of the principles of justice presuppose a certain theory of social
institutions. Indeed, one cannot avoid assumptions about general facts
any more than one can do without a conception of the good on the basis
of which the parties rank alternatives. If these assumptions are true and
suitably general, everything is in order, for without these elements the
whole scheme would be pointless and empty.

It is evident from these remarks that both general facts as well as moral
conditions are needed even in the argument for the first principles of
justice. (Of course, it has always been obvious that secondary moral rules
and particular ethical judgments depend upon factual premises as well as
normative principles.) In a contract theory, these moral conditions take
the form of a description of the initial contractual situation. It is also clear
that there is a division of labor between general facts and moral conditions
in arriving at conceptions of justice, and this division can be different
from one theory to another. As I have noted before, principles differ in
the extent to which they incorporate the desired moral ideal. It is

characteristic of utilitarianism that it leaves so much to arguments from general facts. The utilitarian tends to meet objections by holding that the laws of society and of human nature rule out the cases offensive to our considered judgments. Justice as fairness, by contrast, embeds the ideals of justice, as ordinarily understood, more directly into its first principles. This conception relies less on general facts in reaching a match with our judgments of justice. It insures this fit over a wider range of possible cases.

There are two reasons that justify this embedding of ideals into first principles. First of all, and most obviously, the utilitarian's standard assumptions that lead to the wanted consequences may be only probably true, or even doubtfully so. Moreover, their full meaning and application may be highly conjectural. And the same may hold for all the requisite general suppositions that support the principle of utility. From the standpoint of the original position it may be unreasonable to rely upon these hypotheses and therefore far more sensible to embody the ideal more expressly in the principles chosen. Thus it seems that the parties would prefer to secure their liberties straightway rather than have them depend upon what may be uncertain and speculative actuarial calculations. These remarks are further confirmed by the desirability of avoiding complicated theoretical arguments in arriving at a public conception of justice (§ 24). In comparison with the reasoning for the two principles, the grounds for the utility criterion trespass upon this constraint. But secondly, there is a real advantage in persons' announcing to one another once and for all that even though theoretical computations of utility always happen to favor the equal liberties (assuming that this is indeed the case here), they do not wish that things had been different. Since in justice as fairness moral conceptions are public, the choice of the two principles is, in effect, such an announcement. And the benefits of this collective profession favor these principles even though the standard utilitarian assumptions should be true. These matters I shall consider in more detail in connection with publicity and stability. The relevant point here is that while, in general, an ethical theory can certainly invoke natural facts, there may nevertheless be good reasons for embedding convictions of justice more directly into first principles than a theoretically complete grasp of the contingencies of the world may actually require.

Notes

1   *Manuel d'économie politique* (Paris, 1909), ch. III, § 23. Pareto says: "L'equilibre résulte précisément de cette opposition des goûts et des obstacles."

2 The veil of ignorance is so natural a condition that something like it must have occurred to many. The closest explicit statement of it known to me is found in J. C. Harsanyi, "Cardinal Utility in Welfare Economics and in the Theory of Risk-Taking," *Journal of Political Economy*, vol. 61 (1953). Harsanyi uses it to develop a utilitarian theory, as I discuss below in §§ 27–8 [not excerpted here].

3 Rousseau, *The Social Contract*, bk. II, ch. IV, par. 5.

4 See R. B. Perry, *The General Theory of Value* (New York, Longmans, Green and Company, 1926), pp. 674–82.

5 An accessible discussion of this and other rules of choice under uncertainty can be found in W. J. Baumol, *Economic Theory and Operations Analysis*, 2nd ed. (Englewood Cliffs, N.J., Prentice-Hall Inc., 1965), ch. 24. Baumol gives a geometric interpretation of these rules, including the diagram used in § 13 to illustrate the difference principle. See pp. 558–62. See also R. D. Luce and Howard Raiffa, *Games and Decisions* (New York, John Wiley and Sons, Inc., 1957), ch. XIII, for a fuller account.

6 Here I borrow from William Fellner, *Probability and Profit* (Homewood, Ill., R. D. Irwin, Inc., 1965), pp. 140–2, where these features are noted.

7 I am indebted to S. A. Marglin for this point.

Chapter IV   Equal Liberty

40   *The Kantian Interpretation of Justice as Fairness*

For the most part I have considered the content of the principle of equal liberty and the meaning of the priority of the rights that it defines. It seems appropriate at this point to note that there is a Kantian interpretation of the conception of justice from which this principle derives. This interpretation is based upon Kant's notion of autonomy. It is a mistake, I believe, to emphasize the place of generality and universality in Kant's ethics. That moral principles are general and universal is hardly new with him; and as we have seen these conditions do not in any case take us very far. It is impossible to construct a moral theory on so slender a basis, and therefore to limit the discussion of Kant's doctrine to these notions is to reduce it to triviality. The real force of his view lies elsewhere.[1]

For one thing, he begins with the idea that moral principles are the object of rational choice. They define the moral law that men can rationally will to govern their conduct in an ethical commonwealth. Moral philosophy becomes the study of the conception and outcome of a suitably defined rational decision. This idea has immediate consequences. For once we think of moral principles as legislation for a kingdom of ends, it is clear that these principles must not only be acceptable to all but public as well. Finally Kant supposes that this moral legislation is to be agreed to under conditions that characterize men as free and equal rational beings. The description of the original position is an attempt to interpret this conception. I do not wish to argue here for this interpretation on the basis of Kant's text. Certainly some will want to read him differently. Perhaps the remarks to follow are best taken as suggestions for relating justice as fairness to the high point of the contractarian tradition in Kant and Rousseau.

Kant held, I believe, that a person is acting autonomously when the principles of his action are chosen by him as the most adequate possible expression of his nature as a free and equal rational being. The principles he acts upon are not adopted because of his social position or natural endowments, or in view of the particular kind of society in which he lives or the specific things that he happens to want. To act on such principles is to act heteronomously. Now the veil of ignorance deprives the persons in the original position of the knowledge that would enable them to choose heteronomous principles. The parties arrive at their choice together as free and equal rational persons knowing only that those circumstances obtain which give rise to the need for principles of justice.

To be sure, the argument for these principles does add in various ways to Kant's conception. For example, it adds the feature that the principles chosen are to apply to the basic structure of society; and premises characterizing this structure are used in deriving the principles of justice. But I believe that this and other additions are natural enough and remain fairly close to Kant's doctrine, at least when all of his ethical writings are viewed together. Assuming, then, that the reasoning in favor of the principles of justice is correct, we can say that when persons act on these principles they are acting in accordance with principles that they would choose as rational and independent persons in an original position of equality. The principles of their actions do not depend upon social or natural contingencies, nor do they reflect the bias of the particulars of their plan of life or the aspirations that motivate them. By acting from these principles persons express their nature as free and equal rational beings subject to the general conditions of human life. For to express one's nature as a being of a particular kind is to act on the principles that would be chosen if this nature were the decisive determining element. Of course, the choice of the parties in the original position is subject to the restrictions of that situation. But when we knowingly act on the principles of justice in the ordinary course of events, we deliberately assume the limitations of the original position. One reason for doing this, for persons who can do so and want to, is to give expression to one's nature.

The principles of justice are also categorical imperatives in Kant's sense. For by a categorical imperative Kant understands a principle of conduct that applies to a person in virtue of his nature as a free and equal rational being. The validity of the principle does not presuppose that one has a particular desire or aim. Whereas a hypothetical imperative by contrast does assume this: it directs us to take certain steps as effective means to achieve a specific end. Whether the desire is for a particular thing, or whether it is for something more general, such as certain kinds of agreeable feelings or pleasures, the corresponding imperative is hypothetical. Its applicability depends upon one's having an aim which one need not have as a condition of being a rational human individual. The argument for the two principles of justice does not assume that the parties have particular ends, but only that they desire certain primary goods. These are things that it is rational to want whatever else one wants. Thus given human nature, wanting them is part of being rational; and while each is presumed to have some conception of the good, nothing is known about his final ends. The preference for primary goods is derived, then, from only the most general assumptions about rationality and the conditions of human life. To act from the principles of justice is to act from categorical imperatives in the sense that they apply to us whatever in particular our aims are. This simply reflects the fact that no such contingencies appear as premises in their derivation.

We may note also that the motivational assumption of mutual disinterest accords with Kant's notion of autonomy, and gives another reason for this condition. So far this assumption has been used to characterize the circumstances of justice and to provide a clear conception to guide the reasoning of the parties. We have also seen that the concept of benevolence, being a second-order notion, would not work out well. Now we can add that the assumption of mutual disinterest is to allow for freedom in the choice of a system of final ends.[2] Liberty in adopting a conception of the good is limited only by principles that are deduced from a doctrine which imposes no prior constraints on these conceptions. Presuming mutual disinterest in the original position carries out this idea. We postulate that the parties have opposing claims in a suitably general sense. If their ends were restricted in some specific way, this would appear at the outset as an arbitrary restriction on freedom. Moreover, if the parties were conceived as altruists, or as pursuing certain kinds of pleasures, then the principles chosen would apply, as far as the argument would have shown, only to persons whose freedom was restricted to choices compatible with altruism or hedonism. As the argument now runs, the principles of justice cover all persons with rational plans of life, whatever their content, and these principles represent the appropriate restrictions on freedom. Thus it is possible to say that the constraints on conceptions of the good are the result of an interpretation of the contractual situation that puts no prior limitations on what men may desire. There are a variety of reasons, then, for the motivational premise of mutual disinterest. This premise is not only a matter of realism about the circumstances of justice or a way to make the theory manageable. It also connects up with the Kantian idea of autonomy.

There is, however, a difficulty that should be clarified. It is well expressed by Sidgwick.[3] He remarks that nothing in Kant's ethics is more striking than the idea that a man realizes his true self when he acts from the moral law, whereas if he permits his actions to be determined by sensuous desires or contingent aims, he becomes subject to the law of nature. Yet in Sidgwick's opinion this idea comes to naught. It seems to him that on Kant's view the lives of the saint and the scoundrel are equally the outcome of a free choice (on the part of the noumenal self) and equally the subject of causal laws (as a phenomenal self). Kant never explains why the scoundrel does not express in a bad life his characteristic and freely chosen selfhood in the same way that a saint expresses his characteristic and freely chosen selfhood in a good one. Sidgwick's objection is decisive, I think, as long as one assumes, as Kant's exposition may seem to allow, both that the noumenal self can choose any consistent set of principles and that acting from such principles, whatever they are, is sufficient to express one's choice as that of a free and equal rational being. Kant's reply must be that though acting on any consistent set of principles could be the outcome of a decision on the part of the noumenal self, not all such action by the phenomenal self expresses this decision as that of a free and equal rational being. Thus if a person realizes his true self by expressing it in his actions, and if he desires above all else to realize this self, then he will choose to act from principles that manifest his nature as a free and equal rational being. The missing part of the argument concerns the concept of expression. Kant did not show that acting from the moral law expresses our nature in identifiable ways that acting from contrary principles does not.

This defect is made good, I believe, by the conception of the original position. The essential point is that we need an argument showing which principles, if any, free and equal rational persons would choose and these principles must be applicable in practice. A definite answer to this question is required to meet Sidgwick's objection. My suggestion is that we think of the original position as the point of view from which noumenal selves see the world. The parties qua noumenal selves have complete freedom to choose whatever principles they wish; but they also have a desire to express their nature as rational and equal members of the intelligible realm with precisely this liberty to choose, that is, as beings who can look at the world in this way and express this perspective in their life as members of society. They must decide, then, which principles when consciously followed and acted upon in everyday life will best manifest this freedom in their community, most fully reveal their independence from natural contingencies and social accident. Now if the argument of the contract doctrine is correct, these principles are indeed those defining the moral law, or more exactly, the principles of justice for institutions and individuals. The description of the original position interprets the point of view of noumenal selves, of what it means to be a free and equal rational being. Our nature as such beings is displayed when we act from the principles we would choose when this nature is reflected in the conditions determining the choice. Thus men exhibit their freedom, their independence from the contingencies of nature and society, by acting in ways they would acknowledge in the original position.

Properly understood, then, the desire to act justly derives in part from the desire to express most fully what we are or can be, namely free and equal rational beings with a liberty to choose. It is for this reason, I believe, that Kant speaks of the failure to act on the moral law as giving rise to shame and not to feelings of guilt. And this is appropriate, since for him acting unjustly is acting in a manner that fails to express our nature as a free and equal rational being. Such actions therefore strike at our self-respect, our sense of our own worth, and the experience of this loss is shame. We have acted as though we belonged to a lower order, as though we were a creature whose first principles are decided by natural contingencies. Those who think of Kant's moral doctrine as one of law and guilt badly misunderstand him. Kant's main aim is to deepen and to justify Rousseau's idea that liberty is acting in accordance with a law that we give to ourselves. And this leads not to a morality of austere command but to an ethic of mutual respect and self-esteem.[4]

The original position may be viewed, then, as a procedural interpretation of Kant's conception of autonomy and the categorical imperative. The principles regulative of the kingdom of ends are those that would be chosen in this position, and the description of this situation enables us to explain the sense in which acting from these principles expresses our nature as free and equal rational persons. No longer are these notions purely transcendent and lacking explicable connections with human conduct, for the procedural conception of the original position allows us to make these ties. It is true that I have departed from Kant's views in several respects. I shall not discuss these matters here; but two points should be noted. The person's choice as a noumenal self I have assumed to be a collective one. The force of the self's being equal is that the principles chosen must be acceptable to other selves. Since all are similarly free and rational, each must have an equal say in adopting the public principles of the ethical commonwealth. This means that as noumenal selves, everyone is to consent to these principles. Unless the scoundrel's principles would be chosen, they cannot express this free choice, however much a single self might be of a mind to opt for them. Later I shall try to define a clear sense in which this unanimous agreement is best expressive of the nature of even a single self. It in no way overrides a person's interests as the collective nature of the choice might seem to imply. But I leave this aside for the present.

Secondly, I have assumed all along that the parties know that they are subject to the conditions of human life. Being in the circumstances of justice, they are situated in the world with other men who likewise face limitations of moderate scarcity and competing claims. Human freedom is to be regulated by principles chosen in the light of these natural restrictions. Thus justice as fairness is a theory of human justice and among its premises are the elementary facts about persons and their place in nature. The freedom of pure intelligences not subject to these constraints, and the freedom of God, are outside the scope of the theory. It might appear that Kant meant his doctrine to apply to all rational beings as such and therefore to God and the angels as well. Men's social situation in the world may seem to have no role in his theory in determining the first principles of justice. I do not believe that Kant held this view, but I cannot discuss this question here. It suffices to say that if I am mistaken, the Kantian interpretation of justice as fairness is less faithful to Kant's intentions than I am presently inclined to suppose.

Notes

1　To be avoided at all costs is the idea that Kant's doctrine simply provides the general, or formal, elements for a utilitarian (or indeed for any other) theory. See, for example, R. M. Hare, *Freedom and Reason* (Oxford, The Clarendon Press, 1963), pp. 123f. One must not lose sight of the full scope of his view, one must take the later works into consideration. Unfortunately, there is no commentary on Kant's moral theory as a whole; perhaps it would prove impossible to write. But the standard works of H. J. Paton, *The Categorical Imperative* (Chicago, University of Chicago Press, 1948), and L. W. Beck, *A Commentary on Kant's*

Critique of Practical Reason (Chicago, University of Chicago Press, 1960), and others need to be further complemented by studies of the other writings. See here M. J. Gregor's *Laws of Freedom* (Oxford, Basil Blackwell, 1963), an account of *The Metaphysics of Morals,* and J. G. Murphy's brief *Kant: The Philosophy of Right* (London, Macmillan, 1970). Beyond this, *The Critique of Judgment, Religion within the Limits of Reason,* and the political writings cannot be neglected without distorting his doctrine. For the last, see *Kant's Political Writings,* ed. Hans Reiss and trans. H. B. Nisbet (Cambridge, The University Press, 1970).

2   For this point I am indebted to Charles Fried.

3   See *The Methods of Ethics,* 7th ed. (London, Macmillan, 1907), Appendix, "The Kantian Conception of Free Will" (reprinted from *Mind,* vol. 13, 1888), pp. 511–16, esp. p. 516.

4   See B. A. O. Williams, 'The Idea of Equality," in *Philosophy, Politics and Society,* Second Series, ed. Peter Laslett and W. G. Runciman (Oxford, Basil Blackwell, 1962), pp. 115f. For confirmation of this interpretation, see Kant's remarks on moral education in *The Critique of Practical Reason,* pt. II. See also Beck, *A Commentary on Kant's Critique of Practical Reason,* pp. 233–6.

8

Kantian Constructivism in Moral Theory

John Rawls

LECTURE I
Rational and Full Autonomy

In these lectures I examine the notion of a constructivist moral conception, or, more exactly, since there are different kinds of constructivism, one Kantian variant of this notion. The variant I discuss is that of justice as fairness, which is presented in my book *A Theory of Justice*.[1] I have two reasons for doing this: one is that it offers me the opportunity to consider certain aspects of the conception of justice as fairness which I have not previously emphasized and to set out more clearly the Kantian roots of that conception. The other reason is that the Kantian form of constructivism is much less well understood than other familiar traditional moral conceptions, such as utilitarianism, perfectionism, and intuitionism. I believe that this situation impedes the advance of moral theory. Therefore, it may prove useful simply to explain the distinctive features of Kantian constructivism, to say what it is, as illustrated by justice as fairness, without being concerned to defend it. To a degree that it is hard for me to estimate, my discussion assumes some acquaintance with *A Theory of Justice*, but I hope that, for the most part, a bare familiarity with its main intuitive ideas will suffice; and what these are I note as we proceed. . . .

I

What distinguishes the Kantian form of constructivism is essentially this: it specifies a particular conception of the person as an element in a rea-

John Rawls, "Kantian Constructivism in Moral Theory," *Journal of Philosophy* 77, 9: 515–24, 528–30, 532, 554–72.

sonable procedure of construction, the outcome of which determines the content of the first principles of justice. Expressed another way: this kind of view sets up a certain procedure of construction which answers to certain reasonable requirements, and within this procedure persons characterized as rational agents of construction specify, through their agreements, the first principles of justice. (I use 'reasonable' and 'rational' to express different notions throughout, notions which will be explained below, in section v, [pp. 196–9].) The leading idea is to establish a suitable connection between a particular conception of the person and first principles of justice, by means of a procedure of construction. In a Kantian view the conception of the person, the procedure, and the first principles must be related in a certain manner – which, of course, admits of a number of variations. Justice as fairness is not, plainly, Kant's view, strictly speaking; it departs from his text at many points. But the adjective 'Kantian' expresses analogy and not identity; it means roughly that a doctrine sufficiently resembles Kant's in enough fundamental respects so that it is far closer to his view than to the other traditional moral conceptions that are appropriate for use as benchmarks of comparison.

On the Kantian view that I shall present, conditions for justifying a conception of justice hold only when a basis is established for political reasoning and understanding within a public culture. The social role of a conception of justice is to enable all members of society to make mutually acceptable to one another their shared institutions and basic arrangements, by citing what are publicly recognized as sufficient reasons, as identified by that conception. To succeed in doing this, a conception must specify admissible social institutions and their possible arrangements into one system, so that they can be justified to all citizens, whatever their social position or more particular interests. Thus, whenever a sufficient basis for agreement among citizens is not presently known, or recognized, the task of justifying a conception of justice becomes: how can people settle on a conception of justice, to serve this social role, that is (most) reasonable for them in virtue of how they conceive of their persons and construe the general features of social cooperation among persons so regarded?

Pursuing this idea of justification, we take our examination of the Kantian conception of justice as addressed to an impasse in our recent political history; the course of democratic thought over the past two centuries, say, shows that there is no agreement on the way basic social institutions should be arranged if they are to conform to the freedom and equality of citizens as moral persons. The requisite understanding of freedom and equality, which is implicit in the public culture of a democratic society, and the most suitable way to balance the claims of these notions, have not been expressed so as to meet general approval. Now a Kantian conception of justice tries to dispel the conflict between the different understandings of freedom and equality by asking: which traditionally recognized principles of freedom and equality, or which natural variations thereof, would free and equal moral persons themselves agree upon, if they were fairly represented solely as such persons and thought of themselves as citizens living a complete life in an on-going society? Their agreement, assuming an agreement would be reached, is conjectured to single out the most appropriate principles of freedom and equality and, therefore, to specify the principles of justice.

An immediate consequence of taking our inquiry as focused on the apparent conflict between freedom and equality in a democratic society is that we are not trying to find a conception of justice suitable for all societies regardless of their particular social or historical circumstances. We want to settle a fundamental disagreement over the just form of basic institutions within a democratic society under modern conditions. We look to ourselves and to our future, and reflect upon our disputes since, let's say, the Declaration of Independence. How far the conclusions we reach are of interest in a wider context is a separate question.

Hence, we should like to achieve among ourselves a practicable and working understanding on first principles of justice. Our hope is that there is a common desire for agreement, as well as a sufficient sharing of certain underlying notions and implicitly held principles, so that the effort to reach an understanding has some foothold. The aim of political philosophy, when it presents itself in the public culture of a democratic society, is to articulate and to make explicit those shared notions and principles thought to be already latent in common sense; or, as is often the case, if common sense is hesitant and uncertain, and doesn't know what to think, to propose to it certain conceptions and principles congenial to its most essential convictions and historical traditions. To justify a Kantian conception within a democratic society is not merely to reason correctly from given premises, or even from publicly shared and mutually recognized premises. The real task is to discover and formulate the deeper bases of agreement which one hopes are embedded in common sense, or even to originate and fashion starting points for common understanding by expressing in a new form the convictions found in the historical tradition by connecting them with a wide range of people's considered convictions: those which stand up to critical reflection. Now, as I have said, a Kantian doctrine joins the content of justice with a certain conception of the person; and this conception regards persons as both free and equal, as capable of acting both reasonably and rationally, and therefore as capable of taking part in social cooperation among persons so conceived. In addressing the public culture of a democratic society, Kantian constructivism hopes to invoke a conception of the person implicitly affirmed in that culture, or else one that would prove acceptable to citizens once it was properly presented and explained.

I should emphasize that what I have called the "real task" of justifying a conception of justice is not primarily an epistemological problem. The search for reasonable grounds for reaching agreement rooted in our conception of ourselves and in our relation to society replaces the search for moral truth interpreted as fixed by a prior and independent order of objects and relations, whether natural or divine, an order apart and distinct from how we conceive of ourselves. The task is to articulate a public conception of justice that all can live with who regard their person and their relation to society in a certain way. And though doing this may involve settling theoretical difficulties, the practical social task is primary. What justifies a conception of justice is not its being true to an order antecedent to and given to us, but its congruence with our deeper understanding of ourselves and our aspirations, and our realization that, given our history and the traditions embedded in our public life, it is the most reasonable doctrine for us. We can find no better basic charter for our social world. Kantian constructivism holds that moral objectivity is to be understood in terms of a suitably constructed social point of view that all can accept. Apart from the procedure of constructing the principles of justice, there are no moral facts. Whether certain facts are to be recognized as reasons of right and justice, or how much they are to count, can be ascertained only from within the constructive procedure, that is, from the undertakings of rational agents of construction when suitably represented as free and equal moral persons.

II

. . .

Justice as fairness tries to uncover the fundamental ideas (latent in common sense) of freedom and equality, of ideal social cooperation and of the person, by formulating what I shall call "model-conceptions." We then reason within the framework of these conceptions, which need be defined only sharply enough to yield an acceptable public understanding of freedom and equality. Whether the doctrine that eventually results fulfills its purpose is then decided by how it works out: once stated, it must articulate a suitable conception of ourselves and of our relation to society, and connect this conception with workable first principles of justice, so that, after due consideration, we can acknowledge the doctrine proposed.

Now the two basic model-conceptions of justice as fairness are those of a *well-ordered society* and of a *moral person*. Their general purpose is to single out the essential aspects of our conception of ourselves as moral persons and of our relation to society as free and equal citizens. They depict certain general features of what a society would look like if its members publicly viewed themselves and their social ties with one another in a certain way. The *original position* is a third and mediating model-conception: its role is to establish the connection between the model-conception of a moral person and the principles of justice that characterize the relations of citizens in the model-conception of a well-ordered society. It serves this role by modeling the way in which the citizens in a well-ordered society, viewed as moral persons, would ideally select first principles of justice for their society. The constraints imposed on the parties in the original position, and the manner in which the parties are described, are to represent the freedom and equality of moral persons as understood in such a society. If certain principles of justice would indeed be agreed to (or if they would belong to a certain restricted family of principles), then the aim of Kantian constructivism to connect definite principles with a particular conception of the person is achieved.

For the present, however, I am concerned with the parties in the original position only as rationally autonomous agents of construction who (as such agents) represent the aspect of rationality, which is part of the conception of a moral person affirmed by citizens in a well-ordered society. The rational autonomy of the parties in the original position contrasts with the full autonomy of citizens in society. Thus *rational* autonomy is that of the parties as agents of construction: it is a relatively narrow notion, and roughly parallels Kant's notion of hypothetical imperatives (or the notion of rationality found in neo-classical economics); *full* autonomy is that of citizens in everyday life who think of themselves in a certain way and affirm and act from the first principles of justice that would be agreed to. In section v, I shall discuss the constraints imposed on the parties which enable the original position to represent the essential elements of full autonomy.

Let us briefly recall the features of a well-ordered society most relevant here.[2] First, such a society is effectively regulated by a public conception of justice; that is, it is a society in which every one accepts, and knows that others likewise accept, the same first principles of right and justice. It is also the case that the basic structure of society, the arrangement of its main institutions into one social scheme, actually satisfies, and is believed by all on good grounds to satisfy, these principles. Finally, the public principles of justice are themselves founded on reasonable beliefs as established by the society's generally accepted methods of inquiry; and the same is true of the application of these principles to judge social institutions.

Second, the members of a well-ordered society are, and view themselves and one another in their political and social relations (so far as these are relevant to questions of justice) as, free and equal moral persons. Here there are three distinct notions, specified independently: freedom, equality, and moral (as applied to) person. The members of a well-ordered society are moral persons in that, once they have reached the age of reason, each has, and views the others as having, an effective sense of justice, as well as an understanding of a conception of their good. Citizens are equal in that they regard one another as having an equal right to determine, and to assess upon due reflection, the first principles of justice by which the basic structure of their society is to be governed. Finally, the members of a well-ordered society are free in that they think they are entitled to make claims on the design of their common institutions in the name of their own fundamental aims and highest-order interests. At the same time, as free persons, they think of themselves not as inevitably tied to the pursuit of the particular final ends they have at any given time, but rather as capable of revising and changing these ends on reasonable and rational grounds. . . .

III

Let us descend from these abstractions, at least a bit, and turn to a summary account of the original position. As I have said, justice as fairness begins from the idea that the most appropriate conception of justice for the basic structure of a democratic society is one that its citizens would adopt in a situation that is fair between them and in which they are represented solely as free and equal moral persons. This situation is the original position: we conjecture that the fairness of the circumstances under which agreement is reached transfers to the principles of justice agreed to; since the original position situates free and equal moral persons fairly with respect to one another, any conception of justice they adopt is likewise fair. Thus the name: 'justice as fairness'.

In order to ensure that the original position is fair between individuals regarded solely as free and equal moral persons, we require that, when adopting principles for the basic structure, the parties be deprived of certain information; that is, they are behind what I shall call a "veil of ignorance." For example, they do not know their place in society, their class position, or social status, nor do they know their fortune in the distribution of natural talents and abilities. It is assumed also that they do not know their conception of the good, that is, their particular final ends; nor finally, their own distinctive psychological dispositions and propensities, and the like. Excluding this information is required if no one is to be advantaged or disadvantaged by natural contingencies or social chance in the adoption of principles. Otherwise the parties would have disparate bargaining advantages that would affect the agreement reached. The original position would represent the parties not solely as free and equal moral persons, but instead as persons also affected by social fortune and natural accident. Thus, these and other limitations on information are necessary to establish fairness between the parties as free and equal moral persons and, therefore, to guarantee that it is as such persons that they agree to society's basic principles of justice. . . .

One reason for describing the original position as incorporating pure procedural justice is that it enables us to explain how the parties, as the rational agents of construction, are also autonomous (as such agents). For the use of pure procedural justice implies that the principles of justice themselves are to be constructed by a process of deliberation, a process visualized as being carried out by the parties in the original position. The appropriate weight of considerations for and against various principles is given by the force of these considerations for the parties, and the force of all reasons on balance is expressed by the agreement made. Pure procedural justice in the original position allows that in their deliberations the parties are not required to apply, nor are they bound by, any antecedently given principles of right and justice. Or, put another way, there exists no standpoint external to the parties' own perspective from which they are constrained by prior and independent principles in questions of justice that arise among them as members of one society.

. . .

V

So much for the notion of rational autonomy of the parties as agents of construction. I now turn to the notion of full autonomy; although this notion is realized only by the citizens of a well-ordered society in the course of their daily lives, the essential features of it must nevertheless be represented in a suitable manner in the original position. For it is by affirming the first principles that would be adopted in this situation and by publicly recognizing the way in which they would be agreed to, as well as by acting from these principles as their sense of justice dictates, that citizens' full autonomy is achieved. We must ask, then, how the original position incorporates the requisite elements of full autonomy.

Now these elements are not expressed by how the parties' deliberations and motivation are described. The parties are merely artificial agents, and are presented not as fully but only as rationally autonomous. To explain full autonomy, let us note two elements of any notion of social cooperation. The first is a conception of the *fair terms of cooperation*, that is, terms each participant may reasonably be expected to accept, provided that everyone else likewise accepts them. Fair terms of cooperation articulate an idea of reciprocity and mutuality: all who cooperate must benefit, or share in common burdens, in some appropriate fashion as judged by a suitable benchmark of comparison. This element in social cooperation I call the *Reasonable*. The other element corresponds to the *Rational*: it expresses a conception of each participant's rational advantage, what, as individuals, they are trying to advance. As we have seen, the rational is interpreted by the original position in reference to the desire of persons to realize and to exercise their moral powers and to secure the advancement of their conception of the good. Given a specification of the parties' highest-order interests, they are rational in their deliberations to the extent that sensible principles of rational choice guide their decisions. Familiar examples of such principles are: the adoption of effective means to ends; the balancing of final ends by their significance for our plan of life as a whole and by the extent to which these ends cohere with and support each other; and finally, the assigning of a greater weight to the more likely consequences; and so on. Although there seems to be no one best interpretation of rationality, the difficulties in explaining Kantian constructivism do not lie here. Thus I ignore these matters, and focus on the more obscure notion of the Reasonable and how it is represented in the original position.

This representing is done essentially by the nature of the constraints within which the parties' deliberations take place and which define their circumstances with respect to one another. The Reasonable is incorporated into the background setup of the original position which frames the discussions of the parties and situates them symmetrically. More specifically, in addition to various familiar formal conditions on first principles, such as generality and universality, ordering and finality, the parties are required to adopt a public conception of justice and must assess its first principles with this condition in mind. (I shall say more about the publicity condition in the next lecture.)

Again, the veil of ignorance implies that persons are represented solely as moral persons and not as persons advantaged or disadvantaged by the contingencies of their social position, the distribution of natural abilities, or by luck and historical accident over the course of their lives. As a result they are situated equally as moral persons, and in this sense fairly. Here I appeal to the idea that, in establishing the truly basic terms of social cooperation, the possession of the minimum adequate powers of moral personality (the powers that equip us to be normally cooperating members of society over a complete life) is the sole relevant characteristic. This presumption, plus the precept that equals in all relevant respects are to be represented equally, ensures that the original position is fair.

The last constraint I shall mention here is this: the stipulation that the first subject of justice is the basic structure of society, that is, the main social institutions and how they cohere together into one system, supports situating the parties equally and restricting their information by the veil of ignorance. For this stipulation requires the parties to assess alternative conceptions as providing first principles of what we may call *background justice*: it is only if the basic structure satisfies the requirements of background justice that a society treats its members as equal moral persons. Otherwise, its fundamental regulative arrangements do not answer to principles its citizens would adopt when fairly represented solely as such persons.

Let us pull together these remarks as follows: the Reasonable presupposes and subordinates the Rational. It defines the fair terms of cooperation acceptable to all within some group of separately identifiable persons, each of whom possesses and can exercise the two moral powers. All have a conception of their good which defines their rational advantage, and everyone has a normally effective sense of justice: a capacity to honor the fair terms of cooperation. The Reasonable presupposes the Rational, because, without conceptions of the good that move members of the group, there is no point to social cooperation nor to notions of right and justice, even though such cooperation realizes values that go beyond what conceptions of the good specify taken alone. The Reasonable subordinates the Rational because its principles limit, and in a Kantian doctrine limit absolutely, the final ends that can be pursued.

Thus, in the original position we view the Reasonable as expressed by the framework of constraints within which the deliberations of the parties (as rationally autonomous agents of construction) take place. Representative of these constraints are the condition of publicity, the veil of ignorance and the symmetry of the parties' situation with respect to one another, and the stipulation that the basic structure is the first subject of justice. Familiar principles of justice are examples of reasonable principles, and familiar principles of rational choice are examples of rational principles. The way the Reasonable is represented in the original position leads to the two principles of justice. These principles are constructed by justice as fairness as the content of the Reasonable for the basic structure of a well-ordered society.

VI

. . . [T]he way in which the Reasonable frames the Rational in the original position represents a feature of the unity of practical reason. In Kant's terms, empirical practical reason is represented by the rational deliberations of the parties; pure practical reason is represented by the constraints within which these deliberations take place. The unity of practical reason is expressed by defining the Reasonable to frame the Rational and to subordinate it absolutely; that is, the principles of justice that are agreed to are lexically prior in their application in a well-ordered society to claims of the good. This means, among other things, that the principles of justice and the rights and liberties they define cannot, in such a society, be overridden by considerations of efficiency and a greater net balance of social well-being. This illustrates one feature of the unity of reason: the Reasonable and the Rational are unified within one scheme of practical reasoning which establishes the strict priority of the Reasonable with respect to the Rational. This priority of the right over the good is characteristic of Kantian constructivism.

Now in a well-ordered society we stipulate that the justification of the principles of justice as the outcome of the original position is publicly understood. So not only do citizens have a highest-order desire, their sense of justice, to act from the principles of justice, but they understand these principles as issuing from a construction in which their conception of themselves as free and equal moral persons who are both reasonable and rational is adequately represented. By acting from these principles, and affirming them in public life, as so derived, they express their full autonomy. The rational autonomy of the parties is merely that of artificial agents who inhabit a construction designed to model this more inclusive conception. It is the inclusive conception which expresses the ideal to be realized in our social world. . . .

Notes

1 Cambridge, Mass.: Harvard University Press, 1971. Hereafter referred to as TJ.
2 These features were not conveniently stated at any one place in TJ. In this and the next lectures I try to give a clearer and more systematic account of this notion and to indicate its basic role as a model-conception.

LECTURE III
Construction and Objectivity

In the preceding lectures I sketched the main idea of Kantian constructivism, which is to establish a connection between the first principles of justice and the conception of moral persons as free and equal. These first principles are used to settle the appropriate understanding of freedom and equality for a modern democratic society. The requisite connection is provided by a procedure of construction in which rationally autonomous agents subject to reasonable conditions agree to public principles of justice. With the sketch of these ideas behind us, I consider in this final lecture how a Kantian doctrine interprets the notion of objectivity in terms of a suitably constructed social point of view that is authoritative with respect to all individual and associational points of view. This rendering of objectivity implies that, rather than think of the principles of justice as true, it is better to say that they are the principles most reasonable for us, given our conception of persons as free and equal, and fully cooperating members of a democratic society. [Here 'reasonable' is used, as explained later (pp. 196–9), in contrast with 'true' as understood in rational intuitionism, and not, as previously (pp. 213–14), with 'rational', as in the notion of rational autonomy.]

I

To fix ideas, let's look back roughly a hundred years to Henry Sidgwick. *The Methods of Ethics* (first edition 1874) is, I believe, the outstanding achievement in modern moral theory.[1] By "moral theory" I mean the systematic and comparative study of moral conceptions, starting with those which historically and by current estimation seem to be the most important. Moral philosophy includes moral theory, but takes as its main question justification and how it is to be conceived and resolved; for example, whether it is to be conceived as an epistemological problem (as in rational intuitionism) or as a practical problem (as in Kantian constructivism).

Sidgwick's *Methods* is the first truly academic work in moral theory, modern in both method and spirit. Treating ethics as a discipline to be studied like any other branch of knowledge, it defines and carries out in exemplary fashion, if not for the first time, some of the comprehensive comparisons that constitute moral theory. By pulling together the work of previous writers, and through its influence on G. E. Moore and others, this work defined much of the framework of subsequent moral philosophy. Sidgwick's originality lies in his conception and mode of presentation of the subject and in his recognition of the significance of moral theory for moral philosophy.

It is natural, then, that the limitations of *Methods* have been as important as its merits. Of these limitations I wish to mention two. First, Sidgwick gives relatively little attention to the conception of the person and the social role of morality as main parts of a moral doctrine. He starts with the idea of a method of ethics as a method specified by certain first principles, principles by which we are to arrive at a judgment about what we ought to do. He takes for granted that these methods aim at reaching true judgments that hold for all rational minds. Of course, he thinks it is best to approach the problem of justification only when a broad understanding of moral theory has been achieved. In the preface of the first edition of *Methods* he explains that he wants to resist the natural urgency to discover the true method of ascertaining what it is right to do. He wishes instead to expound, from a neutral position and as impartially as possible, the different methods found in the moral consciousness of humankind and worked into familiar historical systems.[2] But these detailed expositions – necessary as they are – are merely preparation for comparing the various methods and evaluating them by criteria that any rational method that aims at truth must satisfy.

But a consequence of starting with methods of ethics defined as methods that seek truth is not only that it interprets justification as an epistemological problem, but also that it is likely to restrict attention to the first principles of moral conceptions and how they can be known. First principles are however only one element of a moral conception; of equal importance are its conception of the person and its view of the social role of morality. Until these other elements are clearly recognized, the ingredients of a constructivist doctrine are not at hand. It is characteristic of Sidgwick's *Methods* that the social role of morality and the conception of the person receive little notice. And so the possibility of constructivism was closed to him.

Sidgwick overlooked this possibility because of a second limitation: he failed to recognize that Kant's doctrine (and perfectionism also for that matter) is a distinctive method of ethics. He regarded the categorical imperative as a purely formal principle, or what he called "the principle of equity": whatever is right for one person is right for all similar persons in relevantly similar circumstances. This principle Sidgwick accepts, but, since it is plainly not a sufficient basis for a moral view, Kant's doctrine could not be counted a substantive method (209/10). This formal reading of Kant, together with the dismissal of perfectionism, led Sidgwick to reduce the traditional moral conceptions essentially to three main methods: rational egoism, (pluralistic) intuitionism, and classical utilitarianism. Surely he was right to restrict himself to a few conceptions so that each could be explored in considerable detail. Only in this way can depth of understanding be achieved. But rational egoism, which he accepted as a method of ethics, is really not a moral conception at all, but rather a challenge to all such conceptions, although no less interesting for that. Left with only (pluralistic) intuitionism and classical utilitarianism as methods of ethics in the usual sense, it is no surprise that utilitarianism seemed superior to Sidgwick, given his desire for unity and system in a moral doctrine.

Since Kant's view is the leading historical example of a constructivist doctrine, the result once again is that constructivism finds no place in *Methods*. Nor is the situation altered if we include another leading representative work, F. H. Bradley's *Ethical Studies* (first edition 1876); following Hegel, Bradley likewise regarded Kant's ethics as purely formal and lacking in content and, therefore, to be assigned to an early stage of the dialectic as an inadequate view.[3] The result of these formal interpretations of Kant is that constructivism was not recognized as a moral conception to be studied and assimilated into moral theory. Nor was this lack made good in the first half of this century; for in this period, beginning with Moore's *Principia Ethica* (1903), interest centered mainly on philosophical analysis and its bearing on justification regarded as an epistemological problem and on the question whether its conclusions support or deny the notion of moral truth. During this time, however, utilitarianism and intuitionism made important advances. A proper understanding of Kantian constructivism, on a par with our grasp of these views, is still to be achieved.

II

Let us now try to deepen our understanding of Kantian constructivism by contrasting it with what I shall call *rational intuitionism*. This doctrine has, of course, been expressed in various ways; but in one form or another it dominated moral philosophy from Plato and Aristotle onwards until it was challenged by Hobbes and Hume, and, I believe, in a very different way by Kant. To simplify matters, I take rational intuitionism to be the view exemplified in the English tradition by Clarke and Price, Sidgwick and Moore, and formulated in its minimum essentials by W. D. Ross.[4] With qualifications, it was accepted by Leibniz and Wolff in the guise of perfectionism, and Kant knows of it in this form.

For our purposes here, rational intuitionism may be summed up by two theses: first, the basic moral concepts of the right and the good, and the moral worth of persons, are not analyzable in terms of nonmoral concepts (although possibly analyzable in terms of one another); and, second, first principles of morals (whether one or many), when correctly stated, are self-evident propositions about what kinds of considerations are good grounds for applying one of the three basic moral concepts, that is, for asserting that something is (intrinsically) good, or that a certain action is the right thing to do, or that a certain trait of character has moral worth. These two theses imply that the agreement in judgment which is so essential for an effective public conception of justice is founded on the recognition of self-evident truths about good reasons. And what these reasons are is fixed by a moral order that is prior to and independent of our conception of the person and the social role of morality. This order is given by the nature of things and is known, not by sense, but by rational intuition. It is with this idea of moral truth that the idea of first principles as reasonable will be contrasted.

It should be observed that rational intuitionism is compatible with a variety of contents for the first principles of a moral conception. Even classical utilitarianism, which Sidgwick was strongly inclined to favor (although he could not see how to eliminate rational egoism as a rival) was sometimes viewed by him as following from three principles each self-evident in its own right.[5] In brief, these three propositions were: the principle of equity so-called: that it cannot be right to treat two different persons differently merely on the ground of their being numerically different individuals; a principle of rational prudence: that mere difference of position in time is not by itself a reasonable ground for giving more regard to well-being at one moment than to well-being at another; and a principle of rational benevolence: the good of one person is of no more importance from the point of view of the universe than the good of any other person. These three principles, when combined with the principle that, as reasonable beings, we are bound to aim at good generally and not at any particular part of it, Sidgwick thought yielded the principle of utility: namely, to maximize the net balance of happiness. And this principle, like those from which it followed, he was tempted to hold as self-evident.

Of all recent versions of rational intuitionism, the appeal to self-evidence is perhaps most striking in Moore's so-called "ideal utilitarianism" in *Principia Ethica* (1903). A consequence of Moore's principle of organic unity is that his view is extremely pluralistic; there are few if any useful first principles, and distinct kinds of cases are to be decided by intuition as they arise. Moore held a kind of Platonic atomism:[6] moral concepts (along with other concepts) are subsisting and independent entities grasped by the mind. That pleasure and beauty are good, and that different combinations of them alone or together with other good things are also good, and to what degree, are truths known by intuition: by seeing with the mind's eye how these separate and distinct objects (universals) are (timelessly) related. This picture is even more vivid in the early philosophy of mathematics of Bertrand Russell, who talks of searching for the indefinable concepts of mathematics with a mental telescope (as one might look for a planet).[7]

Now my aim in recalling these matters is to point out that rational intuitionism, as illustrated by Sidgwick, Moore, and Ross, is sharply opposed to a constructivist conception along Kantian lines. That Kant would have rejected Hume's psychological naturalism as heteronomous is clear.[8] I believe that the contrast with rational intuitionism, no matter what the content of the view (whether utilitarian, perfectionist, or pluralist) is even more instructive. It is less obvious that for Kant rational intuitionism is also heteronomous. The reason is that from the first thesis of rational intuitionism, the basic moral concepts are conceptually independent of natural concepts, and first principles are independent of the natural world and, as grasped by rational intuition, are regarded as synthetic a priori. This may seem to make these principles not heteronomous. Yet it suffices for heteronomy that these principles obtain in virtue of relations among objects the nature of which is not affected or determined by the conception of the person. Kant's idea of autonomy requires that there exist no such order of given objects determining the first principles of right and justice among free and equal moral persons. Heteronomy obtains not only when first principles are fixed by the special psychological constitution of human nature, as in Hume, but also when they are fixed by an order of universals or concepts grasped by rational intuition, as in Plato's realm of forms or in Leibniz's hierarchy of perfections.[9] Perhaps I should add, to prevent misunderstanding, that a Kantian doctrine of autonomy need not deny that the procedures by which first principles are selected are synthetic a priori. This thesis, however, must be properly interpreted. The essential idea is that such procedures must be suitably founded on practical reason, or, more exactly, on notions which characterize persons as reasonable and rational and which are incorporated into the way in which, as such persons, they represent to themselves their free and equal moral personality. Put another way, first principles of justice must issue from a conception of the person through a suitable representation of that conception as illustrated by the procedure of construction in justice as fairness.

Thus in a Kantian doctrine a relatively complex conception of the person plays a central role. By contrast, rational intuitionism requires but a sparse notion of the person, founded on the self as knower. This is because the content of first principles is already fixed, and the only requirements on the self are to be able to know what these principles are and to be moved by this knowledge. A basic assumption is that the recognition of first principles as true and self-evident gives rise, in a being capable of rationally intuiting these principles, to a desire to act from them for their own sake. Moral motivation is defined by reference to desires that have a special kind of cause, namely, the intuitive grasp of first principles.[10] This sparse conception of the person joined with its moral psychology characterizes the rational intuitionism of Sidgwick, Moore, and Ross, although there is nothing that forces rational intuitionism to so thin a notion. The point is rather that, in rational intuitionism in contrast to a Kantian view, since the content of first principles is already given, a more complex conception of the person, of a kind adequate to determine the content of these principles, together with a suitable moral psychology, is simply unnecessary.

III

Having contrasted Kantian constructivism to rational intuitionism with respect to the idea of a moral order that is prior to and independent from our conception of the person, I now consider a second contrast, namely, how each regards the inevitable limitations that constrain our moral deliberations. The constructionist view accepts from the start that a moral conception can establish but a loose framework for deliberation which must rely very considerably on our powers of reflection and judgment. These powers are not fixed once and for all, but are developed by a shared public culture and hence shaped by that culture. In justice as fairness this means that the principles adopted by the parties in the original position are designed by them to achieve a public and workable agreement on matters of social justice which suffices for effective and fair social cooperation. From the standpoint of the parties as agents of construction, the first principles of justice are not thought to represent, or to be true of, an already given moral order, as rational intuitionism supposes. The essential point is that a conception of justice fulfills its social role provided that citizens equally conscientious and sharing roughly the same beliefs find that, by affirming the framework of deliberation set up by it, they are normally led to a sufficient convergence of opinion. Thus a conception of justice is framed to meet the practical requirements of social life and to yield a public basis in the light of which citizens can justify to one another their common institutions. Such a conception need be only precise enough to achieve this result.

On the constructivist view, the limitations that constrain our moral deliberations affect the requirements of publicity and support the use of priority rules. These limitations also lead us to take the basic structure of a well-ordered society as the first subject of justice and to adopt the primary goods as the basis of interpersonal comparisons. To begin with publicity: at the end of the preceding lecture I mentioned why in a constructivist view first principles are to satisfy the requirements of publicity. The moral conception is to have a wide social role as a part of public culture and is to enable citizens to appreciate and accept the conception of the person as free and equal. Now if it is to play this wide role, a conception's first principles cannot be so complex that they cannot be generally understood and followed in the more important cases. Thus, it is desirable that knowing whether these principles are satisfied, at least with reference to fundamental liberties and basic institutions, should not depend on information difficult to obtain or hard to evaluate. To incorporate these desiderata in a constructivist view, the parties are assumed to take these considerations into account and to prefer (other things equal) principles that are easy to understand and simple to apply. The gain in compliance and willing acceptance by citizens more than makes up for the rough and ready nature of the guiding framework that results and its neglect of certain distinctions and differences. In effect, the parties agree to rule out certain facts as irrelevant in questions of justice concerning the basic structure, even though they recognize that in regard to other cases it may be appropriate to appeal to them. From the standpoint of the original position, eliminating these facts as reasons of social justice sufficiently increases the capacity of the conception to fulfill its social role. Of course, we should keep in mind that the exclusion of such facts as reasons of social justice does not alone entail that they are not reasons in other kinds of situation where different moral notions apply. Indeed, it is not even ruled out that the account of some notions should be constructivist, whereas the account of others is not.

It is evident, then, why a constructivist view such as justice as fairness incorporates into the framework of moral deliberation a number of schematic and practical distinctions as ways that enable us to deal with the inevitable limitations of our moral capacities and the complexity of our social circumstances. The need for such distinctions supports and helps to account for the use of certain priority rules to settle the relative weight of particular kinds of grounds in extremely important cases. Two such rules in justice as fairness are: first, the priority of justice over efficiency (in the sense of Pareto) and the net balance of advantages (summed over all individuals in society), and second, the priority of the principle of equal liberty (understood in terms of certain enumerated basic liberties) over the second principle of justice.[11] These rules are introduced to handle the complexity of the many prima facie reasons we are ready to cite in everyday life; and their plausibility depends in large part on the first principles to which they are adjoined. But although these rules are intended to narrow the scope of judgment in certain fundamental questions of justice, this scope can never be entirely eliminated, and for many other questions sharp and definite conclusions cannot usually be derived. Sharp and definite conclusions are not needed, however, if sufficient agreement is still forthcoming (TJ 44/5).

Similar considerations apply in beginning with the basic structure of a well-ordered society as the first subject of justice and trying to develop a conception of justice for this case alone. The idea is that this structure plays a very special role in society by establishing what we may call *background justice*; and if we can find suitable first principles of background justice, we may be able to exclude enough other considerations as irrelevant for this case, so as to develop a reasonably simple and workable conception of justice for the basic structure. The further complexities of everyday cases that cannot be ignored in a more complete moral conception may be dealt with later in the less general situations that occur within the various associations regulated by the basic structure, and in that sense subordinate to it.[12]

Finally, parallel observations hold in finding a feasible basis for interpersonal comparisons of well-being relevant for questions of justice that arise in regard to the basic structure. These comparisons are to be made in terms of primary goods (as defined in the first lecture), which are, so far as possible, certain public features of social institutions and of people's situations with respect to them, such as their rights, liberties, and opportunities, and their income and wealth, broadly understood. This has the consequence that the comparison of citizens' shares in the benefits of social cooperation is greatly simplified and put on a footing less open to dispute.

Thus the reason why a constructivist view uses the schematic or practical distinctions we have just noted is that such distinctions are necessary if a workable conception of justice is to be achieved. These distinctions are incorporated into justice as fairness through the description of the parties as agents of construction and the account of how they are to deliberate. Charged with the task of agreeing to a workable conception of justice designed to achieve a sufficient convergence of opinion, the parties can find no better way in which to carry out this task. They accept the limitations of human life and recognize that at best a conception of justice can establish but a guiding framework for deliberation.

A comparison with classical utilitarianism will highlight what is involved here. On that view, whether stated as a form of rational intuitionism (Sidgwick) or as a form of naturalism (Bentham), every question of right and justice has an answer: whether an institution or action is right depends upon whether it will produce the greatest net balance of satisfaction. We may never be in a position to know the answer, or even to come very near to it, but, granting that a suitable measure of satisfaction exists, there is an answer: a fact of the matter. Of course, utilitarianism recognizes the needs of practice: working precepts and secondary rules are necessary to guide deliberation and coordinate our actions. These norms may be thought of as devised to bring our actions as close as possible to those which would maximize utility, so far as this is feasible. But of course, such rules and precepts are not first principles; they are at best directives that when followed make the results of our conduct approximate to what the principle of utility enjoins. In this sense, our working norms are approximations to something given.

By contrast, justice as fairness, as a constructivist view, holds that not all the moral questions we are prompted to ask in everyday life have answers. Indeed, perhaps only a few of them can be settled by any moral conception that we can understand and apply. Practical limitations impose a more modest aim upon a reasonable conception of justice, namely, to identify the most fundamental questions of justice that can be dealt with, in the hope that, once this is done and just basic institutions established, the remaining conflicts of opinion will not be so deep or widespread that they cannot be compromised. To accept the basic structure as the first subject of justice together with the account of primary goods is a step toward achieving this more modest goal. But in addition, the idea of approximating to moral truth has no place in a constructivist doctrine: the parties in the original position do not recognize any principles of justice as true or correct and so as antecedently given; their aim is simply to select the conception most rational for them, given their circumstances. This conception is not regarded as a workable approximation to the moral facts: there are no such moral facts to which the principles adopted could approximate.

As we have just seen, the differences between constructivism and classical utilitarianism are especially sharp in view of the content of the principle of utility: it always yields an answer that we can at least verbally describe. With the rational (pluralistic) intuitionism of Ross, however, the contrast is less obvious, since Ross's list of self-evident prima facie principles that identify good reasons also specifies but a loose guiding framework of moral deliberation which shares a number of the features of the framework provided by constructivism. But though these resemblances are real, the underlying idea of Ross's view is still essentially different from constructivism. His pluralistic intuitionism rejects utilitarianism (even an ideal utilitarianism) as oversimplifying the given moral facts, especially those concerning the correct weight of special duties and obligations. The complexity of the moral facts in particular kinds of cases is said to force us to recognize that no family of first principles that we can formulate characterizes these facts sufficiently accurately to lead to a definite conclusion. Decision and judgment are almost always to some degree uncertain and must rest with "perception,"[13] that is, with our intuitive estimate of where the greatest balance of prima facie reasons lies in each kind of case. And this perception is that of a balance of reasons each of which is given by an independent moral order known by intuition. The essential contrast with constructivism remains.

IV

Having examined several contrasts between Kantian constructivism and rational intuitionism, we are now in a position to take up a fundamental point suggested by the discussion so far: an essential feature of a constructivist view, as illustrated by justice as fairness, is that its first principles single out what facts citizens in a well-ordered society are to count as reasons of justice. Apart from the procedure of constructing these principles, there are no reasons of justice. Put in another way, whether certain facts are to count as reasons of justice and what their relative force is to be can be ascertained only on the basis of the principles that result from the construction. This connects with the use of pure procedural justice at the highest level. It is, therefore, up to the parties in the original position to decide how simple or complex the moral facts are to be, that is, to decide on the number and complexity of the principles that identify which facts are to be accepted as reasons of justice by citizens in society (see TJ 45). There is nothing parallel to this in rational intuitionism.

This essential feature of constructivism may be obscured by the fact that in justice as fairness the first principles of justice depend upon those general beliefs about human nature and how society works which are allowed to the parties in the original position. First principles are not, in a constructivist view, independent of such beliefs, nor, as some forms of rational intuitionism hold, true in all possible worlds. In particular, they depend on the rather specific features and limitations of human life that give rise to the circumstances of justice.[14] Now, given the way the original position is set up, we can allow, in theory, that, as the relevant general beliefs change, the beliefs we attribute to the parties likewise change, and conceivably also the first principles that would be agreed to. We can say, if we like that *the* (most reasonable) principles of justice are those which would be adopted if the parties possessed all relevant general information and if they were properly to take account of all the practical desiderata required for a workable public conception of justice. Though these principles have a certain preeminence, they are still the outcome of construction. Furthermore, it is important to notice here that no assumptions have been made about a theory of truth. A constructivist view does not require an idealist or a verificationist, as opposed to a realist, account of truth. Whatever the nature of truth in the case of general beliefs about human nature and how society works, a constructivist moral doctrine requires a distinct procedure of construction to identify the first principles of justice. To the extent that Kant's moral doctrine depends upon what to some may appear to be a constructivist account of truth in the *First Critique* (I don't mean to imply that such an interpretation is correct), justice as fairness departs from that aspect of Kant's view and seeks to preserve the over-all structure of his moral conception apart from that background.

In the preceding paragraph I said that the way justice as fairness is set up allows the possibility that, as the general beliefs ascribed to the parties in the original position change, the first principles of justice may also change. But I regard this as a mere possibility noted in order to explain the nature of a constructivist view. To elaborate: at the end of the first lecture I distinguished between the roles of a conception of the person and of a theory of human nature, and I remarked that in justice as fairness these are distinct elements and enter at different places. I said that a conception of the person is a companion moral ideal paired with the ideal of a well-ordered society. A theory of human nature and a view of the requirements of social life tell us whether these ideals are feasible, whether it is possible to realize them under normally favorable conditions of human life. Changes in the theory of human nature or in social theory generally which do not affect the feasibility of the ideals of the person and of a well-ordered society do not affect the agreement of the parties in the original position. It is hard to imagine realistically any new knowledge that should convince us that these ideals are not feasible, given what we know about the general nature of the world, as opposed to our particular social and historical circumstances. In fact, the relevant information on these matters must go back a long time and is available to the common sense of any thoughtful and reflective person. Thus such advances in our knowledge of human nature and society as may take place do not affect our moral conception, but rather may be used to implement the application of its first principles of justice and suggest to us institutions and policies better designed to realize them in practice.[15]

In justice as fairness, then, the main ideals of the conception of justice are embedded in the two model-conceptions of the person and of a well-ordered society. And, granting that these ideals are allowed by the theory of human nature and so in that sense feasible, the first principles of justice to which they lead, via the constructivist procedure of the original position, determine the long-term aim of social change. These principles are not, as in rational intuitionism, given by a moral order prior to and independent from our conception of the person and the social role of morality; nor are they, as in some naturalist doctrines, to be derived from the truths of science and adjusted in accordance with advances in human psychology and social theory. (These remarks are admittedly too brief, but we must return to the main line of discussion.)

V

The rational intuitionist may object that an essential feature of constructivism – the view that the facts to count as reasons of justice are singled out by the parties in the original position as agents of construction and that, apart from such construction, there are no reasons of justice – is simply incoherent.[16] This view is incompatible not only with the notion of truth as given by a prior and independent moral order, but also with the notions of reasonableness and objectivity, neither of which refer to what can be settled simply by agreement, much less by choice. A constructivist view, the objection continues, depends on the idea of adopting or choosing first principles, and such principles are not the kind of thing concerning which it makes sense to say that their status depends on their being chosen or adopted. We cannot "choose" them; what we can do is choose whether to follow them in our actions or to be guided by them in our reasoning, just as we can choose whether to honor our duties, but not what our duties are.

In reply, one must distinguish the three points of view that we noted at the end of the first lecture (in section VII [not excerpted]): that of the parties in the original position, that of the citizens in a well-ordered society, and that of you and me who are examining justice as fairness to serve as a basis for a conception that may yield a suitable understanding of freedom and equality. It is, of course, the parties in the original position whose agreement singles out the facts to count as reasons. But their agreement is subject to all the conditions of the original position which represent the Reasonable and the Rational. And the facts singled out by the first principles count as reasons not for the parties, since they are moved by their highest-order interests, but for the citizens of a well-ordered society in matters of social justice. As citizens in society we are indeed bound by first principles and by what our duties are, and must act in the light of reasons of justice. Constructivism is certain to seem incoherent unless we carefully distinguish these points of view.

The parties in the original position do not agree on what the moral facts are, as if there already were such facts. It is not that, being situated impartially, they have a clear and undistorted view of a prior and independent moral order. Rather (for constructivism), there is no such order, and therefore no such facts apart from the procedure of construction as a whole; the facts are identified by the principles that result. Thus the rational intuitionists' objection, properly expressed, must be that no hypothetical agreement by rationally autonomous agents, no matter how circumscribed by reasonable conditions in a procedure of construction, can determine the reasons that settle what we as citizens should consider just and unjust; right and wrong are not, even in that way, constructed. But this is merely to deny what constructivism asserts. If, on the other hand, such a construction does yield the first principles of a conception of justice that matches more accurately than other views our considered convictions in general and wide reflective equilibrium, then constructivism would seem to provide a suitable basis for objectivity.

The agreement of the parties in the original position is not a so-called "radical" choice: that is, a choice not based on reasons, a choice that simply fixes, by sheer fiat, as it were, the scheme of reasons that we, as citizens, are to recognize, at least until another such choice is made. The notion of radical choice, commonly associated with Nietzsche and the existentialists, finds no place in justice as fairness. The parties in the original position are moved by their preference for primary goods, which preference in turn is rooted in their highest-order interests in developing and exercising their moral powers. Moreover, the agreement of the parties takes place subject to constraints that express reasonable conditions.

In the model-conception of a well-ordered society, citizens affirm their public conception of justice because it matches their considered convictions and coheres with the kind of persons they, on due reflection, want to be. Again, this affirmation is not radical choice. The ideals of the person and of social cooperation embedded in the two model-conceptions mediated by the original position are not ideals that, at some moment in life, citizens are said simply to choose. One is to imagine that, for the most part, they find on examination that they hold these ideals, that they have taken them in part from the culture of their society.

The preceding paragraph ties in with what I said at the beginning of the first lecture, except that there I was talking about us and not about a well-ordered society. Recall that a Kantian view, in addressing the public culture of a democratic society, hopes to bring to awareness a conception of the person and of social cooperation conjectured to be implicit in that culture, or at least congenial to its deepest tendencies when properly expressed and presented. Our society is not well-ordered: the public conception of justice and its understanding of freedom and equality are in dispute. Therefore, for us – you and me – a basis of public justification is still to be achieved. In considering the conception of justice as fairness we have to ask whether the ideals embedded in its model-conceptions are sufficiently congenial to our considered convictions to be affirmed as a practicable basis of public justification. Such an affirmation would not be radical choice (if choice at all); nor should it be confused with the adoption of principles of justice by the parties in the original position. To the contrary, it would be rooted in the fact that this Kantian doctrine as a whole, more fully than other views available to us, organized our considered convictions.

Given the various contrasts between Kantian constructivism and rational intuitionism, it seems better to say that in constructivism first principles are reasonable (or unreasonable) than that they are true (or false) – better still, that they are most reasonable for those who conceive of their person as it is represented in the procedure of construction. And here 'reasonable' is used instead of 'true' not because of some alternative theory of truth, but simply in order to keep to terms that indicate the constructivist standpoint as opposed to rational intuitionism. This usage, however, does not imply that there are no natural uses for the notion of truth in moral reasoning. To the contrary, for example, particular judgments and secondary norms may be considered true when they follow from, or are sound applications of, reasonable first principles. These first principles may be said to be true in the sense that they would be agreed to if the parties in the original position were provided with all the relevant true general beliefs.

Nor does justice as fairness exclude the possibility of there being a fact of the matter as to whether there is a single most reasonable conception. For it seems quite likely that there are only a few viable conceptions of the person both sufficiently general to be part of a moral doctrine and congruent with the ways in which people are to regard themselves in a democratic society. And only one of these conceptions may have a representation in a procedure of construction that issues in acceptable and workable principles, given the relevant general beliefs.[17] Of course, this is conjecture, intended only to indicate that constructivism is compatible with there being, in fact, only one most reasonable conception of justice, and therefore that constructivism is compatible with objectivism in this sense. However, constructivism does not presuppose that this is the case, and it may turn out that, for us, there exists no reasonable and workable conception of justice at all. This would mean that the practical task of political philosophy is doomed to failure.

VI

My account of Kantian constructivism in moral theory (as illustrated by justice as fairness) is now concluded. I should stress, however, that for all I have said it is still open to the rational intuitionist to reply that I have not shown that rational intuitionism is false or that it is not a possible basis for the necessary agreement in our judgments of justice. It has been my intention to describe constructivism by contrast and not to defend it, much less to argue that rational intuitionism is mistaken. In any case, Kantian constructivism, as I would state it, aims to establish only that the rational intuitionist notion of objectivity is unnecessary for objectivity. Of course, it is always possible to say, if we ever do reach general and wide reflective equilibrium, that now at last we intuit the moral truths fixed by a given moral order; but the constructivist will say instead that our conception of justice, by all the criteria we can think of to apply, is now the most reasonable for us.

We have arrived at the idea that objectivity is not given by "the point of view of the universe," to use Sidgwick's phrase. Objectivity is to be understood by reference to a suitably constructed social point of view, an example of which is the framework provided by the procedure of the original position. This point of view is social in several respects. It is the publicly shared point of view of citizens in a well-ordered society, and the principles that issue from it are accepted by them as authoritative with regard to the claims of individuals and associations. Moreover, these principles regulate the basic structure of society within which the activities of individuals and associations take place. Finally, by representing the person as a free and equal citizen of a well-ordered society, the constructivist procedure yields principles that further everyone's highest-order interests and define the fair terms of social cooperation among persons so understood. When citizens invoke these principles they speak as members of a political community and appeal to its shared point of view either in their own behalf or in that of others. Thus, the essential agreement in judgments of justice arises not from the recognition of a prior and independent moral order, but from everyone's affirmation of the same authoritative social perspective.

The central place of the conception of the person in these lectures prompts me to conclude with a note of warning, addressed as much to me as to anyone else: ever since the notion of the person assumed a central place in moral philosophy in the latter part of the eighteenth century, as seen in Rousseau and Kant and the philosophy of idealism, its use has suffered from excessive vagueness and ambiguity. And so it is essential to devise an approach that disciplines our thought and suitably limits these defects. I view the three model-conceptions that underlie justice as fairness as having this purpose.

To elucidate: suppose we define the concept of a person as that of a human being capable of taking full part in social cooperation, honoring its ties and relationships over a complete life. There are plainly many specifications of this capacity, depending, for example, on how social cooperation or a complete life is understood; and each such specification yields another conception of the person falling under the concept. Moreover, such conceptions must be distinguished from specifications of the concept of the self as knower, used in epistemology and metaphysics, or the concept of the self as the continuant carrier of psychological states: the self as substance, or soul. These are prima facie distinct notions, and questions of identity, say, may well be different for each; for these notions arise in connection with different problems. This much is perhaps obvious. The consequence is that there are numerous conceptions of the person as the basic unit of agency and responsibility in social life, and of its requisite intellectual, moral, and active powers. The specification of these conceptions by philosophical analysis alone, apart from any background theoretical structure or general requirements, is likely to prove fruitless. In isolation these notions play no role that fixes or limits their use, and so their features remain vague and indeterminate.

One purpose of a model-conception like that of the original position is that, by setting up a definite framework within which a binding agreement on principles must be made, it serves to fix ideas. We are faced with a specific problem that must be solved, and we are forced to describe the parties and their mutual relations in the process of construction so that appropriate principles of justice result. The context of the problem guides us in removing vagueness and ambiguity in the conception of the person, and tells us how precise we need to be. There is no such thing as absolute clarity or exactness; we have to be only clear or exact enough for the task at hand. Thus the structure defined by the original position may enable us to crystallize our otherwise amorphous notion of the person and to identify with sufficient sharpness the appropriate characterization of free and equal moral personality.

The constructivist view also enables us to exploit the flexibility and power of the idea of rational choice subject to appropriate constraints. The rational deliberations of the parties in the original position serve as a way to select among traditional or other promising conceptions of justice. So understood, the original position is not an axiomatic (or deductive) basis from which principles are derived but a procedure for singling out principles most fitting to the conception of the person most likely to be held, at least implicitly, in a modern democratic society. To exaggerate, we compute via the deliberations of the parties and in this way hope to achieve sufficient rigor and clarity in moral theory. Indeed, it is hard to see how there could be any more direct connection between the conception of free and equal moral persons and first principles of justice than this construction allows. For here persons so conceived and moved by their highest-order interests are themselves, in their rationally autonomous deliberations, the agents who select the principles that are to govern the basic structure of their social life. What connection could be more intimate than this?

Finally, if we ask, what is clarity and exactness enough? the answer is: enough to find an understanding of freedom and equality that achieves workable public agreement on the weight of their respective claims. With this we return to the current impasse in the understanding of freedom and equality which troubles our democratic tradition and from which we started. Finding a way out of this impasse defines the immediate practical task of political philosophy. Having come full circle, I bring these lectures to a close.

Notes

1 On Sidgwick now, see the comprehensive work by J. B. Schneewind, *Sidgwick's Ethics and Modern Victorian Moral Philosophy* (New York: Oxford, 1977).

2 *The Methods of Ethics* (London: Macmillan, 1907), 7th ed., pp. v–vi; parenthetical page references to Sidgwick are to this book, this edition.

3 See Essay IV: "Duty for Duty's Sake," 2nd ed. (New York: Oxford, 1927).

4 See *The Right and the Good* (Oxford: The Clarendon Press, 1930), esp. chs. 1–2. I shall adopt Ross's characterization of rational intuitionism, adjusted to allow for any number of first principles and, thus, as fitting either single-principle or pluralistic intuitionism. I should add that, for my purposes here, I interpret Aristotle's view as combining teleological and metaphysical perfectionism. Although this may not be a sound interpretation in the light of contemporary scholarship, it suits well enough how Aristotle was interpreted up to Kant's time.

5 *Methods*, Book III, ch. 13, pp. 379–89. See Schneewind's discussion in J. B. Schneewind, *Sidgwick's Ethics and Victorian Moral Philosophy* (Oxford: Clarendon Press, 1977), ch. 10, pp. 286–309.

6 I borrow this expression from Peter Hylton's discussion. *The Origins of Analytic Philosophy*, ch. 3 (Dissertation: Harvard University, 1978).

7 See *The Principles of Mathematics* (London: Allen & Unwin, 1937), 2nd ed. (1st ed. 1903), pp. xv–xvi. The analogy of the mental telescope is Russell's.

8 Because it formulates definitions of the basic moral concepts in terms of nonmoral concepts, this being the mode of identifying those facts which are to count as good reasons in applying the basic moral concepts, naturalism is a form of heteronomy from the Kantian standpoint. The various definitions, presumably arrived at by the analysis of concepts, convert moral judgments into statements about the world on all fours with those of science and common sense. Therefore, these definitions, combined with the natural order itself, now come to constitute the moral order, which is prior to and independent from our conception of ourselves as free and equal moral persons. If time permitted, this could be substantiated by setting out, for example, the details of Hume's view (as often interpreted) and of Bentham's hedonistic utilitarianism, at least once these views are expressed in the requisite naturalistic format. (Rational intuitionism tries to secure a kind of independence of the moral order from the order of nature.)

9   This fundamental contention is unfortunately obscured by the fact that although in the *Grundlegung* Kant classifies the view of Leibniz and Wolff as a form of heteronomy, his criticism of it is that it is circular and therefore empty. See Academy Edition, p. 443. Much the same happens in the *Second Critique*, Academy Edition, p. 41, where Kant argues that the notion of perfection in practical reasoning means fitness for any given ends and therefore is again empty until these ends are specified independently. These arguments give the erroneous impression that, if perfectionism had sufficient content, it would be compatible with autonomy.

10 See, for example, *Methods*, pp. 23–8, 34–7, 39 f, read together with the discussion of the self-evident basis of the principle of utility, cited in note 5 above.

11 For a statement of these principles and priority rules, see TJ, pp. 60–2, 250, 302/3.

12 See "The Basic Structure as Subject," in A. I. Goldman and Jaegwon Kim, eds., *Values and Morals* (Boston: Reidel, 1978), especially secs. IV–V, pp. 52–7.

13 See *The Right and the Good*, pp. 41/2. Ross refers to Aristotle's remark: "The decision rests with perception" (*Nicomachean Ethics* 1109 b 23, 1126 b 4).

14 See Lecture II, section I [not excerpted here].

15 Therefore these advances in our knowledge of human psychology and social theory might be relevant at the constitutional, legislative, and judicial stages in the application of the principles of justice, as opposed to the adoption of principles in the original position. For a brief account of these stages, see TJ, § 31.

16 For this and other objections to what I call "constructivism" in this lecture, see the review of TJ by Marcus Singer, *Philosophy of Science*, XLIV, 4 (December 1977): 594–618, pp. 612–15. I am grateful to him for raising this objection, which I here try to meet. Singer's criticism starts from the passage on page 45 of TJ (also referred to above, pp. 209–10). It should not be assumed that Singer's own position is that of rational intuitionism. I simply suppose that a rational intuitionist would make this objection.

17 I am indebted to Samuel Scheffler for valuable discussion on this point.

9

Contractualism and Utilitarianism

T. M. Scanlon

Utilitarianism occupies a central place in the moral philosophy of our time. It is not the view which most people hold; certainly there are very few who would claim to be act utilitarians. But for a much wider range of people it is the view towards which they find themselves pressed when they try to give a theoretical account of their moral beliefs. Within moral philosophy it represents a position one must struggle against if one wishes to avoid it. This is so in spite of the fact that the implications of act utilitarianism are wildly at variance with firmly held moral convictions, while rule utilitarianism, the most common alternative formulation, strikes most people as an unstable compromise.

The wide appeal of utilitarianism is due, I think, to philosophical considerations of a more or less sophisticated kind which pull us in a quite different direction than our first-order moral beliefs. In particular, utilitarianism derives much of its appeal from alleged difficulties about the foundations of rival views. What a successful alternative to utilitarianism must do, first and foremost, is to sap this source of strength by providing a clear account of the foundations of non-utilitarian moral reasoning. In what follows I will first describe the problem in more detail by setting out the questions which a philosophical account of the foundations of morality must answer. I will then put forward a version of contractualism which, I will argue, offers a better set of responses to these questions than that supplied by straightforward versions of utilitarianism. Finally I will explain why contractualism, as I understand it, does not lead back to some utilitarian formula as its normative outcome.

T. M. Scanlon, "Contractualism and Utilitarianism," *Utilitarianism and Beyond*, Amartya Sen and Bernard Williams, eds. (Cambridge: Cambridge University Press, 1982), pp. 103–28.

Contractualism has been proposed as the alternative to utilitarianism before, notably by John Rawls in *A Theory of Justice* (Rawls 1971). Despite the wide discussion which this book has received, however, I think that the appeal of contractualism as a foundational view has been underrated. In particular, it has not been sufficiently appreciated that contractualism offers a particularly plausible account of moral motivation. The version of contractualism that I shall present differs from Rawls' in a number of respects. In particular, it makes no use, or only a different and more limited kind of use, of his notion of choice from behind a veil of ignorance. One result of this difference is to make the contrast between contractualism and utilitarianism stand out more clearly.

I

There is such a subject as moral philosophy for much the same reason that there is such a subject as the philosophy of mathematics. In moral judgements, as in mathematical ones, we have a set of putatively objective beliefs in which we are inclined to invest a certain degree of confidence and importance. Yet on reflection it is not at all obvious what, if anything, these judgements can be about, in virtue of which some can be said to be correct or defensible and others not. This question of subject matter, or the grounds of truth, is the first philosophical question about both morality and mathematics. Second, in both morality and mathematics it seems to be possible to discover the truth simply by thinking or reasoning about it. Experience and observation may be helpful, but observation in the normal sense is not the standard means of discovery in either subject. So, given any positive answer to the first question – any specification of the subject matter or ground of truth in mathematics or morality – we need some compatible epistemology explaining how it is possible to discover the facts about this subject matter through something like the means we seem to use.

Given this similarity in the questions giving rise to moral philosophy and to the philosophy of mathematics, it is not surprising that the answers commonly given fall into similar general types. If we were to interview students in a freshman mathematics course many of them would, I think, declare themselves for some kind of conventionalism. They would hold that mathematics proceeds from definitions and principles that are either arbitrary or instrumentally justified, and that mathematical reasoning consists in perceiving what follows from these definitions and principles. A few others, perhaps, would be realists or platonists according to whom mathematical truths are a special kind of non-empirical fact that we can perceive through some form of intuition. Others might be naturalists who hold that mathematics, properly understood, is just the most abstract empirical science. Finally there are, though perhaps not in an average freshman course, those who hold that there are no mathematical facts in the world 'outside of us', but that the truths of mathematics are objective truths about the mental constructions of which we are capable. Kant held that pure mathematics was a realm of objective mind-dependent truths, and Brouwer's mathematical Intuitionism is another theory of this type (with the important difference that it offers grounds for the warranted assertability of mathematical judgements rather than for their truth in the classical sense). All of these positions have natural correlates in moral philosophy. Intuitionism of the sort espoused by W. D. Ross is perhaps the closest analogue to mathematical platonism, and Kant's theory is the most familiar version of the thesis that morality is a sphere of objective, mind-dependent truths.

All of the views I have mentioned (with some qualification in the case of conventionalism) give positive (i.e. non-sceptical) answers to the first philosophical question about mathematics. Each identifies some objective, or at least intersubjective, ground of truth for mathematical judgements. Outright scepticism and subjective versions of mind-dependence (analogues of emotivism or prescriptivism) are less appealing as philosophies of mathematics than as moral philosophies. This is so in part simply because of the greater degree of intersubjective agreement in mathematical judgement. But it is also due to the difference in the further questions that philosophical accounts of the two fields must answer.

Neither mathematics nor morality can be taken to describe a realm of facts existing in isolation from the rest of reality. Each is supposed to be connected with other things. Mathematical judgements give rise to predictions about those realms to which mathematics is applied. This connection is something that a philosophical account of mathematical truth must explain, but the fact that we can observe and learn from the correctness of such predictions also gives support to our belief in objective mathematical truth. In the case of morality the main connection is, or is generally supposed to be, with the will. Given any candidate for the role of subject matter of morality we must explain why anyone should care about it, and the need to answer this question of motivation has given strong support to subjectivist views.

But what must an adequate philosophical theory of morality say about moral motivation? It need not, I think, show that the moral truth gives anyone who knows it a reason to act which appeals to that person's present desires or to the advancement of his or her interests. I find it entirely intelligible that moral requirement might correctly apply to a person even though that person had no reason of either of these kinds for complying with it. Whether moral requirements give those to whom they apply reasons for compliance of some third kind is a disputed question which I shall set aside. But what an adequate moral philosophy must do, I think, is to make clearer to us the nature of the reasons that morality does provide, at least to those who are concerned with it. A philosophical theory of morality must offer an account of these reasons that is, on the one hand, compatible with its account of moral truth and moral reasoning and, on the other, supported by a plausible analysis of moral experience. A satisfactory moral philosophy will not leave concern with morality as a simple special preference, like a fetish or a special taste, which some people just happen to have. It must make it understandable why moral reasons are ones that people can take seriously, and why they strike those who are moved by them as reasons of a special stringency and inescapability.

There is also a further question whether susceptibility to such reasons is compatible with a person's good or whether it is, as Nietzsche argued, a psychological disaster for the person who has it. If one is to defend morality one must show that it is not disastrous in this way, but I will not pursue this second motivational question here. I mention it only to distinguish it from the first question, which is my present concern.

The task of giving a philosophical explanation of the subject matter of morality differs both from the task of analysing the meaning of moral terms and from that of finding the most coherent formulation of our first-order moral beliefs. A maximally coherent ordering of our first-order moral beliefs could provide us with a valuable kind of explanation: it would make clear how various, apparently disparate moral notions, precepts and judgements are related to one another, thus indicating to what degree conflicts between them are fundamental and to what degree, on the other hand, they can be resolved or explained away. But philosophical inquiry into the subject matter of morality takes a more external view. It seeks to explain what kind of truths moral truths are by describing them in relation to other things in the world and in relation to our particular concerns. An explanation of how we can come to know the truth about morality must be based on such an external explanation of the kind of things moral truths are rather than on a list of particular moral truths, even a maximally coherent list. This seems to be true as well about explanations of how moral beliefs can give one a reason to act.[1]

Coherence among our first-order moral beliefs – what Rawls has called narrow reflective equilibrium[2] – seems unsatisfying[3] as an account of moral truth or as an account of the basis of justification in ethics just because, taken by itself, a maximally coherent account of our moral beliefs need not provide us with what I have called a philosophical explanation of the subject matter of morality. However internally coherent our moral beliefs may be rendered, the nagging doubt may remain that there is nothing to them at all. They may be merely a set of socially inculcated reactions, mutually consistent perhaps but not judgements of a kind which can properly be said to be correct or incorrect. A philosophical theory of the nature of morality can contribute to our confidence in our first-order moral beliefs chiefly by allaying these natural doubts about the subject. Insofar as it includes an account of moral epistemology, such a theory may guide us towards new forms of moral argument, but it need not do this. Moral argument of more or less the kind we have been familiar with may remain as the only form of justification in ethics. But whether or not it leads to revision in our modes of justification, what a good philosophical theory should do is to give us a clearer understanding of what the best forms of moral argument amount to and what kind of truth it is that they can be a way of arriving at. (Much the same can be said, I believe, about the contribution which philosophy of mathematics makes to our confidence in particular mathematical judgements and particular forms of mathematical reasoning.)

Like any thesis about morality, a philosophical account of the subject matter of morality must have some connection with the meaning of moral terms: it must be plausible to claim that the subject matter described is in fact what these terms refer to at least in much of their normal use. But the current meaning of moral terms is the product of many different moral beliefs held by past and present speakers of the language, and this meaning is surely compatible with a variety of moral views and with a variety of views about the nature of morality. After all, moral terms are used to express many different views of these kinds, and people who express these views are not using moral terms incorrectly, even though what some of them say must be mistaken. Like a first-order moral judgement, a philosophical characterisation of the subject matter of morality is a substantive claim about morality, albeit a claim of a different kind.

While a philosophical characterisation of morality makes a kind of claim that differs from a first-order moral judgement, this does not mean that a philosophical theory of morality will be neutral between competing normative doctrines. The adoption of a philosophical thesis about the nature of morality will almost always have some effect on the plausibility of particular moral claims, but philosophical theories of morality vary widely in the extent and directness of their normative implications. At one extreme is intuitionism, understood as the philosophical thesis that morality is concerned with certain non-natural properties. Rightness, for example, is held by Ross[4] to be the property of 'fittingness' or 'moral suitability'. Intuitionism holds that we can identify occurrences of these properties, and that we can recognise as self-evident certain general truths about them, but that they cannot be further analysed or explained in terms of other notions. So understood, intuitionism is in principle compatible with a wide variety of normative positions. One could, for example, be an intuitionistic utilitarian or an intuitionistic believer in moral rights, depending on the general truths about the property of moral rightness which one took to be self-evident.

The other extreme is represented by philosophical utilitarianism. The term 'utilitarianism' is generally used to refer to a family of specific normative doctrines – doctrines which might be held on the basis of a number of different philosophical theses about the nature of morality. In this sense of the term one might, for example, be a utilitarian on intuitionist or on contractualist grounds. But what I will call 'philosophical utilitarianism' is a particular philosophical thesis about the subject matter of morality, namely the thesis that the only fundamental moral facts are facts about individual well-being.[5] I believe that this thesis has a great deal of plausibility for many people, and that, while some people are utilitarians for other reasons, it is the attractiveness of philosophical utilitarianism which accounts for the widespread influence of utilitarian principles.

It seems evident to people that there is such a thing as individuals' being made better or worse off. Such facts have an obvious motivational force; it is quite understandable that people should be moved by them in much the way that they are supposed to be moved by moral considerations. Further, these facts are clearly relevant to morality as we now understand it. Claims about individual well-being are one class of valid starting points for moral argument. But many people find it much harder to see how there could be any other, independent starting points. Substantive moral requirements independent of individual well-being strike people as intuitionist in an objectionable sense. They would represent 'moral facts' of a kind it would be difficult to explain. There is no problem about recognising it as a fact that a certain act is, say, an instance of lying or of promise breaking. And a utilitarian can acknowledge that such facts as these often have (derivative) moral significance:

they are morally significant because of their consequences for individual well-being. The problems, and the charge of 'intuitionism', arise when it is claimed that such acts are wrong in a sense that is not reducible to the fact that they decrease individual well-being. How could this independent property of moral wrongness be understood in a way that would give it the kind of importance and motivational force which moral considerations have been taken to have? If one accepts the idea that there are no moral properties having this kind of intrinsic significance, then philosophical utilitarianism may seem to be the only tenable account of morality. And once philosophical utilitarianism is accepted, some form of normative utilitarianism seems to be forced on us as the correct first-order moral theory. Utilitarianism thus has, for many people, something like the status which Hilbert's Formalism and Brouwer's Intuitionism have for their believers. It is a view which seems to be forced on us by the need to give a philosophically defensible account of the subject. But it leaves us with a hard choice: we can either abandon many of our previous first-order beliefs or try to salvage them by showing that they can be obtained as derived truths or explained away as useful and harmless fictions.

It may seem that the appeal of philosophical utilitarianism as I have described it is spurious, since this theory must amount either to a form of intuitionism (differing from others only in that it involves just one appeal to intuition) or else to definitional naturalism of a kind refuted by Moore and others long ago. But I do not think that the doctrine can be disposed of so easily. Philosophical utilitarianism is a philosophical thesis about the nature of morality. As such, it is on a par with intuitionism or with the form of contractualism which I will defend later in this paper. None of these theses need claim to be true as a matter of definition; if one of them is true it does not follow that a person who denies it is misusing the words 'right', 'wrong' and 'ought'. Nor are all these theses forms of intuitionism, if intuitionism is understood as the view that moral facts concern special non-natural properties, which we can apprehend by intuitive insight but which do not need or admit of any further analysis. Both contractualism and philosophical utilitarianism are specifically incompatible with this claim. Like other philosophical theses about the nature of morality (including, I would say, intuitionism itself), contractualism and philosophical utilitarianism are to be appraised on the basis of their success in giving an account of moral belief, moral argument and moral motivation that is compatible with our general beliefs about the world: our beliefs about what kinds of things there are in the world, what kinds of observation and reasoning we are capable of, and what kinds of reasons we have for action. A judgement as to which account of the nature of morality (or of mathematics) is most plausible in this general sense is just that: a judgement of overall plausibility. It is not usefully described as an insight into concepts or as a special intuitive insight of some other kind.

If philosophical utilitarianism is accepted then some form of utilitarianism appears to be forced upon us as a normative doctrine, but further argument is required to determine which form we should accept. If all that counts morally is the well-being of individuals, no one of whom is singled out as counting for more than the others, and if all that matters in the case of each individual is the degree to which his or her well-being is affected, then it would seem to follow that the basis of moral appraisal is the goal of maximising the *sum*[6] of individual well-being. Whether this standard is to be applied to the criticism of individual actions, or to the selection of rules or policies, or to the inculcation of habits and dispositions to act is a further question, as is the question of how 'well-being' itself is to be understood. Thus the hypothesis that much of the appeal of utilitarianism as a normative doctrine derives from the attractiveness of philosophical utilitarianism explains how people can be convinced that some form of utilitarianism must be correct while yet being quite uncertain as to which form it is, whether it is 'direct' or 'act' utilitarianism or some form of indirect 'rule' or 'motive' utilitarianism. What these views have in common, despite their differing normative consequences, is the identification of the same class of fundamental moral facts.

II

If what I have said about the appeal of utilitarianism is correct, then what a rival theory must do is to provide an alternative to philosophical utilitarianism as a conception of the subject matter of morality. This is what the theory which I shall call contractualism seeks to do. Even if it succeeds in this, however, and is judged superior to philosophical utilitarianism as an account of the nature of morality, normative utilitarianism will not have been refuted. The possibility will remain that normative utilitarianism can be established on other grounds, for example as the normative outcome of contractualism itself. But one direct and, I think, influential argument for normative utilitarianism will have been set aside.

To give an example of what I mean by contractualism, a contractualist account of the nature of moral wrongness might be stated as follows.

An act is wrong if its performance under the circumstances would be disallowed by any system of rules for the general regulation of behaviour which no one could reasonably reject as a basis for informed, unforced general agreement.

This is intended as a characterisation of the kind of property which moral wrongness is. Like philosophical utilitarianism, it will have normative consequences, but it is not my present purpose to explore these in detail. As a contractualist account of one moral notion, what I have set out here is only an approximation, which may need to be modified considerably. Here I can offer a few remarks by way of clarification.

The idea of 'informed agreement' is meant to exclude agreement based on superstition or false belief about the consequences of actions, even if these beliefs are ones which it would be reasonable for the person in question to have. The intended force of the qualification 'reasonably', on the other hand, is to exclude rejections that would be unreasonable *given* the aim of finding principles which could be the basis of informed, unforced general agreement. Given this aim, it would be unreasonable, for example, to reject a principle because it imposed a burden on you when every alternative principle would impose much greater burdens on others. I will have more to say about grounds for rejection later in the paper.

The requirement that the hypothetical agreement which is the subject of moral argument be unforced is meant not only to rule out coercion, but also to exclude being forced to accept an agreement by being in a weak bargaining position, for example because others are able to hold out longer and hence to insist on better terms. Moral argument abstracts from such considerations. The only relevant pressure for agreement comes from the desire to find and agree on principles which no one who had this desire could reasonably reject. According to contractualism, moral argument concerns the possibility of agreement among persons who are all moved by this desire, and moved by it to the same degree. But this counter-factual assumption characterises only the agreement with which morality is concerned, not the world to which moral principles are to apply. Those who are concerned with morality look for principles for application to their imperfect world which they could not reasonably reject, and which others in this world, who are not now moved by the desire for agreement, could not reasonably reject should they come to be so moved.[7]

The contractualist account of moral wrongness refers to principles 'which no one could reasonably reject' rather than to principles 'which everyone could reasonably accept' for the following reason.[8] Consider a principle under which some people will suffer severe hardships, and suppose that these hardships are avoidable. That is, there are alternative principles under which no one would have to bear comparable burdens. It might happen, however, that the people on whom these hardships fall are particularly self-sacrificing, and are willing to accept these burdens for the sake of what they see as the greater good of all. We would not say, I think, that it would be unreasonable of them to do this. On the other hand, it might not be unreasonable for them to refuse these burdens, and, hence, not unreasonable for someone to reject a principle requiring him to bear them. If this rejection would be reasonable, then the principle imposing these burdens is put in doubt, despite the fact that some particularly self-sacrificing people could (reasonably) accept it. Thus it is the reasonableness of rejecting a principle, rather than the reasonableness of accepting it, on which moral argument turns.

It seems likely that many non-equivalent sets of principles will pass the test of non-rejectability. This is suggested, for example, by the fact that there are many different ways of defining important duties, no one of which is more or less 'rejectable' than the others. There are, for example, many different systems of agreement-making and many different ways of assigning responsibility to care for others. It does not follow, however, that any action allowed by at least one of these sets of principles cannot be morally wrong according to contractualism. If it is important for us to have *some* duty of a given kind (some duty of fidelity to agreements, or some duty of mutual aid) of which there are many morally acceptable forms, then one of these forms needs to be established by convention. In a setting in which one of these forms *is* conventionally established, acts disallowed by it will be wrong in the sense of the definition given. For, given the need for such conventions, one thing that could not be generally agreed to would be a set of principles allowing one to disregard conventionally established (and morally acceptable) definitions of important duties. This dependence on convention introduces a degree of cultural relativity into contractualist morality. In addition, what a person can reasonably reject will depend on the aims and conditions that are important in his life, and these will also depend on the society in which he lives. The definition given above allows for variation of both of these kinds by making the wrongness of an action depend on the circumstances in which it is performed.

The partial statement of contractualism which I have given has the abstract character appropriate in an account of the subject matter of morality. On its face, it involves no specific claim as to which principles could be agreed to or even whether there is a unique set of principles which could be the basis of agreement. One way, though not the only way, for a contractualist to arrive at substantive moral claims would be to give a technical definition of the relevant notion of agreement, e.g. by specifying the conditions under which agreement is to be reached, the parties to this agreement and the criteria of reasonableness to be employed. Different contractualists have done this in different ways. What must be claimed for such a definition is that (under the circumstances in which it is to apply) what it describes is indeed the kind of unforced, reasonable agreement at which moral argument aims. But contractualism can also be understood as an informal description of the subject matter of morality on the basis of which ordinary forms of moral reasoning can be understood and appraised without proceeding via a technical notion of agreement.

Who is to be included in the general agreement to which contractualism refers? The scope of morality is a difficult question of substantive morality, but a philosophical theory of the nature of morality should provide some basis for answering it. What an adequate theory should do is to provide a framework within which what seem to be relevant arguments for and against particular interpretations of the moral boundary can be carried out. It is often thought that contractualism can provide no plausible basis for an answer to this question. Critics charge either that contractualism provides no answer at all, because it must begin with some set of contracting parties taken as given, or that contractualism suggests an answer which is obviously too restrictive, since a contract requires parties who are able to make and keep agreements and who are each able to offer the others some benefit in return for their cooperation. Neither of these objections applies to the version of contractualism that I am defending. The general specification of the scope of morality which it implies seems to me to be this: morality applies to a being if the notion of justification to a being of that kind makes sense. What is required in order for this to be the case? Here I can only suggest some necessary conditions. The first is that the being have a good, that is, that there be a clear sense in which things can be said to go better or worse for that being. This gives partial sense to the idea of what it would be reasonable for a trustee to accept on the being's behalf. It would be reasonable for a trustee to accept at least those things that are good, or not bad, for the being in question. Using this idea of trusteeship we can extend the notion of acceptance to apply to beings that are incapable of literally agreeing to anything. But this minimal notion of trusteeship is too weak to provide a basis for morality, according to contractualism. Contractualist morality relies on notions of what it would be reasonable to accept, or reasonable to reject, which are essentially comparative. Whether it would be unreasonable for me to reject a certain principle, given the aim of finding principles which no one with this aim could reasonably reject, depends not only on how much actions allowed by that principle might hurt me in absolute terms but also on how that potential loss compares with other potential losses to others under this principle and alternatives to it. Thus, in order for a being to stand in moral relations with us it is not enough that it have a good, it is also necessary that its good be sufficiently similar to our own to provide a basis for some system of comparability. Only on the basis of such a system can we give the proper kind of sense to the notion of what a trustee could reasonably reject on a being's behalf.

But the range of possible trusteeship is broader than that of morality. One could act as a trustee for a tomato plant, a forest or an ant colony, and such entities are not included in morality. Perhaps this can be explained by appeal to the requirement of comparability: while these entities have a good, it is not comparable to our own in a way that provides a basis for moral argument. Beyond this, however, there is in these cases insufficient foothold for the notion of justification *to* a being. One further minimum requirement for this notion is that the being constitute a point of view; that is, that there be such a thing as what it is like to be that being, such a thing as what the world seems like to it. Without this, we do not stand in a relation to the being that makes even hypothetical justification *to it* appropriate.

On the basis of what I have said so far contractualism can explain why the capacity to feel pain should have seemed to many to count in favour of moral status: a being which has this capacity seems also to satisfy the three conditions I have just mentioned as necessary for the idea of justification to it to make sense. If a being can feel pain, then it constitutes a centre of consciousness to which justification can be addressed. Feeling pain is a clear way in which the being can be worse off; having its pain alleviated a way in which it can be benefited; and these are forms of weal and woe which seem directly comparable to our own.

It is not clear that the three conditions I have listed as necessary are also sufficient for the idea of justification to a being to make sense. Whether they are, and, if they are not, what more may be required, are difficult and disputed questions. Some would restrict the moral sphere to those to whom justifications could in principle be communicated, or to those who can actually agree to something, or to those who have the capacity to understand moral argument. Contractualism as I have stated it does not settle these issues at once. All I claim is that it provides a basis for argument about them which is at least as plausible as that offered by rival accounts of the nature of morality. These proposed restrictions on the scope of morality are naturally understood as debatable claims about the conditions under which the relevant notion of justification makes sense, and the arguments commonly offered for and against them can also be plausibly understood on this basis.

Some other possible restrictions on the scope of morality are more evidently rejectable. Morality might be restricted to those who have the capacity to observe its constraints, or to those who are able to confer some reciprocal benefit on other participants. But it is extremely implausible to suppose that the beings excluded by these requirements fall entirely outside the protection of morality. Contractualism as I have formulated it[9] can explain why this is so: the absence of these capacities alone does nothing to undermine the possibility of justification to a being. What it may do in some cases, however, is to alter the justifications which are relevant. I suggest that whatever importance the capacities for deliberative control and reciprocal benefit may have is as factors altering the duties which beings have and the duties others have towards them, not as conditions whose absence suspends the moral framework altogether.

III

I have so far said little about the normative content of contractualism. For all I have said, the act utilitarian formula might turn out to be a theorem of contractualism. I do not think that this is the case, but my main thesis is that whatever the normative implications of contractualism may be it still has distinctive content as a philosophical thesis about the nature of morality. This content – the difference, for example, between being a utilitarian because the utilitarian formula is the basis of general agreement and being a utilitarian on other grounds – is shown most clearly in the answer that a contractualist gives to the first motivational question.

Philosophical utilitarianism is a plausible view partly because the facts which it identifies as fundamental to morality – facts about individual well-being – have obvious motivational force. Moral facts can motivate us, on this view, because of our sympathetic identification with the good of others. But as we move from philosophical utilitarianism to a specific utilitarian formula as the standard of right action, the form of motivation that utilitarianism appeals to becomes more abstract. If classical utilitarianism is the correct normative doctrine then the natural source of moral motivation will be a tendency to be moved by changes in aggregate well-being, however these may be composed. We must be moved in the same way by an aggregate gain of the same magnitude whether it is obtained by relieving the acute suffering of a few people or by bringing tiny benefits to a vast number, perhaps at the expense of moderate discomfort for a few. This is very different from sympathy of the familiar kind toward particular individuals, but a utilitarian may argue that this more abstract desire is what natural sympathy becomes when it is corrected by rational reflection. This desire has the same content as sympathy – it is a concern for the good of others – but it is not partial or selective in its choice of objects.

Leaving aside the psychological plausibility of this even-handed sympathy, how good a candidate is it for the role of moral motivation? Certainly sympathy of the usual kind is one of the many motives that can sometimes impel one to do the right thing. It may be the dominant motive, for example, when I run to the aid of a suffering child. But when I feel convinced by Peter Singer's article[10] on famine, and find myself crushed by the recognition of what seems a clear moral requirement, there is something else at work. In addition to the thought of how much good I could do for people in drought-stricken lands, I am overwhelmed by the further, seemingly distinct thought that it would be wrong for me to fail to aid them when I could do so at so little cost to myself. A utilitarian may respond that his account of moral motivation cannot be faulted for not capturing this aspect of moral experience, since it is just a reflection of our non-utilitarian moral upbringing. Moreover, it must be groundless. For what kind of fact could this supposed further fact of moral wrongness be, and how could it give us a further, special reason for acting? The question for contractualism, then, is whether it can provide a satisfactory answer to this challenge.

According to contractualism, the source of motivation that is directly triggered by the belief that an action is wrong is the desire to be able to justify one's actions to others on grounds they could not reasonably[11] reject. I find this an extremely plausible account of moral motivation – a better account of at least my moral experience than the natural utilitarian alternative – and it seems to me to constitute a strong point for the contractualist view. We all might like to be in actual agreement with the people around us, but the desire which contractualism identifies as basic to morality does not lead us simply to conform to the standards accepted by others whatever these may be. The desire to be able to justify one's actions to others on grounds they could not reasonably reject will be satisfied when we know that there is adequate justification for our action even though others in fact refuse to accept it (perhaps because they have no interest in finding principles which we and others could not reasonably reject). Similarly, a person moved by this desire will not be satisfied by the fact that others accept a justification for his action if he regards this justification as spurious.

One rough test of whether you regard a justification as sufficient is whether you would accept that justification if you were in another person's position. This connection between the idea of 'changing places' and the motivation which underlies morality explains the frequent occurence of 'Golden Rule' arguments within different systems of morality and in the teachings of various religions. But the thought experiment of changing places is only a rough guide; the fundamental question is what would it be unreasonable to reject as a basis for informed, unforced, general agreement. As Kant observed,[12] our different individual points of view, taken as they are, may in general be simply irreconcilable. 'Judgemental harmony' requires the construction of a genuinely interpersonal form of justification which is nonetheless something that each individual could agree to. From this interpersonal standpoint, a certain amount of how things look from another person's point of view, like a certain amount of how they look from my own, will be counted as bias.

I am not claiming that the desire to be able to justify one's actions to others on grounds they could not reasonably reject is universal or 'natural'. 'Moral education' seems to me plausibly understood as a process of cultivating this desire and shaping it, largely by learning what justifications others are in fact willing to accept, by finding which ones you yourself find acceptable as you confront them from a variety of perspectives, and by appraising your own and others' acceptance or rejection of these justifications in the light of greater experience.

In fact it seems to me that the desire to be able to justify one's actions (and institutions) on grounds one takes to be acceptable is quite strong in most people. People are willing to go to considerable lengths, involving quite heavy sacrifices, in order to avoid admitting the unjustifiability of their actions and institutions. The notorious insufficiency of moral motivation as a way of getting people to do the right thing is not due to simple weakness of the underlying motive, but rather to the fact that it is easily deflected by self-interest and self-deception.

It could reasonably be objected here that the source of motivation I have described is not tied exclusively to the contractualist notion of moral truth. The account of moral motivation which I have offered refers to the idea of a justification which it would be unreasonable to reject, and this idea is potentially broader than the contractualist notion of agreement. For let M be some non-contractualist account of moral truth. According to M, we may suppose, the wrongness of an action is simply a moral characteristic of that action in virtue of which it ought not to be done. An act which has this characteristic, according to *M*, has it quite independently of any tendency of informed persons to come to agreement about it. However, since informed persons are presumably in a position to recognise the wrongness of a type of action, it would seem to follow that if an action is wrong then such persons would agree that it is not to be performed. Similarly, if an act is not morally wrong, and there is adequate moral justification to perform it, then there will presumably be a moral justification for it which an informed person would be unreasonable to reject. Thus, even if *M*, and not contractualism, is the correct account of moral truth, the desire to be able to justify my actions to others on grounds they could not reasonably reject could still serve as a basis for moral motivation.

What this shows is that the appeal of contractualism, like that of utilitarianism, rests in part on a qualified scepticism. A non-contractualist theory of morality can make use of the source of motivation to which contractualism appeals. But a moral argument will trigger this source of motivation only in virtue of being a good justification for acting in a certain way, a justification which others would be unreasonable not to accept. So a non-contractualist theory must claim that there are moral properties which have justificatory force quite independent of their recognition in any ideal agreement. These would represent what John Mackie has called instances of intrinsic 'to-be-doneness' and 'not-to-be-doneness'.[13] Part of contractualism's appeal rests on the view that, as Mackie puts it, it is puzzling how there could be such properties 'in the world'. By contrast, contractualism seeks to explain the justificatory status of moral properties, as well as their motivational force, in terms of the notion of reasonable agreement. In some cases the moral properties are themselves to be understood in terms of this notion. This is so, for example, in the case of the property of moral wrongness, considered above. But there are also right- and wrong-making properties which are themselves independent of the contractualist notion of agreement. I take the property of being an act of killing for the pleasure of doing so to be a wrong-making property of this kind. Such properties are wrong-making because it would be reasonable to reject any set of principles which permitted the acts they characterise. Thus, while there are morally relevant properties 'in the world' which are independent of the contractualist notion of agreement, these do not constitute instances of intrinsic 'to-be-doneness' and 'not-to-be-doneness': their moral relevance – their force in justifications as well as their link with motivation – is to be explained on contractualist grounds.

In particular, contractualism can account for the apparent moral significance of facts about individual well-being, which utilitarianism takes to be fundamental. Individual well-being will be morally significant, according to contractualism, not because it is intrinsically valuable or because promoting it is self-evidently a right-making characteristic, but simply because an individual could reasonably reject a form of argument that gave his well-being no weight. This claim of moral significance is, however, only approximate, since it is a further difficult question exactly how 'well-being' is to be understood and in what ways we are required to take account of the well-being of others in deciding what to do. It does not follow from this claim, for example, that a given desire will always and everywhere have the same weight in determining the rightness of an action that would promote its satisfaction, a weight proportional to its strength or 'intensity'. The right-making force of a person's desires is specified by what might be called a conception of morally legitimate interests. Such a conception is a product of moral argument; it is not given, as the notion of individual well-being may be, simply by the idea of what it is rational for an individual to desire. Not everything for which I have a rational desire will be something in which others need concede me to have a legitimate interest which they undertake to weigh in deciding what to do. The range of things which may be objects of my rational desires is very wide indeed, and the range of claims which others could not reasonably refuse to recognise will almost certainly be narrower than this. There will be a tendency for interests to conform to rational desire – for those conditions making it rational to desire something also to establish a legitimate interest in it – but the two will not always coincide.

One effect of contractualism, then, is to break down the sharp distinction, which arguments for utilitarianism appeal to, between the status of individual well-being and that of other moral notions. A framework of moral argument is required to define our legitimate interests and to account for their moral force. This same contractualist framework can also account for the force of other moral notions such as rights, individual responsibility and procedural fairness.

IV

It seems unlikely that act utilitarianism will be a theorem of the version of contractualism which I have described. The positive moral significance of individual interests is a direct reflection of the contractualist requirement that actions be defensible to each person on grounds he could not reasonably reject. But it is a long step from here to the conclusion that each individual must agree to deliberate always from the point of view of maximum aggregate benefit and to accept justifications appealing to this consideration alone. It is quite possible that, according to contractualism, *some* moral questions may be properly settled by appeal to maximum aggregate well-being, even though this is not the sole or ultimate standard of justification.

What seems less improbable is that contractualism should turn out to coincide with some form of 'two-level' utilitarianism. I cannot fully assess this possibility here. Contractualism does share with these theories the important features that the defence of individual actions must proceed via a defence of principles that would allow those acts. But contractualism differs from *some* forms of two level utilitarianism in an important way. The role of principles in contractualism is fundamental; they do not enter merely as devices for the promotion of acts that are right according to some other standard. Since it does not establish two potentially conflicting forms of moral reasoning, contractualism avoids the instability which often plagues rule utilitarianism.

The fundamental question here, however, is whether the principles to which contractualism leads must be ones whose general adoption (either ideally or under some more realistic conditions) would promote maximum aggregate well-being. It has seemed to many that this must be the case. To indicate why I do not agree I will consider one of the best known arguments for this conclusion and explain why I do not think it is successful. This will also provide an opportunity to examine the relation between the version of contractualism I have advocated here and the version set forth by Rawls.

The argument I will consider, which is familiar from the writings of Harsanyi[14] and others, proceeds via an interpretation of the contractualist notion of acceptance and leads to the principle of maximum average utility. To think of a principle as a candidate for unanimous agreement I must think of it not merely as acceptable to *me* (perhaps in virtue of my particular position, my tastes, etc.) but as acceptable[15] to others as well. To be relevant, my judgement that the principle is acceptable must be impartial. What does this mean? To judge impartially that a principle is acceptable is, one might say, to judge that it is one which you would have reason to accept no matter who you were. That is, and here is the interpretation, to judge that it is a principle which it would be rational to accept if you did not know which person's position you occupied and believed that you had an equal chance of being in any of these positions. ('Being in a person's position' is here understood to mean being in his objective circumstances and evaluating these from the perspective of his tastes and preferences.) But, it is claimed, the principle which it would be rational to prefer under these circumstances – the one which would offer the chooser greatest expected utility – would be that principle under which the average utility of the affected parties would be highest.

This argument might be questioned at a number of points, but what concerns me at present is the interpretation of impartiality. The argument can be broken down into three stages. The first of these is the idea that moral principles must be impartially acceptable. The second is the idea of choosing principles in ignorance of one's position (including one's tastes, preferences, etc.). The third is the idea of rational choice under the assumption that one has an equal chance of occupying anyone's position. Let me leave aside for the moment the move from stage two to stage three, and concentrate on the first step, from stage one to stage two. There is a way of making something like this step which is, I think, quite valid, but it does not yield the conclusion needed by the argument. If I believe that a certain principle, P, could not reasonably be rejected as a basis for informed, unforced general agreement, then I must believe not only that it is something which it would be reasonable for me to accept but something which it would be reasonable for others to accept as well, insofar as we are all seeking a ground for general agreement. Accordingly, I must believe that I would have reason to accept P no matter which social position I were to occupy (though, for reasons mentioned above, I may not believe that I *would* agree to P if I were in some of these positions). Now it may be thought that no sense can be attached to the notion of choosing or agreeing to a principle in ignorance of one's social position, especially when this includes ignorance of one's tastes, preferences, etc. But there is at least a minimal sense that might be attached to this notion. If it would be reasonable for everyone to choose or agree to P, then my knowledge that I have reason to do so need not depend on my knowledge of my particular position, tastes, preferences, etc. So, insofar as it makes any sense at all to speak of choosing or agreeing to something in the absence of this knowledge, it could be said that I have reason to choose or agree to those things which everyone has reason to choose or agree to (assuming, again, the aim of finding principles on which all could agree). And indeed, this same reasoning can carry us through to a version of stage three. For if I judge P to be a principle which everyone has reason to agree to, then it could be said that I would have reason to agree to it if I thought that I had an equal chance of being anybody, or indeed, if I assign any other set of probabilities to being one or another of the people in question.

But it is clear that this is not the conclusion at which the original argument aimed. That conclusion concerned what it would be rational for a self-interested person to choose or agree to under the assumption of ignorance or equal probability of being anyone. The conclusion we have reached appeals to a different notion: the idea of what it would be unreasonable for people to reject given that they are seeking a basis for general agreement. The direction of explanation in the two arguments is quite different. The original argument sought to explain the notion of impartial acceptability of an ethical principle by appealing to the notion of rational self-interested choice under special conditions, a notion which appears to be a clearer one. My revised argument explains how *a* sense might be attached to the idea of choice or agreement in ignorance of one's position given some idea of what it would be unreasonable for someone to reject as a basis for general agreement. This indicates a problem for my version of contractualism: it may be charged with failure to explain the central notion on which it relies. Here I would reply that my version of contractualism does not seek to explain this notion. It only tries to describe it clearly and to show how other features of morality can be understood in terms of it. In particular, it does not try to explain this notion by reducing it to the idea of what would maximise a person's self-interested expectations if he were choosing from a position of ignorance or under the assumption of equal probability of being anyone.

The initial plausibility of the move from stage one to stage two of the original argument rests on a subtle transition from one of these notions to the other. To believe that a principle is morally correct one must believe that it is one which all could reasonably agree to and none could reasonably reject. But my belief that this is the case may often be distorted by a tendency to take its advantage to me more seriously than its possible costs to others. For this reason, the idea of 'putting myself in another's place' is a useful corrective device. The same can be said for the thought experiment of asking what I could agree to in ignorance of my true position. But both of these thought experiments are devices for considering more accurately the question of what *everyone* could reasonably agree to or what no one could reasonably reject. That is, they involve the pattern of reasoning exhibited in my revised form of the three-stage argument, not that of the argument as originally given. The question, what would maximise the expectations of a single self-interested person choosing in ignorance of his true position, is a quite different question. This can be seen by considering the possibility that the distribution with the highest average utility, call it *A*, might involve extremely low utility levels for some people, levels much lower than the minimum anyone would enjoy under a more equal distribution.

Suppose that *A* is a principle which it would be rational for a self-interested chooser with an equal chance of being in anyone's position to select. Does it follow that no one could reasonably reject *A*? It seems evident that this does not follow.[16] Suppose that the situation of those who would fare worst under *A*, call them the Losers, is extremely bad, and that there is an alternative to *A*, call it *E*, under which no one's situation would be nearly as bad as this. Prima facie, the losers would seem to have a reasonable ground for complaint against *A*. Their objection may be rebutted, by appeal to the sacrifices that would be imposed on some other individual by the selection of *E* rather than *A*. But the mere fact that *A* yields higher average utility, which might be due to the fact that many people do very slightly better under *A* than under *E* while a very few do much worse, does not settle the matter.

Under contractualism, when we consider a principle our attention is naturally directed first to those who would do worst under it. This is because if anyone has reasonable grounds for objecting to the principle it is *likely* to be them. It does not follow, however, that contractualism always requires us to select the principle under which the expectations of the worse off are highest. The reasonableness of the Losers' objection to *A* is not established simply by the fact that they are worse off under *A* and no one would be this badly off under *E*. The force of their complaint depends also on the fact that their position under *A* is, in absolute terms, very bad, and would be significantly better under *E*. This complaint must be weighed against those of individuals who would do worse under *E*. The question to be asked is, is it unreasonable for someone to refuse to put up with the Losers' situation under *A* in order that someone else should be able to enjoy the benefits which he would have to give up under *E*? As the supposed situation of the Loser under *A* becomes better, or his gain under *E* smaller in relation to the sacrifices required to produce it, his case is weakened.

One noteworthy feature of contractualist argument as I have presented it so far is that it is non-aggregative: what are compared are individual gains, losses and levels of welfare. How aggregative considerations can enter into contractualist argument is a further question too large to be entered into here.

I have been criticising an argument for Average Utilitarianism that is generally associated with Harsanyi, and my objections to this argument (leaving aside the last remarks about maximin) have an obvious similarity to objections raised by Rawls.[17] But the objections I have raised apply as well against some features of Rawls' own argument. Rawls accepts the first step of the argument I have described. That is, he believes that the correct principles of justice are those which 'rational persons concerned to advance their interests' would accept under the conditions defined by

his Original Position, where they would be ignorant of their own particular talents, their conception of the good, and the social position (or generation) into which they were born. It is the second step of the argument
which Rawls rejects, i.e. the claim that it would be rational for persons
so situated to choose those principles which would offer them greatest
expected utility under the assumption that they have an equal chance of
being anyone in the society in question. I believe, however, that a mistake
has already been made once the first step is taken.

This can be brought out by considering an ambiguity in the idea of
acceptance by persons 'concerned to advance their interests'. On one
reading, this is an essential ingredient in contractual argument; on another
it is avoidable and, I think, mistaken. On the first reading, the interests in
question are simply those of the members of society to whom the principles of justice are to apply (and by whom those principles must ultimately be accepted). The fact that they have interests which may conflict,
and which they are concerned to advance, is what gives substance to questions of justice. On the second reading, the concern 'to advance their
interests' that is in question is a concern of the parties to Rawls' Original
Position, and it is this concern which determines, in the first instance,[18]
what principles of justice they will adopt. Unanimous agreement among
these parties, each motivated to do as well for himself as he can, is to be
achieved by depriving them of any information that could give them
reason to choose differently from one another. From behind the veil of
ignorance, what offers the best prospects for one will offer the best
prospects for all, since no one can tell what would benefit him in particular. Thus the choice of principles can be made, Rawls says, from the point
of view of a single rational individual behind the veil of ignorance.

Whatever rules of rational choice this single individual, concerned to
advance his own interests as best he can, is said to employ, this reduction
of the problem to the case of a single person's self-interested choice should
arouse our suspicion. As I indicated in criticising Harsanyi, it is important to ask whether this single individual is held to accept a principle
because he judges that it is one he could not reasonably reject whatever
position he turns out to occupy, or whether, on the contrary, it is supposed
to be acceptable to a person in any social position because it would be the
rational choice for a single self-interested person behind the veil of ignorance. I have argued above that the argument for average utilitarianism involves a covert transition from the first pattern of reasoning to the
second. Rawls' argument also appears to be of this second form; his
defence of his two principles of justice relies, at least initially, on claims
about what it would be rational for a person, concerned to advance

his own interests, to choose behind a veil of ignorance. I would claim, however, that the plausibility of Rawls' arguments favouring his two principles over the principle of average utility is preserved, and in some cases enhanced, when they are interpreted as instances of the first form of contractualist argument.

Some of these arguments are of an informal moral character. I have already mentioned his remark about the unacceptability of imposing lower expectations on some for the sake of the higher expectations of others. More specifically, he says of the parties to the Original Position that they are concerned 'to choose principles the consequences of which they are prepared to live with whatever generation they turn out to belong to'[19] or, presumably, whatever their social position turns out to be. This is a clear statement of the first form of contractualist argument. Somewhat later he remarks, in favour of the two principles, that they 'are those a person would choose for the design of a society in which his enemy is to assign him a place'.[20] Rawls goes on to dismiss this remark, saying that the parties 'should not reason from false premises',[21] but it is worth asking why it seemed a plausible thing to say in the first place. The reason, I take it, is this. In a contractualist argument of the first form, the object of which is to find principles acceptable to each person, assignment by a malevolent opponent is a thought experiment which has a heuristic role like that of a veil of ignorance: it is a way of testing whether one really does judge a principle to be acceptable from all points of view or whether, on the contrary, one is failing to take seriously its effect on people in social positions other than one's own.

But these are all informal remarks, and it is fair to suppose that Rawls' argument, like the argument for average utility, is intended to move from the informal contractualist idea of principles 'acceptable to all' to the idea of rational choice behind a veil of ignorance, an idea which is, he hopes, more precise and more capable of yielding definite results. Let me turn then to his more formal arguments for the choice of the Difference Principle by the parties to the Original Position. Rawls cites three features of the decision faced by parties to the Original Position which, he claims, make it rational for them to use the maximin rule and, therefore, to select his Difference Principle as a principle of justice. These are (1) the absence of any objective basis for estimating probabilities, (2) the fact that some principles could have consequences for them which 'they could hardly accept' while (3) it is possible for them (by following maximin) to ensure themselves of a minimum prospect, advances above which, in comparison, matter very little.[22] The first of these features is slightly puzzling, and I leave it aside. It seems clear, however, that the other considerations mentioned have at least as much force in an informal contractualist argument about what all could reasonably agree to as they do in determining the rational choice of a single person concerned to advance his interests. They express the strength of the objection that the losers' might have to a scheme that maximised average utility at their expense, as compared with the counter-objections that others might have to a more egalitarian arrangement.

In addition to this argument about rational choice, Rawls invokes among 'the main grounds for the two principles' other considerations which, as he says, use the concept of contract to a greater extent.[23] The parties to the Original Position, Rawls says, can agree to principles of justice only if they think that this agreement is one that they will actually be able to live up to. It is, he claims, more plausible to believe this of his two principles than of the principle of average utility, under which the sacrifices demanded ('the strains of commitment') could be much higher. A second, related claim is that the two principles of justice have greater psychological stability than the principle of average utility. It is more plausible to believe, Rawls claims, that in a society in which they were fulfilled people would continue to accept them and to be motivated to act in accordance with them. Continuing acceptance of the principle of average utility, on the other hand, would require an exceptional degree of identification with the good of the whole on the part of those from whom sacrifices were demanded.

These remarks can be understood as claims about the 'stability' (in a quite practical sense) of a society founded on Rawls' two principles of justice. But they can also be seen as an attempt to show that a principle arrived at via the second form of contractualist reasoning will also satisfy the requirements of the first form, i.e. that it is something no one could reasonably reject. The question 'Is the acceptance of this principle an agreement you could actually live up to?' is, like the idea of assignment by one's worst enemy, a thought experiment through which we can use our own reactions to test our judgement that certain principles are ones that no one could reasonably reject. General principles of human psychology can also be invoked to this same end.

Rawls' final argument is that the adoption of his two principles gives public support to the self-respect of individual members of society, and that they 'give a stronger and more characteristic interpretation of Kant's idea'[24] that people must be treated as ends, not merely as means to the greater collective good. But, whatever difference there may be here between Rawls' two principles of justice and the principle of average utility, there is at least as sharp a contrast between the two patterns of contractualist reasoning distinguished above. The connection with self-respect, and with the Kantian formula, is preserved by the requirement that principles of justice be ones which no member of the society could reasonably reject. This connection is weakened when we shift to the idea of a choice which advances the interests of a single rational individual for whom the various individual lives in a society are just so many different possibilities. This is so whatever decision rule this rational chooser is said to employ. The argument from maximin seems to preserve this connection because it reproduces as a claim about rational choice what is, in slightly different terms, an appealing moral argument.

The 'choice situation' that is fundamental to contractualism as I have described it is obtained by beginning with 'mutually disinterested' individuals with full knowledge of their situations and adding to this (not, as is sometimes suggested, benevolence but) a desire on each of their parts to find principles which none could reasonably reject insofar as they too have this desire. Rawls several times considers such an idea in passing.[25] He rejects it in favour of his own idea of mutually disinterested choice from behind a veil of ignorance on the ground that only the latter enables us to reach definite results: 'if in choosing principles we required unanimity even where there is full information, only a few rather obvious cases could be decided'.[26] I believe that this supposed advantage is questionable. Perhaps this is because my expectations for moral argument are more modest than Rawls'. However, as I have argued, almost all of Rawls' own arguments have at least as much force when they are interpreted as arguments within the form of contractualism which I have been proposing. One possible exception is the argument from maximin. If the Difference Principle were taken to be generally applicable to decisions of public policy, then the second form of contractualist reasoning through which it is derived would have more far reaching implications than the looser form of argument by comparison of losses, which I have employed. But these wider applications of the principle are not always plausible, and I do not think that Rawls intends it to be applied so widely. His intention is that the Difference Principle should be applied only to major inequalities generated by the basic institutions of a society, and this limitation is a reflection of the special conditions under which he holds maximin to be the appropriate basis for rational choice: some choices have outcomes one could hardly accept, while gains above the minimum one can assure one's self matter very little, and so on. It follows, then, that in applying the Difference Principle – in identifying the limits of its applicability – we must fall back on the informal comparison of losses which is central to the form of contractualism I have described.

V

I have described this version of contractualism only in outline. Much more needs to be said to clarify its central notions and to work out its normative implications. I hope that I have said enough to indicate its appeal as a philosophical theory of morality and as an account of moral motivation. I have put forward contractualism as an alternative to utilitarianism, but the characteristic feature of the doctrine can be brought out by contrasting it with a somewhat different view.

It is sometimes said[27] that morality is a device for our mutual protection. According to contractualism, this view is partly true but in an important way incomplete. Our concern to protect our central interests will have an important effect on what we could reasonably agree to. It will thus have an important effect on the content of morality if contractualism is correct. To the degree that this morality is observed, these interests will gain from it. If we had no desire to be able to justify our actions to others on grounds they could reasonably accept, the hope of gaining this protection would give us reason to try to instil this desire in others, perhaps through mass hypnosis or conditioning, even if this also meant acquiring it ourselves. But given that we have this desire already, our concern with morality is less instrumental.

The contrast might be put as follows. On one view, concern with protection is fundamental, and general agreement becomes relevant as a means or a necessary condition for securing this protection. On the other, contractualist view, the desire for protection is an important factor determining the content of morality because it determines what can reasonably be agreed to. But the idea of general agreement does not arise as a means of securing protection. It is, in a more fundamental sense, what morality is about.

Notes

1   Though here the ties between the nature of morality and its content are more important. It is not clear that an account of the nature of morality which left its content *entirely* open could be the basis for a plausible account of moral motivation.
2   See Rawls 1974–5, p. 8; and Daniels 1979, pp. 257–8. How closely the process of what I am calling philosophical explanation will coincide with the search for 'wide reflective equilibrium' as this is understood by Rawls and by Daniels is a further question which I cannot take up here.

3   For expression of this dissatisfaction see Singer 1974 and Brandt 1979, pp. 16–21.

4   Ross 1939, pp. 52–4, 315.

5   For purposes of this discussion I leave open the important questions of which individuals are to count and how 'well-being' is to be understood. Philosophical utilitarianism will retain the appeal I am concerned with under many different answers to these questions.

6   'Average Utilitarianism' is most plausibly arrived at through quite a different form of argument, one more akin to contractualism. I discuss one such argument in section IV below.

7   Here I am indebted to Gilbert Harman for comments which have helped me to clarify my statement of contractualism.

8   A point I owe to Derek Parfit.

9   On this view (as contrasted with some others in which the notion of a contract is employed) what is fundamental to morality is the desire for reasonable agreement, not the pursuit of mutual advantage. See section V below. It should be clear that this version of contractualism can account for the moral standing of future persons who will be better or worse off as a result of what we do now. It is less clear how it can deal with the problem presented by future people who would not have been born but for actions of ours which also made the conditions in which they live worse. Do such people have reason to reject principles allowing these actions to be performed? This difficult problem, which I cannot explore here, is raised by Derek Parfit in Parfit 1976.

10 Singer 1972.

11 Reasonably, that is, given the desire to find principles which others similarly motivated could not reasonably reject.

12 Kant 1785, section 2, footnote 14.

13 Mackie 1977, p. 42.

14 See Harsanyi 1955, sec. IV. He is there discussing an argument which he presented earlier in Harsanyi 1953.

15 In discussing Harsanyi and Rawls I will generally follow them in speaking of the acceptability of principles rather than their unrejectability. The difference between these, pointed out above, is important only within the version of contractualism I am presenting; accordingly, I will speak of rejectability only when I am contrasting my own version with theirs.

16 The discussion which follows has much in common with the contrast between majority principles and unanimity principles drawn by Thomas Nagel in 'Equality', Chapter 8 of Nagel 1979. I am indebted to Nagel's discussion of this idea.

17 For example, the intuitive argument against utilitarianism on page 14 of Rawls 1971 and his repeated remark that we cannot expect some people to accept lower standards of life for the sake of the higher expectations of others.

18   Though they must then check to see that the principles they have chosen will be stable, not produce intolerable strains of commitment, and so on. As I argue below, these further considerations can be interpreted in a way that brings Rawls' theory closer to the version of contractualism presented here.
19   Rawls 1971, p. 137.
20   Rawls 1971, p. 152.
21   Rawls 1971, p. 153.
22   Rawls 1971, p. 154.
23   Rawls 1971, sec. 29, pp. 175ff.
24   Rawls 1971, p. 183.
25   E.g. Rawls 1971, pp. 141, 148, although these passages may not clearly distinguish between this alternative and an assumption of benevolence.
26   Rawls 1971, p. 141.
27   In different ways by G. J. Warnock in Warnock 1971, and by J. L. Mackie in Mackie 1977. See also Richard Brandt's remarks on justification in Chapter X of Brandt 1979.

References

Richard Brandt, *A Theory of the Good and the Right* (Oxford: Oxford University Press, 1979).

Norman Daniels, "Wide Reflective Equilibrium and Theory Acceptance in Ethics," *Journal of Philosophy* 76 (1979): 256–82.

John C. Harsanyi, "Cardinal Utility in Welfare Economics and in the Theory of Risk-Taking," *Journal of Political Economy* 61 (1953): 434–5.

John C. Harsanyi, "Cardinal Welfare, Individualistic Ethics, and Interpersonal Comparisons of Utility," *Journal of Political Economy* 63 (1955): 309–21.

Immanuel Kant, *Groundwork of the Metaphysics of Morals*, ed. by Mary Gregor (Cambridge: Cambridge University Press, 1998 [1785]).

John Mackie, *Ethics: Inventing Right and Wrong* (Harmondsworth: Pelican, 1977).

Thomas Nagel, *Mortal Questions* (Cambridge: Cambridge University Press, 1979).

Derek Parfit, "On Doing the Best for Our Children," in *Ethics and Population*, edited by M. Bayles (Cambridge, MA: Schnenkman Publishing Company Inc., 1976), pp. 100–15.

John Rawls, *A Theory of Justice* (Cambridge, MA: Harvard University Press, 1971).

John Rawls, "The Independence of Moral Theory," *Proceedings and Addresses of the American Philosophical Association* 47 (1974–5).

W. D. Ross, *The Foundations of Ethics* (Oxford: Oxford University Press, 1939).

Peter Singer, "Famine, Affluence, and Morality," *Philosophy and Public Affairs* 1 (1972): 229–43.

Peter Singer, "Sidgwick and Reflective Equilibrium," *The Monist* 58 (1974): 490–517.

G. J. Warnock, *The Object of Morality* (London: Methuen & Co., 1971).

Part V

Contemporary Discussion

Some Considerations in Favor of Contractualism

Gary Watson

The rights and responsibilities that we recognize in our critical moral practices serve human interests in deep and pervasive ways; that is part of their point. At the same time, they do this by constraining our pursuit of those interests; that is how they work. These utterly familiar features of our practices turn out to be troublesome for moral philosophy; they have seemed in serious tension with one another. One of the chief appeals of contractualist moral theory is its capacity to accommodate these features in a straightforward manner. In this essay, I want to articulate this theoretical virtue more fully.

I

The connection between morality and general human well-being gives some credibility to the long-standing notion that morality is in some sense an expression of love or benevolence.[1] This notion belongs, of course, to one strand of Christian teaching, but utilitarians have traded on this truth as well, especially when seeking to put their doctrine in a high-minded light. "In the golden rule of Jesus of Nazareth," John Stuart Mill assures us, "we read the complete spirit of the ethics of utility. 'To do as you would be done by,' and 'to love your neighbor as yourself,' constitute the ideal perfection of utilitarian morality."[2] More recently, J. J. C. Smart put utilitarianism forward as the unique theoretical expression of "generalized benevolence," the outlook of those who have the "welfare of humanity at

Gary Watson, "Some Considerations in Favor of Contractualism," *Rational Commitment, and Morality*, Christopher Morris and Jules Coleman, eds. (Cambridge: Cambridge University Press, 1998), pp. 168–85.

heart."[3] The idea is given a more ghastly twist by Joseph Fletcher, who speaks of the "vast scale of 'agapeic calculus' [on which] President Truman made his decision about [dropping] the A-bombs on Hiroshima and Nagasaki."[4]

However, utilitarians are not the only secular moralists to embrace this notion. Schopenhauer, for example, held that morality could be codified by a two-part principle: "Injure no one; help others as much as you can." Each part of this principle corresponds to one of the two cardinal moral virtues, justice and "loving-kindness," both of which are rooted, according to Schopenhauer, in "compassion."[5] Rodger Beehler and A. I. Melden are contemporary nonutilitarians who see benevolence as, in some sense, underlying moral practice. Beehler declares: "if human beings did not care about one another there could not be what we speak of as morality, for the reason that morality is a manifestation of that caring."[6] Melden connects benevolence with rights in particular: "Far from it being the case that a consideration of the rights of persons occupies a separate moral domain from that of benevolence, it depends on it; for in the absence of a concern for the well being of others there could be no sense of the important role that the rights of persons ... play in our lives."[7] The truly just person cares about rights at least partly because of a concern for the human good that rights foster and protect. Without such concern, the concern for justice lacks sense.

Thus, any satisfactory moral theory must provide for the connection of rights with vital human goods.[8] Respect for certain rights (for example, the right to be secure against aggression, the right to pursue one's ends without interference, rights arising from special relationships or undertakings) is essential to human cooperation and (hence) to flourishing. This truth is acknowledged every day in moral casuistry, where disputes about the existence or interpretation of rights often turn on the interests at stake. To illustrate, judgments about the content of the right to privacy inescapably involve balancing interests protected by that right with other concerns. We do not recognize a right not to be viewed as one walks down the street, since that would be too invasive of other interests.[9] (Privacy is not just a legal matter. Other things being equal, it would be wrong of you knowingly to look at my diary without permission, even though I might have no legal recourse.)

Furthermore, the relative gravity of rights corresponds to the importance of the interests concerned. Killing or assaulting another is generally worse than failing to repay a small loan. Hence the corresponding rights are relatively more stringent, their violation a graver matter.

The connections between rights and goods, then, do not appear to be accidental; they are part of the *function* of rights and responsibilities. The moral justification of rights and responsibilities depends upon their manifold connections to central human ends. I will call this the *teleological connection*.

Philippa Foot has suggested that what makes utilitarianism so "compelling" is its consequentialism, the "thought that it can never be right to prefer a worse state of affairs to a better."[10] But I think that the teleological connection is the source of its specific appeal; in contrast both to nonconsequentialist views and to other forms of consequentialism, utilitarianism takes the link between morality and well-being as its starting point. The teleological connection is, as T. M. Scanlon puts it, "the incontrovertible insight of the classical utilitarians."[11]

But as we will see, this connection is a theorem of any plausible form of contractualism as well. I want, in what follows, to consider the teleological connection from a contractualist point of view. What initially seems a strength of utilitarianism is, I shall argue, better accommodated by a nonconsequentialist theory.

II

Although utilitarianism seems to handle the teleological connection in a straightforward way, it comes to grief, notoriously, over another and equally conspicuous feature of our moral practice: its *deontological character*. Rights not only foster goods but constrain our pursuit of them. This feature of rights has been explored by many writers.[12] Much of modern moral philosophy has been an attempt to articulate a theory that can accommodate both of these features of rights. This is not a simple task. It is arguably not even coherent, for they appear to be in tension with one another.

Despite the teleological connection, rights are not reducible to reasons of beneficence, that is, to considerations of the benefits to be achieved and the harms to be avoided in particular actions. This point does not depend upon the rare case in which respecting a right does no good at all. Even if reasons of beneficence typically stand against the infringement of rights, they do not explain the moral force of rights in specific circumstances.

Although we might agree with Beehler that morality is in *some* sense a "manifestation" of a concern for human well-being, we should not accept his explanation of why "lies ought not to be told or promises broken," namely that "pain will be given."[13] For avoiding the pain to one person caused by a second person's lie, theft, or broken promise is equally a reason for a third person to prevent these things or to do what was promised herself, if possible. If I do not keep my promise to help you move on Saturday, you might be in a serious jam. But avoiding that consequence is equally a reason for a third person to help you move when she notices your plight. So to invoke the pain I would cause you will not explain *my* special obligation. To promise is to grant rights, and to do this is to grant moral authority over a limited range of one's life. In promising to help you, I thereby forswear (within limits) the appeal to considerations that would otherwise have been available to me – for instance, that I might help another just as much.[14]

Similarly, any bystander has a moral reason to warn you of the banana peel in your path, namely, to prevent your injury. But if I negligently drop a banana peel and create the risk, my reason has a different source (and perhaps weight); it derives from my causal responsibility, and hence is not a consideration that is neutral for all agents.

Rights, then, are not reducible to reasons of beneficence. They place constraints on one's response to such reasons. It is these features of rights and responsibilities that I am calling *deontological constraints*. Such constraints are ubiquitous in everyday life. They appear throughout legal and other institutional contexts of authoritative regulation. Laws against assault say "Do not attack others," not "Minimize physical attacks on others." Your obligation is to pay your tax bill, not to use that money in whatever way is best designed to minimize tax evasion (say, by evading your tax payments and using the money you owe to hire a detective to expose more serious evasions). When such laws have legitimate authority over us, they are sources of deontological reasons. So are legislators, judges, military commanders, department chairs, parents, teachers, mayors, employers, police officers, when they have rightful jurisdiction over us. It is essential to the role of these rules and the function of these offices that they yield such constraints.

Less institutionalized contexts are saturated with nonconsequentialist reasoning as well. As bearers of moral rights, we each hold a moral office, as it were, and as such each is a source of deontological reasons. To have a moral right is to have a certain kind of authority, a sphere of discretion in which what others may properly do depends upon one's consent.[15] (This is not to say that one may not wrongly consent.) The notion of authority bears its deontological character on its face.

III

These familiar points about moral practice give rise, then, to a theoretical problem. On the one hand, the connections between rights and goods are deep and pervasive. They exert a strong teleological pull on moral theory. On the other hand, rights restrict our pursuit of human good in distinctive ways. The problem is to make these connections perspicuous without reducing rights to reasons of beneficence in particular cases. The problem is to accommodate the teleological connection in a theory that at the same time accounts for the deontological character of moral rights. I shall call this the *problem of accommodation*.[16]

This problem is exacerbated by the fact that we do not in general take most deontological constraints to be *absolute*; they may sometimes be overridden not only to prevent the infringement of more serious rights, but to prevent sufficiently bad consequences of other kinds. Most deontological theorists would agree, for example, that one may lie to protect innocent lives. Although this position seems morally correct, it enhances the initial obscurity of the phenomenon. For how can reasons of beneficence interact in this manner with deontological considerations? How can such disparate considerations be "balanced" in an intelligible way? Doesn't this balancing require ordering principles that are ultimately teleological? Once again, the pressure is to collapse deontological constraints into reasons of beneficence or to deny that deontological constraints can be overridden. Though it seems to be true of our practice, the mixed position seems difficult, in theory, to occupy.[17]

A perpetual philosophical temptation is to try to dissolve the problem by abandoning one of its elements. At one extreme, we find proposals to view rights as merely useful rules of thumb or else to reject deontological constraints as somehow paradoxical. At the other extreme, we find philosophers[18] who would repudiate the teleological connection altogether.

Both responses seem unsatisfactory. The teleological connection is too deep and important to ignore, but the deontological aspect of our thought cannot be dismissed just because it is theoretically inconvenient. One of the greatest achievements of contractualism is its capacity to bring these two features of rights together in a coherent and straightforward way.

IV

First, let me say more about the possibilities for utilitarianism. My aim in these remarks is not to advance original objections but to set up the discussion of contractualism as an attractive alternative treatment of the problem of accommodation.

Clearly, this problem has been the primary theoretical impetus of rule utilitarianism and other two-level consequentialist views. The idea is to accommodate the teleological and deontological character of rights by distinguishing different levels of justification and evaluation.[19] Systems of rules and rights are justified by their "general acceptance utility" relative to other systems. The connection between rights and human well-being appears at this level. However, particular actions or policies are justified by reference to the applicable rules. The set of rules with the greatest acceptance utility is likely to call for conduct in isolated cases that differs from the dictates of act utilitarianism. Therefore, complying with the best set of rules will constrain one's pursuit of benefits in particular cases. Hence deontological constraints are explained as well.

Rule utilitarianism has not, however, succeeded in explaining how these two levels of justification cohere with one another.[20] If what justifies the rule or the right are just the effects on well-being of general compliance, then the effects on well-being should be decisive in deciding whether or not to comply in particular cases. To follow the rules in these counterutilitarian cases looks like "rule worship,"[21] in which one's concern for consequences has become fixated on general compliance.

Therefore, rule utilitarians face a dilemma: either the requirements of the rule completely coincide with what has the most utility, in which case rule utilitarianism is equivalent to act utilitarianism and deontological constraints are denied, or else those requirements diverge from straightforward utilitarian reasoning in some instances, in which case obedience has no consequentialist justification. Either rule utilitarianism collapses into act utilitarianism, or it ceases to be utilitarian.[22]

Other responses to the problem of accommodation have been inspired by Henry Sidgwick's observation that it is probably best, from a utilitarian point of view, that most people are not utilitarians. The rule-utilitarian insight was that the observance of deontological constraints is very useful because of the abuses to which utilitarian thought is liable in practice. The best results are most likely to ensue if we are not wholehearted utilitarians. The best means of accomplishing this is to take rule worship (within limits) as a virtue, something to foster and encourage. In this way, utilitarianism endorses its own rejection.

This argument is said to be coherent because the endorsement and rejection take place at different levels of moral thought. One question concerns the ideal form of reasoning for beings who are fully informed, impartial, and rational. A different question is how we are to raise children, who never will be perfect in these respects. We need to inculcate moral sensibilities and dispositions for beings who are imperfect in these ways. Since we never fully outgrow these liabilities, we are never in a position to kick over the deontological traces altogether.[23]

Perhaps this is the most coherent utilitarian response to deontological constraints. And it *is* a kind of accommodation. But it remains troubling. The chief trouble, in my view, concerns the gap between theory and practice; practice must be to a significant degree benighted. There is much to be said on this question.[24] I will emphasize just one point. The reason why the gap is disturbing is not that it requires too much psychological complexity on the part of moral agents, but that it precludes the realization of a certain kind of value in the moral life. Just people (those who among other things are deontologically sensitive) must be to a certain extent deluded about the grounds of their own virtue.[25] The charge of rule worship is not so much evaded as turned into a form of praise. But the praise is faint; attachments that are necessarily deluded cannot be fully admirable in a mature human being, and therefore the trait that involves that attachment cannot be affirmed unambivalently as a virtue.

This criticism concerns the moral adequacy of two-level utilitarianism, not its conceptual or psychological coherence. The complaint is that it excludes some of our deepest moral aspirations. We might live with this implication, if this were the best philosophy we could get. But contractualism can do better.

V

Contractualism comes in both a Hobbesian and a Kantian form.[26] Hobbesian versions attempt to explain moral constraints in terms of individual advantage. It is to the advantage of each of us to submit to agreements that constrain our individual pursuit of advantage. Morality is thereby derived from nonmoral interests.[27] In contrast, on Kantian versions, morality involves a form of practical reason that is independent of the rationality of maximal advantage. Practical reason expresses itself as a fundamental commitment to act in accordance with principles to which all rational beings could agree.

These preliminary characterizations allow for significant refinements within each type. For now, I wish to bring out some common issues and advantages.

One issue is whether a determinate content can be given to morality just by appealing to the relevant notion of agreement. There must be a solution, or at least a definite range of solutions, to the hypothetical choice problem as the theory defines it. Call this the problem of content.

Moreover, the theory must justify its definition of the choice situation without invoking moral considerations of the kind the theory is designed to explain; that definition cannot be justified merely by the fact that it leads to such and such (intuitively plausible) moral principles. This point is related to the second issue, which is how the fact that certain principles would be agreed to can be a reason for endorsing those principles in the actual world. Call this the problem of compliance.

These issues will be more difficult for some versions of contractualism than for others; I shall take up some aspects of them shortly. However, we can already see the connection between these issues and the problem of accommodation. For, any contractualist theory that has a reasonable response to these issues will thereby accommodate both the teleological connection and deontological constraints. To begin with the former, in a contractualist account, each individual is to agree upon principles at least partly from the standpoint of her own interests. (On some types, that will be the parties' only concern; on others, this concern will be qualified in certain respects.) The resultant set of principles is bound to reflect some concern for each person's well-being; the agreement point will necessarily represent something like the common good. Therefore, on any plausible contractualist view, the rights, duties, and responsibilities that are the product of the agreement will serve to protect certain central interests.

At the same time, on any plausible view, the agreement will include rights-conferring principles restricting how we may treat others without their consent. That is, they entail deontological constraints. Therefore, contractualism of either form will support two claims: that rights are pervasively and nonaccidentally linked to human good, and that the moral reasons to which rights give rise do not all reduce to reasons of beneficence.

The problem of commensurability that we identified in our examination of mixed positions (section III) also seems manageable on a contractualist view. There are obvious reasons why it would not be in the common interest to adopt principles that accorded absolute rights; rather, the adopted principles would likely contain provisos for their permissible infringement. This conclusion would have to be shown in detail. But it can be seen why reasons of beneficence and deontological constraints are not incommensurably disparate, as they might initially appear.

What gives force to the problem of accommodation and the subsidiary problem of commensurability is the idea that teleological reasons must be explained by some version of *outcome* ethics, according to which moral reasons come from the value of particular outcomes, in this case the enhancement of human good. In contrast, on a contractualist approach, considerations of beneficence, deontological constraints, and the conditions of their infringement all have a common source in the principles defining the basic agreement. (I take up a related point in section IX.)

For the same reasons, contractualism has no difficulty with the "self–other asymmetry" discussed by Michael Slote, who takes this asymmetry to cast suspicion on ordinary morality.[28] Given the circumstances that define the hypothetical choice situation, namely the need for a framework for interpersonal cooperation, it is not surprising that moral requirements would include mutual aid but not self-regard.[29] This asymmetry will seem puzzling only on a theory that derives all moral reasons from the value of outcomes.

VI

If any form of contractualism is adequate, then the problem of accommodation is resolved. That is, of course, a very large "if." Any acceptable form of contractualism must deal with the issue of compliance as well. Why should we be concerned to comply with principles that have the feature of being choiceworthy under certain hypothetical circumstances? How does the reason for choosing principles in the hypothetical situation transfer to one's choices here and now? This issue is worrisome in different respects to the two general forms of contractualism we have distinguished.

The main worry for Hobbesian views is the "free-rider" problem. The reason for agreement – namely, long-term advantage – is not necessarily a reason for compliance with the agreement. The agreement will include deontological constraints only if it restricts individuals' pursuit of their long-term advantage. It is clear that a concern for one's long-term advantage could rationally motivate one to agree to limit one's pursuit of one's long-term advantage if others did so as well. But that reason cannot intelligibly lead one to comply with deontological constraints when doing so can be expected to frustrate one's interests overall.

Note the instructive parallel here to the problem of rule utilitarianism. Hobbesianism and utilitarianism are rival interpretations of the same truth: that moral constraints serve the common good. In the common good, the ends of both benevolence and self-interest are realized. Nonetheless, in order to explain reasons for compliance with moral constraints, we must go beyond the austere resources of both theories; we must appeal, apparently, to fairness or some similar moral concern.

To continue the parallel, Hobbesians can also respond to the problem of compliance by recourse to a two-tier view, a kind of character "egoism"; it can be rational, in terms of one's own advantage, to develop character traits that lead one to comply with deontological constraints. The parallel objection would be that such self-sacrificing compliance would still be irrational, on Hobbesian criteria. So a two-tier theory would not succeed in explaining how moral conduct can be rational; it would show at most that it might be rational to become the kind of person who is disposed to behave irrationally in certain contexts.

This problem is what makes David Gauthier's appeal to constrained maximization tempting. Gauthier argues against the received Hobbesian interpretation of practical rationality. The rationality of an action is not a simple function of its expected utility. It is enough if the action manifests a "disposition" that it is rational (in terms of expected utility) to acquire and maintain. The rationality of acquiring and maintaining the disposition to limit the pursuit of one's advantage in accordance with deontological constraints transfers to the actions that exercise those dispositions. Thus, a choice can be rational not because it maximizes expected utility but because it is an exercise of a disposition that it is rational to have. Thus Gauthier proposes to "identif[y] practical rationality with utility-maximization at the level of dispositions to choose."[30]

This view agrees with Kantians that compliance with moral constraints cannot plausibly be motivated in particular cases by a concern to maximize one's advantage. But to explain such compliance we need not invoke a distinctly moral interest nor appeal to a form of practical reason other than rational advantage. All that is needed is rational consistency, where this is understood to include consistency with the dispositions that it is advantageous for one to possess.

VII

Gauthier's proposal has turned out to be very controversial. It seems clear, in any case, that a Hobbesian solution will invoke some kind of two-level view.[31] On the other hand, compliance is not an issue for Kantian versions of contractualism. Actions are right or wrong, on this approach, if they are allowed or disallowed by principles that it would be unreasonable to reject as a basis for cooperative arrangements.[32] The reason for compliance with such principles is not the advancement of one's ends (though that concern is important in determining what principles one could reasonably reject); it is, rather, the concern to pursue one's ends only in ways that can be justified by reasons that others can accept as free and rational persons. I shall call this concern *respect*.[33] It involves a readiness to acknowledge the points of view of others, which in turn involves a concern to take others' aims and interests into account. This attitude is an acknowledgment of others as in this way moral equals.

Thus, Kantian contractualism works with two motivational assumptions. It assumes that individuals are motivated both by self-regard and by respect for others. It assumes (1) that each individual is concerned to advance his or her own ends, but (2) that moral persons will do this only in ways that can be justified to others on the basis of reasons the others can accept from their own points of view (assuming that they too respect others).[34] Respect delimits the form of practical reason, but the content of judgments of right and wrong is determined by the agreement of individuals so conceived. Determinate moral principles and judgments are constructed by mutual deliberation, not given directly by the notion of respect. Hence, the fact that respect is a moral notion does not entail that the notion of a hypothetical agreement is a dispensable expository device.[35]

These assumptions distinguish this form of contractualism from both Hobbesianism and utilitarianism. Self-regard[36] is not the sole source of practical reasons. Nor is there any foundational commitment here to general benevolence. "Individual well-being will be morally significant," as Scanlon puts it, "not because it is intrinsically valuable or because promoting it is self-evidently a right-making characteristic, but simply because an individual could reasonably reject a form of argument that gave his well-being no weight."[37] Self-regard, rather than benevolence, makes the teleological connection a theorem of contractualism.

VIII

The appeal to respect enables Kantians to avoid the compliance problem. But to Hobbesians, the appeal is a cheat. To understand this complaint, we must distinguish two general forms that a Kantian doctrine can take. In what might be called the "classical" or stronger version, the readiness to submit to impartial constraints is somehow a constitutive commitment of practical reason; to lack this virtue is a failure of reason. In contrast, neo-Kantians (such as Scanlon) view respect as a rationally more contingent matter. On both views, one has a (nonhypothetical) reason to take the interests of others into account. The concern to conform one's conduct to the hypothetical-choice situation – to reason morally – is part of what it is to be "reasonable." But whereas classical Kantians think that the commitment to moral virtue can be derived from a more general account of reason, neo-Kantians do not take reasonableness to be something that can be demonstrated outside the moral point of view.

Hobbesians find these versions of Kantianism objectionable in different respects. Ironically, perhaps, the Hobbesian shares the classical Kantian ambition to find a universal and "sure grounding" for morality in reason. As Gauthier puts it, the Hobbesian wants to "demonstrate the rationality of impartial constraints on the pursuit of individual interest to persons who may take no interest in others' interests." But this demonstration must rely on "a weak and widely accepted conception of rationality,"[38] not on the notoriously controversial notion favored by Kantians. Hobbesians suspect that this notion depends for its appeal upon an antecedent commitment to impartial morality.

The Hobbesian complaint against the neo-Kantians is precisely that they abandon the classical project. They take as basic what ought to be securely grounded: moral rationality. They give us no reply to the Foole.

My own sympathies lie with the neo-Kantians here. I suspect that the Hobbesian project can support at best a seriously revisionist conception of moral practice. Nor am I optimistic about the Kantian version of the project. The Hobbesian worries, however, bring out an important truth: that Kantianism cannot be contractualist at its foundations.

A moral theory is contractualist at its foundations, I take it, if it claims to account for the significance of all moral phenomena in terms of the notion of agreement.[39] But the moral significance of respect cannot itself be understood in this manner. For respect – the readiness to act only on principles to which others could agree – is itself something we demand of one another. It might be called an *ur*-demand, a metarequirement to deliberate from a point of view from which all other moral requirements are constructed. The demand to submit to the standpoint of impartial deliberation (what Scanlon himself calls the "most general moral demand")[40] cannot itself derive its authority from that standpoint.[41]

So contractualism on its own does not get to the bottom of things. The *ur*-demand itself must be understood in a different way. On classical Kantian theories, as I have said, respect will be founded in the commitments of rational agency more generally. That theory will be contractualist if moral requirements (other than respect itself) are understood in terms of an interpersonal hypothetical choice situation.[42]

There are a number of possibilities for neo-Kantian theories. For example, respect might be based on a widely shared and deeply rooted cultural ideal[43] or tradition. A neo-Kantian account could even be grounded in a theory of virtue, in which respect was explained as just one among a number of central virtues.[44] In any case, a satisfactory neo-Kantian view must explain why respect has a deep motivational place in our lives and further how (and in what sense) it is something that we can demand of one another.[45]

IX

I have tried to show how a contractualist view (or any view that includes contractualism) can readily accommodate both the deontological and the teleological features of rights. Some philosophers have argued that any moral outlook that includes deontological constraints will have an "air of paradox." In this concluding section, I want to respond to this argument.

This challenge to deontological constraints has been pressed especially forcefully by Samuel Scheffler. Moral requirements can claim our allegiance, Scheffler argues, only if their violation is highly "objectionable" and "undesirable" from a moral point of view. Then how, Scheffler asks, "can it be rational to forbid the performance of a morally objectionable action that would have the effect of minimizing the total number of comparably objectionable actions that were performed and would have no other morally relevant consequences? How can the minimization of morally objectionable conduct be morally unacceptable?"[46] One may not kill an innocent person just because that would prevent two other deaths, or even two other murders. The usual "rationales" for these restrictions do not dispel the puzzle, Scheffler claims. To say that deception or homicide violates the victim's autonomy, for example, does not explain why we recognize deontological limits rather than the aim of minimizing violations of autonomy.

Of course, it is no objection to say that deontological constraints restrict one's pursuit of various outcomes. That is what they are supposed to do. To take this as an objection is already to assume a consequentialist position. Scheffler's argument is rather that deontological theories cannot do without goals, and that this threatens their coherence.[47] In order to have sufficient authority to override our own interests, Scheffler thinks, moral violations must be seen as "objectionable or undesirable" in the sense that "it is morally preferable that no such actions should occur than that any should."[48] So, deontological theories are committed to at least one agent-neutral, impersonal goal: the nonviolation of the restrictions they imply. To have a goal is to have a reason, *ceteris paribus*, to choose those options that promise to realize that goal. These reasons reflect an elementary commitment of practical rationality, not an antecedent commitment to a particular moral theory.

Although this argument helps to bring out what is at stake, it does not establish a presumptive case against deontological theories. What it shows, at most, is this: if deontological theories are coherent, then they must explain how maximizing rationality interacts with other alleged features of practical reason. But this is of course the starting point of anti-consequentialist theories since Kant, who took the main task of moral philosophy to be to show how the hypothetical and categorical imperatives can be unified in practical reason. That Scheffler takes his conclusion to present an apparent "paradox" rather than to describe a philosophical project simply expresses his pessimism about the enterprise. By itself, it is no argument against it.

To be sure, Scheffler's challenge raises interesting questions for contractualism. A theory that admits deontological goals (that is, to minimize violations of constraints) must explain why they should in general be subordinate to the constraints. One could view the constraints as themselves agent-relative *goals*,[49] but as Scheffler says, it is hard to see why agent-relative deontological goals should generate stronger reasons than the impersonal ones.

But I am not convinced that contractualism is committed to deontological goals, or that such a commitment would be a problem. This issue recalls the problems of mixed theories we considered in section III. Everything depends on how these goals are construed. If the point is that the theory must have a foundational commitment to the idea that moral violations constitute intrinsically bad states of affairs and are therefore "objectionable" or "undesirable," the reply is that contractualism need have no such commitment.[50] If instead the question is whether there is a *derivable* commitment to minimize violations, the answer depends on the upshot of moral deliberation. Arguably, if no one could reasonably reject principle P, then no one could reasonably reject a *ceteris paribus* commitment to prevent violations of P. The same contractualist reasoning that establishes a constraint against homicide, for example, would establish a general reason to prevent others from violating this principle. So the answer is plausibly yes.

The weight of this reason (and the permissible means by which it could be acted upon) would probably vary somewhat with the principle in question (would be stronger in the case of homicide, say, than in the case of deception). More importantly, the reasons would operate like moral goals rather than restrictions. They correspond to what were traditionally called "imperfect duties." Although we are required to give some weight to these goals in our decisions, we may choose to forego them in particular circumstances if their pursuit would violate a constraint or would seriously interfere with our attaining important personal ends.

The crucial point here is to distinguish the status of moral goals in a contractualist view from their role in outcome ethics. On the former view, I have a reason to minimize moral violations, not *because* they are morally objectionable or impersonally undesirable, but because no one could reasonably reject a principle that gave some deliberative importance to this consideration.[51] To be sure, moral violations *are* morally undesirable and impersonally objectionable, on this view, but that is to say that the prohibitions in question are derivable from the hypothetical choice situation. This judgment is an implication, rather than a ground, of my contractualist duties.[52]

X

Our practical and theoretical lives might be simpler if a concern to maximize valued outcomes were the sole determinant of moral reasoning. But it appears not to be. Morality both enjoins and restricts the pursuit of goals. This complexity is not puzzling from a (Kantian) contractualist point of view. It is just what we should expect of the practice of human beings who are concerned to advance their good under conditions of mutual respect. This constitutes, I have argued, a considerable theoretical merit.

Notes

1 Of course, to Nietzsche and some others, this connection is a mere pretense.
2 John Stuart Mill, *Utilitarianism* ([1861] Indianapolis: Hackett, 1979), ch. 2, p. 16. To treat these two ideals as equivalent is, as we will see, problematic. The contractualist sees the Golden Rule as an expression of a concern for reciprocity rather than love.
3 J. J. C. Smart, *Utilitarianism: For and Against* (Cambridge: Cambridge University Press, 1973).
4 Joseph Fletcher, *Situation Ethics* (Philadelphia: Westminster, 1966), p. 98.
5 Arthur Schopenhauer, *On the Basis of Morality* ([1841] Indianapolis: Bobbs-Merrill, 1965), pp. 135–8.
6 Rodger Beehler, *Moral Life* ([1848] Oxford: Blackwell Publisher, 1978), p. 1.
7 A. I. Melden, *Rights and Persons* (Berkeley and Los Angeles: University of California Press, 1977), p. 145.

8   My discussion in the next few paragraphs of the role of rights follows T. M. Scanlon, "Rights, Goals and Fairness," in *Public and Private Morality*, ed. Stuart Hampshire (Cambridge: Cambridge University Press, 1978), pp. 93–111; reprinted in *Consequentialism and Its Critics*, ed. Samuel Scheffler (New York: Oxford University Press, 1988). For further remarks on Scanlon's relation to utilitarianism, see note 32 in the present chapter.

9   Some will insist that these rights are restricted not by interests but by others' rights – your right to privacy by my right to noninterference. This response is suggested by John Hospers' declaration: "Every human being has the right to act in accordance with his own choices, unless those actions infringe on the equal liberty of other human beings to act in accordance with *their* choices." "What Libertarianism Is," in *The Libertarian Alternative*, ed. Tibor Machan (Chicago: Nelson Hall, 1974), p. 3. Presumably this principle is meant to restrict my right to punch you when I feel like it. But it can be applied in a noncircular manner only when it is supplemented by background assumptions about what interests are more worthy of protection. For your claim not to be punched also interferes with my liberty to punch. We do not consider that an infringement, because we do not take the right to punch someone to be a general interest worth protecting.

10   Philippa Foot, "Utilitarianism and the Virtues," *Mind* 94 (1985), 196–209. The quoted passage is from the reprinted version in Scheffler, *Consequentialism*, p. 227.

11   Scanlon, "Rights, Goals and Fairness," p. 93. One of the best discussions of these connections from a utilitarian point of view is in chapter 5 of Mill's *Utilitarianism*.

12   My account follows especially Thomas Nagel, *The View from Nowhere* (New York: Oxford University Press, 1986), ch. 9. See also Robert Nozick, *Anarchy, State and Utopia* (New York: Basic Books, 1974), pp. 28–35.

13   Beehler, *Moral Life*, p. 17.

14   On this feature of promising, see John Rawls, "Two Concepts of Rules," *Philosophical Review* 64 (1955), 3–32.

15   To characterize rights in terms of authority will be circular, if authority cannot be explained without invoking rights. Nevertheless, a circular characterization can be philosophically helpful by locating a term in its conceptual network.

16   The problem of accommodation is relevant to what Gregory Kavka called "the reconciliation project," "The Reconciliation Project," in *Morality, Reason, and Truth: New Essays on the Foundations of Ethics*, ed. David Copp and David Zimmerman (Totowa, NJ: Rowman & Allanheld, 1984), pp. 279–319. In one version, this is the project of showing that morality is compatible with "self-interest." Because self-interest is then identified with (practical) rationality, this project is transformed into the attempt to reconcile morality with rationality. The problem of accommodation is related but distinct; it is not to reconcile morality with the independent claims of reason, but to accommodate

two features *of* morality, neither of which is on its face self-interested. Nevertheless, the problem can also be seen as arising from a tension within practical reason: that morality at once requires and restricts "maximizing rationality." I return to this notion later in this essay.

17   For an attack on the mixed position, see Shelly Kagan, *The Limits of Morality* (New York: Oxford University Press, 1989).

18   For instance, H. A. Prichard. Because he identifies morality with the realm of deontological constraints (in his term, the realm of "obligation"), Prichard takes the search for the "role" of such constraints to be a misguided attempt to ground morality in nonmoral considerations. Since moral philosophy is conceived to be the theory of such constraints, the very enterprise "rests on a mistake." See "Does Moral Philosophy Rest on a Mistake?", *Mind* (1912), reprinted in Prichard's *Moral Obligation* (New York: Oxford University Press, 1949). For a valuable discussion of Prichard's view, see James Wallace, *Virtues and Vices* (Ithaca: Cornell University Press, 1978), ch. 4.

19   For a related attempt to "reconcile deontological intuitions with consequentialist insights," see the very suggestive essay by Conrad D. Johnson, "The Authority of the Moral Agent," *Journal of Philosophy* 82 (1985), 260, reprinted in Scheffler, *Consequentialism*, pp. 261–87. As an alternative to two-level views, Johnson proposes a "division of labor" view, which distinguishes judicial and legislative points of view within morality. He appears to think that his view remains fundamentally consequentialist; he speaks of reconciling "consequentialism with agent-centered constraints" (p. 263) rather than developing an alternative to consequentialism.

20   My discussion abstracts from substantial differences among versions of rule utilitarianism. A valuable discussion of rule utilitarianism and its varieties is to be found in David Lyons, *The Forms and Limits of Utilitarianism* (Oxford: Clarendon Press, 1965). See also Donald Regan, *Utilitarianism and Co-operation* (Oxford: Clarendon Press, 1980), Rawls, "Two Concepts," and Wallace, *Virtues and Vices*.

21   This is Smart's criticism of what he calls "indirect utilitarianism" in *Utilitarianism: For and Against*.

22   Hence, as Scanlon puts it, rule utilitarianism "strikes most people as an unstable compromise." See "Contractualism and Utilitarianism," in *Utilitarianism and Beyond*, ed. A. Sen and B. Williams (Cambridge: Cambridge University Press, 1982), pp. 103–28.

23   R. M. Hare defends a view like this in *Moral Thinking* (Oxford: Clarendon Press, 1981). A similar view is expounded, though not endorsed, by Robert Adams, "Motive Utilitarianism," *Journal of Philosophy* 73 (1976), 467–81.

A subtle version of consequentialism has been advanced by Peter Railton. See "Alienation, Consequentialism, and the Demands of Morality," *Philosophy and Public Affairs* 13 (1984).

24   See, e.g., Michael Stocker, "The Schizophrenia of Modern Ethical Theories," *Journal of Philosophy* 73 (1976), 453–66; Thomas Nagel, "The Limits of

Objectivity," in *The Tanner Lectures on Human Values*, ed. S. McMurrin (Salt Lake City: University of Utah Press, 1980), esp. pp. 129ff.; and various contributions to *Hare and Critics: Essays on Moral Thinking*, ed. D. Seanor and N. Fotion (Oxford: Clarendon Press, 1990).

25 Hare responds to some of these worries in *Moral Thinking* and in "Ethical Theory and Utilitarianism," in *Utilitarianism and Beyond*, ed. Sen and Williams, pp. 23–38. See also his replies in Seanor and Fotion, *Hare and Critics*.

26 Hobbesian and Kantian theories are so different at their foundations that they might better be treated as generically different. For this point, see Will Kymlicka, "The Social Contract Tradition," in *A Companion to Ethics*, ed. Peter Singer (Oxford: Blackwell Publisher, 1993). I would propose "consentualism" as an apt term for Kantian-type theories. I treat them together just the same, because each promises to resolve the problem of accommodation via some notion of agreement.

27 I shall assume that Hobbesian theories aspire (with David Gauthier) to generate morality as "a rational constraint from the non-moral premises of rational choice." David Gauthier, *Morals by Agreement* (Oxford: Clarendon Press, 1986), p. 4. This book contains an excellent presentation of the two forms of contractualism; see esp. chapter 1. See also Jean Hampton, "Two Faces of Contractarian Thought," in *Contractarianism and Rational Choice: Essays on Gauthier*, ed. P. Vallentyne (Cambridge: Cambridge University Press, 1990), pp. 31–55, and Christopher Morris, "A Contractarian Account of Moral Justification," in *Moral Knowledge? New Essays in Moral Epistemology*, ed. Walter Sinnott-Armstrong and Mark Simmons (New York: Oxford University Press, 1996), pp. 215–42.

28 In "Morality and Self–Other Asymmetry," *Journal of Philosophy* 81 (1984), 179–92. In "The Authority of the Moral Agent," p. 284, Johnson notes the capacity of two-level views to accommodate this asymmetry.

29 Conversely, it is arguably a problem that self-neglect and self-development cannot even be regarded as moral issues by contractualism. This points to one of the ways in which contractualism can be at most an adequate theory for a part of morality, the part having to do with moral requirement. (I return to a related issue at the end of this essay.)

30 Gauthier, *Morals by Agreement*, p. 187.

31 See the essays by Michael E. Bratman and Daniel M. Farrell in this volume [Christopher Morris and Jules Coleman (eds.), *Rational Commitment and Morality* (Cambridge: Cambridge University Press, 1998)]. See also Gregory S. Kavka, "A Paradox of Deterrence Revisited," in his *Moral Paradoxes of Nuclear Deterrence* (Cambridge: Cambridge University Press, 1987), pp. 33–56, esp. 43–7. For a development of a two-tier view that does not rely on a revision of maximizing rationality, see Eric M. Cave, *Preferring Justice: Rationality, Self-transformation, and the Sense of Justice* (Boulder, CO: Westview, 1997).

32 Here I follow Scanlon, "Contractualism and Utilitarianism." It is a reasonable conjecture, I think, that Scanlon's transitions from an earlier Kantian stage,

through his flirtation with a two-tier consequentialism in "Rights, Goals and Fairness," to the contractualism of this essay are influenced by his evolving assessment of the capacities of these theories to handle the problem of accommodation.

33 Scanlon himself does not use this term, but it is a fair characterization of what he has in mind. In certain contexts, at least, the refusal to consider one's actions from the perspective of others is called "unreasonable." We call the opposite "fair-mindedness." The connection between these notions is brought out by Rawls, who links being reasonable (as distinct from rational) with a concern for "fair terms of cooperation," that is, "terms which participants may reasonably be expected to accept provided that everyone else likewise accepts them." "Kantian Constructivism (The Dewey Lectures)," *Journal of Philosophy* 77 (1980), 515–72, at p. 528.

Cp. Rawls, in *A Theory of Justice* (Cambridge, MA: Harvard University Press, 1971): "respect for persons is shown by treating them in ways that they can see to be justified" (p. 586). Respect is shown in "our willingness to see the situation of others from their points of view, from the perspective of their conception of the good; and in our being prepared to give reasons whenever the interests of others are materially affected" (p. 337).

34 A circularity problem looms here. Respect is the concern to justify one's actions to others, assuming that they have the same attitude. But what is the content of that attitude? This arises for Scanlon's formulation as well. He characterizes the contractualist motivation as the "desire to be able to justify one's actions to others on grounds they could not reasonably reject." "Contractualism and Utilitarianism," p. 116. He goes on to explain: "The intended force of . . . 'reasonably' . . . is to exclude rejections that would be unreasonable *given* the aim of finding principles which could be the basis of informed, unforced general agreement . . . The only pressure for agreement comes from the desire to find and agree on principles which no one who had this desire could reasonably reject." Ibid., p. 111. Scanlon addresses this and other issues in his manuscript "What We Owe to Others."

35 Contrary to Alan Donagan, *The Theory of Morality* (Chicago: University of Chicago Press, 1977), sec. 7.2. Cp. Rawls once again: "While the principles of justice will be effective only if men . . . respect one another, the notion of respect . . . is not a suitable basis for arriving at these principles. It is precisely these ideas that call for interpretation." *A Theory of Justice*, p. 337.

In Rawls's terms, because respect frames the structure of the original position, it gives the outcome of otherwise self-regarding reasoning a moral significance. But the frame does not by itself supply the content. Similarly, in Scanlon's version, the concern to satisfy the terms of reasonable cooperation frames the concern to find principles that will advance one's interests.

36 The term "self-regard" is meant to refer to a concern to advance one's ends, whatever they may be; the term does not imply that one's ends themselves are specifically self-regarding or "egoistic." The same goes for talk of

"advantage." The issue between Kantians and Hobbesians is whether self-regard in this sense is directly or indirectly (as with Gauthier) the ultimate standard of practical reason.

37 Scanlon, "Contractualism and Utilitarianism," p. 119.

38 Gauthier, *Morals by Agreement*, p. 17.

39 See Scanlon, "Contractualism and Utilitarianism," pp. 118–19.

40 T. M. Scanlon, "The Significance of Choice," in *The Tanner Lectures on Human Values*, ed. Sterling McMurrin (Salt Lake City: University of Utah Press, 1988), pp. 149–216, at p. 174.

41 That is not to say that this requirement would not itself be endorsed from that standpoint. It is plausible to suppose that the requirement to constrain one's deliberations by the hypothetical-choice situation would itself be chosen in that situation.

42 Thomas Nagel's enterprise in *The Possibility of Altruism* (Oxford: Clarendon Press, 1970) is a contemporary example of a "classical" Kantian theorist in my loose sense. His view might also be given a contractualist turn. He argues that prudential reasoning involves a conception of objective reasons that yield impartial other-regarding reasons as well. To put the claim in explicitly Kantian terms, the force of the hypothetical imperative as a principle of practical reason depends upon a point of view that implies "categorical reasons." Objective reasons do not depend on any notion of hypothetical agreement, but Nagel entertains the suggestion that conflicts among objective reasons are properly decided by recourse to a hypothetical-choice situation; thus, all-things-considered moral "ought" judgments would have, on this suggestion, a contractualist interpretation.

In a bold new work, *The Sources of Normativity* (Cambridge: Cambridge University Press, 1996), Christine Korsgaard pursues the classical project without making any foundational use of contractualist notions.

43 This idea is congenial to a Rawlsian view. Samuel Scheffler elaborates a view of this sort in "Moral Skepticism and Ideals of the Person," *Monist* 62 (1979), 288–303, though he does not give it contractualist construal.

44 Foot's "Utilitarianism and the Virtues" suggests to me the possibility of a view of this kind.

If contractualism were grounded in a theory of virtue in this manner, then it might be committed to benevolence (as a virtue) after all. Although respect would be a virtue distinct from benevolence, it would not follow that respect is intelligible *as* a virtue independently of the concerns of benevolence. For, on this theory, the account of what makes respect a virtue (say, its role in human flourishing) might entail that benevolence (a concern for the well-being of individuals) is a virtue as well. See section VII in the present chapter.

45 The latter requirement is not met by showing that a failure of respect involves a failure of reason, as the classical Kantians would have it. To say that someone is under a moral demand is not just to say that she has acted contrary to reason; it is to say that she is *answerable* to us in certain ways.

46 Samuel Scheffler, "Agent-centred Restrictions, Rationality, and the Virtues," reprinted in his *Consequentialism*, pp. 243–60 at p. 244.
47 Ibid., p. 254.
48 Ibid., p. 252.
49 For the development of this idea, see Amartya Sen's important essay "Rights and Agency," *Philosophy and Public Affairs* 11 (1982), 3–39 (also reprinted in Scheffler, *Consequentialism*).
50 It is possible that a commitment to goals should appear in the foundations of a particular version of contractualism, but there is no general reason to suppose that it must.
51 This remark parallels what Scanlon says about duties of beneficence; see section VII of the present chapter.
52 This reverses Scheffler's claim that agent-relative deontological goals would be "derivative from, and given life by" the impersonal deontological goal, a claim that betrays his predilection for outcome theories. "Agent-centred Restrictions," p. 256.

Index